W9-BTL-118

USING DATA

TO IMPROVE

STUDENT LEARNING

IN MIDDLE SCHOOLS

VICTORIA L. BERNHARDT, Ph.D.
Executive Director
Education for the Future Initiative

Professor
Department of Professional Studies in Education
College of Communication and Education
California State University, Chico, CA

EYE ON EDUCATION
6 Depot Way West
Larchmont, NY 10538
(914) 833-0551
(914) 833-0761 Fax
www.eyeoneducation.com

Copyright © 2004 Eye on Education, Inc.
All Rights Reserved.

For information about permission to reproduce selections from this book, write:
EYE ON EDUCATION
Permission Dept.
6 Depot Way West
Larchmont, NY 10538

Library of Congress Cataloging—in—Publication Data

Bernhardt, Victoria L., 1952-
    Using data to improve student learning in middle schools / Victoria L. Bernhardt.
        p. cm.
    Includes bibliographical references.
    ISBN 1-930556-87-X
    1. Educational evaluation--United States. 2. Middle school students--
United States. 3. School improvement programs--United States. I. Title.

    LB2822.75.B44 2004
    373.12--dc22

                                                              2004050614

10 9 8 7 6 5 4 3 2

Also Available from Eye on Education

USING DATA TO IMPROVE STUDENT LEARNING IN ELEMENTARY SCHOOLS
(With CD-Rom)
Victoria L. Bernhardt

THE SCHOOL PORTFOLIO TOOLKIT:
A Planning, Implementation, and Evaluation Guide for
Continuous School Improvement (With CD-Rom)
Victoria L. Bernhardt

DATA ANALYSIS FOR COMPREHENSIVE SCHOOLWIDE IMPROVEMENT
Victoria L. Bernhardt

DESIGNING AND USING DATABASES FOR SCHOOL IMPROVEMENT
Victoria L. Bernhardt

THE EXAMPLE SCHOOL PORTFOLIO
Victoria L. Bernhardt, et. al.

THE SCHOOL PORTFOLIO:
A Comprehensive Framework for School Improvement, Second Edition
Victoria L. Bernhardt

SCHOOL LEADER'S GUIDE TO ROOT CAUSE ANALYSIS:
Using Data to Dissolve Problems
Paul Preuss

NAVIGATING COMPREHENSIVE SCHOOL CHANGE:
A Guide for the Perplexed
Thomas Chenoweth and Robert Everhart

BETTER INSTRUCTION THROUGH ASSESSMENT:
What Your Students are Trying to Tell You
Leslie Wilson

ACHIEVEMENT NOW!
How to Assure No Child is Left Behind
Donald J. Fielder

DROPOUT PREVENTION TOOLS
Franklin Schargel

STRATEGIES TO HELP SOLVE OUR SCHOOL DROPOUT PROBLEM
Franklin Schargel and Jay Smink

TEACHING MATTERS:
Motivating and Inspiring Yourself
Todd and Beth Whitaker

Acknowledgements

I am so lucky to have many wonderful, dedicated colleagues and friends all over the world who keep me going, and help me improve each day. I am particularly grateful for special colleagues from Arizona, California, Colorado, Georgia, Iowa, Indiana, Michigan, Missouri, Montana, North Dakota, Nevada, New Jersey, New York, Ohio, South Carolina, Vermont, Washington, Japan, Kuwait, and Brazil who have helped make this book factual and useful. These dedicated reviewers read a very, very drafty first draft and then encouraged me to keep going! They also gave me powerful information for making the content more useful and user-friendly. These reviewers were critical in the writing of this book for probably more reasons than they know. They gave me the confidence and sense of urgency to finish. Our very specialized list of final reviewers of *Using Data to Improve Student Learning in Middle Schools* included (I apologize if I left anyone out): Sue Clayton, Laurel Eisinger, Bill Johnston, Andy Mark, Toni Norris, Paul Preuss and Joy Rose.

Andy Mark gave additional time and energy by reviewing more than one draft, and for carefully looking over table and graph titles, labels, messages, and findings. Joy Rose read and edited the manuscript in every phase. Joy, as always, made herself available to help with any task, any time. Joy, my editor "extraordinaire," is unsurpassed as a supporter and encourager of high-quality work. The nature of her editing goes beyond the proper uses of verbs and commas—her knowledge of continuous school improvement provides insights and revelations that I do not always see. I know the final product is so much better because of her input. Thank you, thank you, and thank you, Joy.

A special thanks to the schools that gave me data to use in the case studies. In concert with our agreements, I will not reveal who you are or your real locations. We all appreciate the opportunity to learn from you. To those who used this case study in early form, thank you for your insights to continuously improve the Azalea story.

I am appreciative and thankful everyday for my outstanding *Education for the Future* staff: Lynn Varicelli, Brad Geise, Alicia Warren, Sally Withuhn, Mary Foard, Diana Castillo, Thiago Jorge, and Marcy Lauck. Brad managed the completion of the CD and graphics with his usual elegance. Alicia, Mary, Sally, Diana, and Thiago do amazing work, every day, to keep us operating and on the cutting edge. They also helped to make this book a reality. Alicia deserves special acknowledgement for help with the references and graphing, and Sally for graphing questionnaire results. Last, but not least, Marcy Lauck, serving as our depth charge in San Jose Unified School District, helps us know that it is possible to do this on a large scale and that it can be sustained over time.

Once again, I am awestruck and indebted to Lynn Varicelli, also an *Education for the Future* staff member, for her careful and artistic work on the book layout and CD files. Her dedication to supporting these publications is unmatched in the history of the world! Thank you, Lynn, for your stellar work, for your commitment, loyalty, and long hours over countless days without a break. These books could never be done without you.

I am also grateful to *MC² Design Group*. Brian Curtis and Vanessa Wolfe created the CD design, artwork, and cover—I highly recommend them—and Tom Devol (that's *loved* spelled backwards), our outstanding professional photographer (even if HE cannot spell backwards).

I thank my husband, Jim Richmond, for again providing his brand of support for my work. He does a lot of what I should be doing around the house so I can pursue these publications and the work I can't not do—with few complaints.

A huge thanks to my publisher, affectionately known as *Cousin Bob*, Mr. Robert Sickles. I am grateful for all you do for us. Thank you.

This *Acknowledgement* section could not be complete without thanking you, the reader, and you, the school personnel working with continuous school improvement, who have believed in and tried *Education for the Future* products and processes.

I do hope this book exceeds your expectations and if it does, it is because of the continuous improvement that has resulted from your insights, direction, assistance, and support all along the way. Thank you.

In appreciation to all interested in continuous quality improvement, enjoy this second in a series of four books on *Using Data to Improve Student Learning*.

Vickie Bernhardt
May 2004

About the Author

Victoria L. Bernhardt, Ph.D., is Executive Director of the *Education for the Future Initiative,* a not-for-profit organization whose mission is to build the capacity of all schools at all levels to gather, analyze, and use data to continuously improve learning for all students. She is also a Professor in the Department of Professional Studies in Education, College of Communication and Education, at California State University, Chico. Dr. Bernhardt is the author of the following books:

▼ A four-book collection of using data to improve student learning—*Using Data to Improve Student Learning in Elementary Schools (2003); Using Data to Improve Student Learning in Middle Schools (2004); Using Data to Improve Student Learning in High Schools (2005);* and *Using Data to Improve Student Learning across School Districts (2005).* Each book shows real analyses focused on one education organizational level and provides templates on an accompanying CD-Rom for leaders to use for gathering, graphing, and analyzing data in their own learning organizations.

▼ *Data Analysis for Comprehensive Schoolwide Improvement* (First Edition, 1998; Second Edition, 2004) helps learning organizations use data to determine where they are, where they want to be, and how to get there—sensibly, painlessly, and effectively.

▼ *The School Portfolio Toolkit: A Planning, Implementation, and Evaluation Guide for Continuous School Improvement,* and CD-Rom (2002), is a compilation of over 500 examples, suggestions, activities, tools, strategies, and templates for producing school portfolios that will lead to continuous school improvement.

▼ *The Example School Portfolio* (2000) shows what a completed school portfolio looks like and further supports schools in developing their own school portfolios.

▼ *Designing and Using Databases for School Improvement* (2000) helps schools and districts think through the issues surrounding the creation and uses of databases established to achieve improved student learning.

▼ *The School Portfolio: A Comprehensive Framework for School Improvement* (First Edition, 1994; Second Edition, 1999). This first book by the author assists schools with clarifying the purpose and vision of their learning organizations as they develop their school portfolios.

Dr. Bernhardt is passionate about her mission of helping all educators continuously improve student learning in their classrooms, their schools, their districts, and states by gathering, analyzing, and using actual data—as opposed to using hunches and "gut-level" feelings. She has made numerous presentations at professional meetings and conducts workshops on the school portfolio, data analysis, datawarehousing, and school improvement at local, state, regional, national, and international levels.

Dr. Bernhardt can be reached at:

Victoria L. Bernhardt
Executive Director, *Education for the Future Initiative*
400 West First Street, Chico, CA 95929-0230
Tel: 530-898-4482 — Fax: 530-898-4484
e-mail: vbernhardt@csuchico.edu
website: *http://eff.csuchico.edu*

Table of Contents

Foreword

TetraData Corporation is a software and services company that focuses on analysis, assessment, and improvement in education. TetraData continues to be proudly associated with Victoria L. Bernhardt, one of the most dedicated, capable, and energetic leaders in school improvement today. Our firm shares a common passion, i.e., that fact-driven decision making can provide each district, each school, and each class with a reliable way to facilitate continuous school improvement. We also share a common vision of a world where education is moving toward increased knowledge, increased caring, and where we focus societal resources on our real future, i.e., the children of our world.

This book in the series of four, *Using Data to Improve Student Learning,* is an excellent addition to Dr. Bernhardt's preceding books that explain how to establish a data-driven environment and how to build the data warehouse to support the needed analysis of data. The four books in this series focus on what to do with a robust data warehouse, i.e., what analyses to prepare and how to interpret the analyses. In the several years that Dr. Bernhardt and TetraData have been building and using education specific data warehouses, the quality of the data and design of the warehouses has grown significantly. Now we have much of the data that we have been seeking to properly assemble, and the next step is addressed by this wonderful publication series.

What I enjoy immensely about these four publications is that Dr. Bernhardt has used real data from real life situations. This brings richness to the examples and the principles that Dr. Bernhardt provides since it is set forth in such a realistic environment. This realism approach has also enabled Dr. Bernhardt to provide both an insightful, as well as practical, description of how to prepare and interpret the analyses. Since there are four books, the publications deliver this information specific to the teachers and staff in elementary, middle, high school, and the district office. That was a wonderful decision by Dr. Bernhardt, as she provides very specific content for each portion of the education spectrum.

One of the major education issues that Dr. Bernhardt addresses is embodied in the word "Focus." One of the first results of the early education data warehousing and data analysis efforts was the *kid in the candy shop* syndrome. What I mean by that is the school data was finally available for examination, and educators started producing queries and analyses, many of which were useful, but not necessarily pertinent to the focus of their educational team. Dr. Bernhardt, in this work, brings focus to all of our data analysis efforts, a focus on what is important to bring about school improvement, a focus on what will bring results in our quality programs, a focus on the real challenges and opportunities, and a focus on what really can effect positive change.

This fine set of works touches the needs of numerous individuals in the education network, from the teacher who needs to understand the demographics and capabilities of her/his individual students to school principals, counselors, instructional coordinators, testing and data analysis coordinators, district researchers, and certainly the district executives. By virtue of her excellent skills, Dr. Bernhardt has given everyone in education, including the non-technologists among us, the opportunity to benefit from this fine edition. I encourage your reading of this newest edition to the library of Dr. Bernhardt's works and welcome you to embrace the passion of improving education by making objective education-enhancement decisions. Enjoy this wonderful rich material and let it drive all of us to focus on our future—our children.

Martin S. Brutosky
Chairman and CEO
TetraData Corporation
150 Executive Center Drive
Box 127
Greenville, SC 29615
Tel: 864-458-8243
http://www.tetradata.com

Preface

With the enactment of *No Child Left Behind,* every school and district in the country need to analyze their data to ensure adequate yearly progress. Sometimes, looking at another's analyses makes it easier to see things you would not have seen while looking only at your own analyses.

When it comes to analyzing student achievement data, the first two questions educators ask are *Now that we have the data, what analyses should we make?* and *What do the analyses tell us?*

These questions are hard to answer on the spot, so I have taken up the challenge to develop a series of books with the purposes of showing what analyses can be made, describing what these analyses are telling us, and illustrating how to use these analyses in continuous school improvement planning. This series of books includes:

▼ *Using Data to Improve Student Learning in Elementary Schools*

▼ *Using Data to Improve Student Learning in Middle Schools*

▼ *Using Data to Improve Student Learning in High Schools*

▼ *Using Data to Improve Student Learning in School Districts*

I believe that most of the time we must look at K-12 data (district level) to ensure a continuum of learning that makes sense for all students. I have purposefully separated building levels so there would be ample space to do a fairly comprehensive job of data analysis at each organizational level and to make the point about needing to understand results beyond one school level.

Each of these four publications uses real data (with some slight alterations to blur identities and to fill gaps where data are missing) and shows the actual descriptive analyses I would perform if I were the person analyzing the data at that particular level. You will see that no matter how much or how little *data* your school or district has, the *data* can tell the story. The study questions at the end of each chapter serve as guides for the reader. I have described what I saw in the analyses following the study questions for readers who want the feedback.

My goal with this book is for anyone to be able to set up these analyses, regardless of the statistical resources available. Therefore, in addition to showing the analyses in the text, the graphing templates, complete narratives, and supplementary tools appear on the accompanying CD.

Intended Audiences

This book is intended for school and district teachers and administrators who want to use data to continuously improve what they do for children; and for college and university professors who teach school administrators, teachers, and support personnel how to analyze school data. It is my belief that all professional educators must learn how to use data in this time of high-stakes accountability. I also believe that these practical and descriptive analyses are more important for practitioners to learn to perform than inferential statistics.

My hope is that you will find this book and the CD to be helpful as you think through the analyses of *your* data to improve learning for all students.

Victoria L. Bernhardt
Executive Director, *Education for the Future Initiative*
400 West First Street, Chico, CA 95929-0230
Tel: 530-898-4482 — Fax: 530-898-4484
e-mail: vbernhardt@csuchico.edu
website: *http://eff.csuchico.edu*

> *Schools that use data understand the effectiveness of their reform efforts; those that do not use data can only assume that effectiveness.*

Schools that gather, analyze, and use information about their school communities make better decisions, not only about what to change but also how to institutionalize systemic change. Schools that understand the needs of their primary customers—the students—are more successful in planning changes and remain more focused during implementation. Schools that simply gather, but make no sustained effort to analyze and use, data, are at a substantial disadvantage. Schools that use data understand the effectiveness of their reform efforts; those that do not use data can only assume that effectiveness.

Schools committed to improving student learning analyze data in order to plan for the future through understanding—

▼ the ways in which the school and the community have changed and are continuing to change

▼ the current and future needs of the students, parents, teachers, school, and community

▼ how well current processes meet these customers' needs

▼ if all subgroups of students are being well-served

▼ the gaps between the results the school is getting and the results it wants

▼ the root causes for the gaps

▼ the types of education programs, expertise, and process adjustments that will be needed to alleviate the gaps and to meet the needs of all customers

▼ how well the new processes being implemented meet the needs of the students, parents, teachers, school, and community

The Importance of Data

Businesses typically use data to determine customers' wants and needs. No matter what occupation we, or our students, aspire to, everyone can appreciate that fact. We can also appreciate the fact that businesses not properly analyzing and using data, more often than not, are not successful. Those of us who work in the business of education, however, may not be as familiar with the ways that *businesses* use *educational* data.

In many states, the prison systems look at the number of students not reading on grade level in grades two, three, or four to determine the number of prison cells to build ten years hence (*Lawmakers Move to Improve Literacy,* 2001). The fact that the prison system can use this prediction formula with great accuracy should make us all cringe, but the critical point is that if businesses can use educational data for predictions, so can educators. Not only can we predict, we can use the same data to *prevent* undesirable results from happening. Nothing would make educators happier than to hear that prison systems do not need as many cells because more students are being successful in school and, therefore, in life.

Schools in the United States have a long history of adopting innovations one after another as they are introduced. Very few schools take the time to understand the needs of the children being served. Few take the time to understand the impact current processes have on these children. Few take the time to determine the root causes of recurring problems, or to measure and analyze the impact of implementing new approaches. Fewer still use sound information to build and stick with a solid long-term plan that will improve learning for all students. Across our country, we have found that schools spend an average of about two years engaged in their school improvement efforts. The sad fact is that most schools are already changing their plans before some schools in their district start implementing all plans. Is it any wonder that nothing seems to generate results for these schools?

We find a different story among the schools that measure and analyze the impact of implementing new approaches. These schools know if what they are doing is working, and if not, why not. These schools also stick with their efforts to create change long after most schools have switched to new efforts. These schools get results.

Using data can make an enormous difference in school reform efforts by improving school processes and student learning. Data can help to—

▼ replace hunches and hypotheses with facts concerning what changes are needed

▼ facilitate a clear understanding of the gaps between where the school is and where the school wants to be

▼ identify the root causes of these gaps, so the school can solve the problem and not just treat the symptom

▼ understand the impact of processes on the student population

▼ ensure equity in program participation

▼ assess needs to target services on important issues

▼ provide information to eliminate ineffective practices

▼ ensure the effective and efficient uses of dollars

▼ show if school goals and objectives are being accomplished

▼ ascertain if the school staffs are *walking the talk*

> *If businesses can use educational data for predictions, so can educators. Not only can we predict, we can use the same data to "prevent" undesirable results from happening.*

▼ promote understanding of the impact of efforts, processes, and progress

▼ generate answers for the community related to: *What are we getting for our children by investing in the school's methods, programs, and processes?*

▼ continuously improve all aspects of the learning organization

▼ predict and prevent failures

▼ predict and ensure successes

Barriers to Using Data

Schools do not deliberately ignore data. Typically, schools say, "We have lots of data; we just do not know what data to use, or how or when to use them." When school personnel first get interested in data and want to do more with the data they have, they often hit the proverbial brick wall.

While many schools gather data, barriers begin with attempts to analyze the data to help improve teaching and learning. Barriers can pop-up anywhere and for a variety of reasons:

▼ In contrast to the work culture in business, the work culture in education usually focuses on programs, and not results data.

▼ Few people in schools and districts are adequately trained to gather and analyze data or to establish and maintain databases.

  ◆ Teachers (and administrators, who are mostly former teachers) have not been trained in data analysis

  ◆ Some teachers see data analysis as another thing that takes away from teaching

▼ Administrators and teachers do not see gathering and analyzing data as part of their jobs.

  ◆ District personnel have job definitions that often do not include, as a priority, helping individual schools with data.

▼ Gathering data is perceived to be a waste of time (after all, we are here every day—we know what the problems are!).

▼ Schools do not have databases that allow for easy access and analysis of data.

  ◆ Computer systems are outdated and inadequate; appropriate, user-friendly software is not available.

- ▼ Professional development for teachers to understand why data are important and how data can make a difference in their teaching is often sorely lacking.

- ▼ Data are not used systematically from the state to the regional and local levels, nor are they used particularly well.

   - ◆ State legislatures keeps changing the rules.

- ▼ School personnel have had only negative experiences with data.

   - ◆ There is a perception that data are collected for someone else's purposes.

   - ◆ Confusion exists regarding which data should be the focus of analyses.

- ▼ There are not enough good examples of schools gathering, maintaining, and benefiting from the use of data.

Whatever it is that keeps us from assessing our progress and products adequately, we must learn to listen, to observe, and to gather data from all sources that will help us *know* how we are doing, where we are going, and how we can get there.

The Purposes of this Book

This book has three purposes. The first is to provide a learning opportunity for readers. The analyses provided in these chapters are laboratories for learning—authentic tasks, if you will. The analyses are case studies, complete with study questions. The second and main purpose is to show real analyses, using a continuous school improvement planning model, that can be used to understand, explain, and continuously improve learning for students in middle schools. The third purpose is to provide tools to do these analyses with your school or district. The analysis tools are found on the accompanying CD.

The Structure of this Book

Using Data to Improve Student Learning in Middle Schools begins with an overview of why data are important to continuous school improvement. Chapter 2 defines what data are important to have in comprehensive data analysis. It also discusses the intersections of four major data measures in terms of different levels of analyses that can be created using these measures. Chapter 3 describes how to get started and how data fit into a continuous school improvement planning model. Chapters 4 through 7 present an example school analysis using this continuous school improvement planning model, and show how the model assists in understanding what the school is doing that is working or not working for its students.

Chapter 4 focuses on the example school's demographic data to answer the question, *Who are we?*, and to establish the context of the school.

Chapter 5 uses the example school's perceptions and process data to answer the question, *How do we do business?*, in terms of its work culture and organizational climate.

Where are we now? is the heart of Chapter 6. Ways to measure student learning are defined; analyses that can be made with different measures and their uses are discussed in this chapter. The example school's data assist us with understanding how to analyze state assessment results.

Chapter 7 discusses and shows gap and root cause analyses, answering the questions, *What are the gaps?* and *What are the root causes of the gaps?*

Chapter 8 synthesizes the analyses conducted in Chapters 4 through 7 and provides implications for the example school's continuous school improvement plan. A plan that grew out of this data analysis example is shown.

Questions to guide the study of the information presented in the chapters are included at the end of chapters 2 through 8, followed by the author's analyses. These files are also found on the CD.

Chapter 9 provides a brief summary and discussion of the example school's results. As the book concludes, typical process issues, such as *who does the analysis work, the role of the administrator, databases,* and *recommendations on how to get student learning increases* are discussed.

The questionnaires, the *Continuous Improvement Continuums,* and related tools used by the example school are found on the CD, along with complete analyses, analysis templates, and questionnaire narratives, as well as other *Education for the Future* questionnaires. Whenever appears in the text, it means that file is on the CD. The specific name of the file (in parenthesis) follows the CD icon. A list of CD files related to each chapter appears at the end of the chapter. A complete index of CD contents appears in the Appendix.

A comprehensive *Glossary of Terms* commonly used in data analysis and assessment, and other terms used in this book, is located just before the references and resources list.

Summary

Using Data to Improve Student Learning in Middle Schools illustrates the basic steps in conducting data analysis to inform continuous school improvement planning in middle schools. Readers will understand what data to gather, how to analyze the data, what the analyses look like, and how the analyses can inform a school's continuous school improvement plan. Tools to help any school do this work, regardless of grade levels, are provided on the accompanying CD.

> *Learning takes place neither in isolation, nor only at school. Multiple measures must be considered and used to understand the multifaceted world of learning from the perspective of everyone involved.*

If the purpose of school is to ensure that all students learn, what data will help schools understand if they are effectively carrying out their purpose? What data analyses will help schools know if all students are learning?

Learning takes place neither in isolation, nor only at school. Multiple measures must be considered and used in an ongoing fashion (formative) to understand the multifaceted world of learning from the perspective of everyone involved. Using more than one method of assessment allows students to demonstrate their full range of abilities, and collecting data on *multiple occasions* provides students several opportunities to demonstrate their various abilities. If you want to know if the school is achieving its purpose and how to continually improve all aspects of the school, multiple measures—gathered from varying points of view—must be used.

The major job of every school is *student learning.* Staff must think through the factors that impact student learning to determine other data requirements. We need to ask students what they like about the way they learn at school and how they learn best. *School processes,* such as programs and instructional strategies, need to be described to understand their impact in helping all staff optimize the learning of all students.

Because students neither learn only at school nor only through teachers, we need to know about the learning environment from the parent and community perspective. Schools may also need to know employer perceptions of the abilities and skills of former students.

But will these data provide enough information to determine how well the school is meeting the needs of all students? Other factors over which we have little or no control, such as background or *demographics,* impact student learning. These data are crucial to our understanding of whom we serve, and whether or not our educational services are meeting the needs of every student.

Analyses of *demographics, perceptions, student learning,* and *school processes* provide a powerful picture that will help us understand the school's impact on student achievement. When used together, these measures give schools the information they need to improve teaching and learning and to get positive results.

In Figure 2.1, these four major categories of data are shown as overlapping circles. (MMgraphic.pdf) This figure illustrates the different types of information one can gain from individual measures and the enhanced levels of analyses that can be gained from the intersections of the measures.

Figure 2.1

Multiple Measures of Data

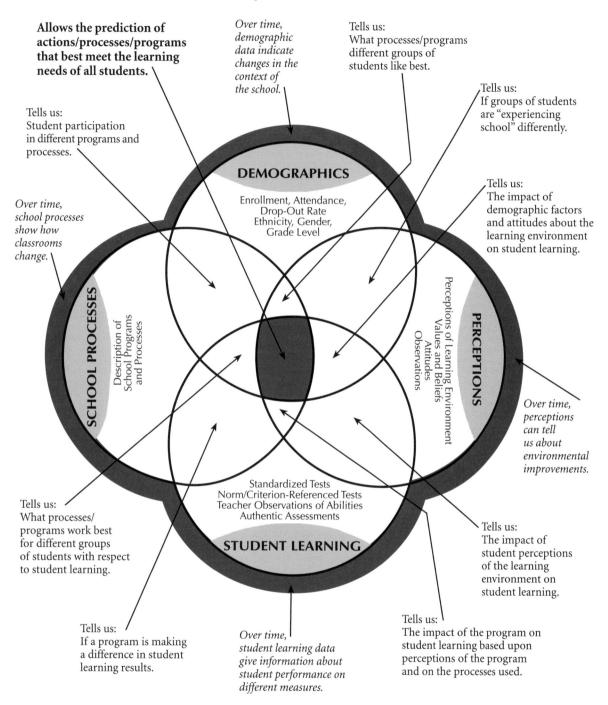

Allows the prediction of actions/processes/programs that best meet the learning needs of all students.

Over time, demographic data indicate changes in the context of the school.

Tells us: What processes/programs different groups of students like best.

Tells us: If groups of students are "experiencing school" differently.

Tells us: Student participation in different programs and processes.

Tells us: The impact of demographic factors and attitudes about the learning environment on student learning.

Over time, school processes show how classrooms change.

DEMOGRAPHICS

Enrollment, Attendance, Drop-Out Rate Ethnicity, Gender, Grade Level

SCHOOL PROCESSES

Description of School Programs and Processes

Perceptions of Learning Environment Values and Beliefs Attitudes Observations

PERCEPTIONS

Over time, perceptions can tell us about environmental improvements.

Standardized Tests
Norm/Criterion-Referenced Tests
Teacher Observations of Abilities
Authentic Assessments

STUDENT LEARNING

Tells us: What processes/ programs work best for different groups of students with respect to student learning.

Tells us: The impact of student perceptions of the learning environment on student learning.

Tells us: If a program is making a difference in student learning results.

Over time, student learning data give information about student performance on different measures.

Tells us: The impact of the program on student learning based upon perceptions of the program and on the processes used.

Copyright © 1991-2004 Education for the Future Initiative, Chico, CA.

If staffs want to know if the school is achieving its purpose and how to continually improve all aspects of the school, multiple measures—gathered from varying points of view—must be used.

One measure, by itself, gives useful information. Comprehensive measures, used together and over time, provide much richer information. Ultimately, schools need to be able to predict what they must do to meet the needs of all the students they have, or will have in the future. The information gleaned from the intersections of these four measures (demographics, perceptions, student learning, and school processes), helps us to define the questions we want to ask, and focuses us on what data are necessary in order to find the answers.

Levels of Analysis

Different levels of analysis reveal answers to questions at varying depths of understanding. Each of the four measures, on its own, gives valuable descriptive information. However, more and better quality information can be found by digging deeper into the data through different levels of analysis in which one type of measure is analyzed and compared with other measures, over time.

We will discuss ten levels of analysis. Each level builds on the previous one to show how past data and intersections of measures provide more comprehensive information than a single measure of data taken one time. If you feel you are only at level one, hang in there; this book and your own work will help you get to level ten.

Note: Unless otherwise specified, *over time* refers to no less than three years. Definitions of terms appear in the Glossary at the back of the book.

Level 1: Snapshots of Measures

Level one refers to the four major measures of data, shown in Figure 2.1, in their current state and independent of each other.

Demographic data provide descriptive information about the school community, such as enrollment, attendance, grade level, ethnicity, gender, and native language. Demographic data are the part of our educational system over which we have no control. From them, however, we can observe trends and glean information for purposes of prediction and planning. Demographic data give us a glimpse of the system and how the school organizes its system.

Perceptions data help us understand what students, parents, staff, and others think about the learning environment. Perceptions can be gathered through questionnaires, interviews, focus groups, and/or observations. Perceptions are important because peoples' actions reflect what they believe, perceive, or think about different topics. Perceptions data can also tell us what is possible.

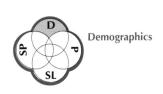
Demographics

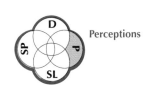
Perceptions

Student Learning describes the outcomes of our educational system in terms of standardized test results, grade point averages, standards assessments, and authentic assessments. Schools often use a variety of student learning measurements separately, sometimes without thinking about how these measurements are interrelated. Schools normally think of multiple measures as looking only at different measures of student learning, rather than including demographics, perceptions, and school processes.

School Processes define what we are doing to help students learn: how we group, teach, and assess students. School processes include programs, instruction and assessment strategies, and other classroom practices. To change the results schools are getting, teachers and school personnel must document these processes and align them with the results they are getting in order to understand what to improve to get different results, and to share their successes with others.

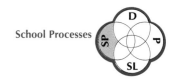

Looking at each of the four measures separately, we get snapshots of data in isolation from any other data at the school level. At this level we can answer questions such as—

▼ How many students are enrolled in the school this year? *(Demographics)*

▼ How satisfied are parents, students, and/or staff with the learning environment? *(Perceptions)*

▼ How did students at the school score on a test? *(Student Learning)*

▼ What programs are operating in the school this year? *(School Processes)*

Level 2: Measures, Over Time

At the second level, we start digging deeper into each of the measures by looking *over time* (i.e., at least three years) to answer questions, such as, but not limited to—

▼ How has enrollment in the school changed over the past five years? *(Demographics)*

▼ How have student perceptions of the learning environment changed, over time? *(Perceptions)*

▼ Are there differences in student scores on standardized tests over the years? *(Student Learning)*

▼ What programs have operated in the school during the past five years? *(School Processes)*

Different levels of analysis reveal answers to questions at varying depths of understanding.

Level 3: Two or More Variables Within Measures

Looking at *more than one type of data* within each of the circles gives us a better view of the learning organization (e.g., one year's standardized test subscores compared with performance assessment measures). We can answer questions such as—

▼ What percentage of the students currently at the school are fluent speakers of languages other than English? *(Demographics)*

▼ Are staff, student, and parent perceptions of the learning environment in agreement? *(Perceptions)*

▼ Are students' standardized test scores consistent with teacher-assigned grades and performance assessment rubrics? *(Student Learning)*

▼ What are the processes in the school's mathematics and science programs? *(School Processes)*

Level 4: Two or More Variables Within One Type of Measure, Over Time

Level 4 takes similar measures as Level 3, *across time* (e.g., standardized test subscores and performance assessment measures compared over the past four years), and allows us to answer deeper questions such as—

▼ How has the enrollment of non-English-speaking seventh graders changed in the past three years? *(Demographics)*

▼ Are staff, students, and parents more or less satisfied with the learning environment now than they were in previous years? *(Perceptions)*

▼ Over the past three years, how do teacher-assigned grades and standardized test scores compare? *(Student Learning)*

▼ How have the processes used in the school's mathematics and science programs changed over time? *(School Processes)*

Level 5: Intersection of Two Types of Measures

Level 5 begins the *intersections across two circles* (e.g., last year's standardized test results by ethnicity). Level 5 helps us to answer questions such as—

Demographics by
Student Learning

▼ Do students who attend school every day perform better on the state assessment than students who miss more than five days per month? *(Demographics by Student Learning)*

▼ How long does it take for non-English-speaking students to be redesignated as fluent English speakers? *(Demographics by School Processes)*

Demographics by
School Processes

▼ Is there a gender difference in students' perceptions of the learning environment? *(Perceptions by Demographics)*

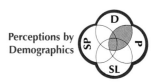

Perceptions by
Demographics

▼ Do students with positive attitudes about school do better academically, as measured by the state assessment? *(Perceptions by Student Learning)*

▼ Are there differences in how students enrolled in different programs perceive the learning environment? *(Perceptions by School Processes)*

Perceptions by
Student Learning

▼ Do students identified as gifted get the highest scores on the state standardized test? *(Student Learning by School Processes)*

Level 6: Intersection of Two Measures, Over Time

Looking at the *intersection of two of the measures over time* allows us to see trends as they develop (e.g., standardized achievement scores disaggregated by ethnicity over the past three years can help us see if the differences between scores, by ethnicity, is truly a trend or an initial fluctuation). This intersection also begins to show the relationship of the multiple measures and why it is so important to look at all the measures together.

Perceptions by
School Processes

Student Learning by
School Processes

At Level 6 we are looking at the intersection of two of the circles over time. The questions we can answer at this level include, as examples—

▼ How have students of different ethnicities scored on standardized tests over the past three years? *(Demographics by Student Learning)*

▼ Are all subgroups of students represented in special education, Title I, and gifted classes? *(Demographics by School Processes)*

▼ Have parent perceptions of the learning environment changed since the implementation of the new mathematics program? *(Perceptions by School Processes)*

Level 7: Intersection of Three Measures

As we *intersect three of the measures* at the school level (e.g., student learning measures disaggregated by ethnicity compared to student questionnaire responses disaggregated by ethnicity), the types of questions that we are able to answer include the following:

Demographics by Perceptions by Student Learning

Perceptions by Demographics by School Processes

Perceptions by Student Learning by School Processes

School Processes by Student Learning by Demographics

▼ Do students of different ethnicities perceive the learning environment differently, and are their scores on standardized achievement tests consistent with these perceptions? (*Demographics by Perceptions by Student Learning*)

▼ What instructional process(es) did the students who were redesignated from English-learners to English-speaking enjoy most in their all-English classrooms this year? (*Perceptions by Demographics by School Processes*)

▼ Is there a difference in students' reports of what they like most about the school by whether or not they participate in extracurricular activities? Do students who participate in extracurricular activities have higher grade-point averages than students who do not participate in extracurricular activities? (*Perceptions by Student Learning by School Processes*)

▼ Which program is making the biggest difference with respect to student achievement for at-risk students this year, and is one group of students responding "better" to the processes? (*School Processes by Student Learning by Demographics*)

Level 8: Intersection of Three Measures, Over Time

Looking at *three measures over time* allows us to see trends, to begin to understand the learning environment from the students' perspectives, and to know how to deliver instruction to get the desired results from and for *all* students.

Level 8 takes Level 7 intersections over time (e.g., standardized achievement scores disaggregated by ethnicity compared to student questionnaires disaggregated by ethnicity, for the past four years). Level 8 allows us to answer the following types of questions:

▼ What programs do all types of students like the most every year? (*Demographics by Perceptions by School Processes*)

▼ Have the processes used to teach English to English-learning students been consistent across grade levels so each student is able to build on her/his abilities? (*Demographics by Student Learning by School Processes*)

Level 9: Intersection of All Four Measures

Our ultimate analysis is the *intersection of all four measures* at the school level (e.g., standardized achievement tests disaggregated by program, by gender, within grade level, compared to questionnaire results for students by program, by gender, within grade level). These intersections allow us to answer questions such as—

▼ Given the population that attends this school, are our programs and strategies meeting their needs in every grade level, as measured by student learning results and everyone's perspective? *(Demographics by Perceptions by School Processes by Student Learning)*

Demographics by
Perceptions by
School Processes by
Student Learning

Level 10: Intersection of All Four Measures, Over Time

It is not until we *intersect all four circles,* at the school level and *over time,* that we are able to answer questions that will predict if the actions, processes, and programs that we are establishing will meet the needs of all students. With this intersection, we can answer the ultimate question:

▼ Based on whom we have as students, how they prefer to learn, and what programs they are in, are all students learning at the same rate? *(Student Learning by Demographics by Perceptions by School Processes)*

Do note that there might not always be a way to display these intersections in one comprehensive table or graph. Often, multiple graphs and/or tables are used together to observe intersection relationships.

It is important to look at each measure by itself to understand where the school is right now and over time. Intersecting the measures can give a broader look at the data and help everyone understand all facets of the school. Figure 2.2 summarizes two, three, and four-way intersections. 💿 (IntrscTbl.pdf) On the CD are a *Data Discovery Activity* and two activities for creating questions from intersecting data, *Intersections Activity* and *Creating Intersections Activity.* 💿 (ACTDiscv.pdf, ACTIntrs.pdf, and ACTCreat.pdf) Also on the CD are the *Data Analysis Presentation,* a *Microsoft PowerPoint* slideshow overview to use with your staffs in getting started analyzing your data, and three articles entitled *Multiple Measures* (Bernhardt, 1998), *Intersections: New Routes Open when One Type of Data Crosses Another* (Bernhardt, 2000), and *No Schools Left Behind* (Bernhardt, 2003). 💿 (DASlides.ppt, MMeasure.pdf, Intersct.pdf, and NoSchls.pdf)

Figure 2.2

Summary of Data Intersections

Intersections	Can tell us —
Two-way Intersections	
• Demographics by student learning	• If subgroups of students perform differently on student learning measures
• Demographics by perceptions	• If subgroups of students are experiencing school differently
• Demographics by school processes	• If all subgroups of students are represented in the different programs and processes offered by the school
• Student learning by school processes	• If different programs are achieving similar student learning results
• Student learning by perceptions	• If student perceptions of the learning environment have an impact on their learning results
• Perceptions by school processes	• If people are perceiving programs and processes differently
Three-way Intersections	
• Demographics by student learning by perceptions	• The impact demographic factors and attitudes about the learning environment have on student learning
• Demographics by student learning by school processes	• What processes or programs work best for different subgroups of students measured by student learning results
• Demographics by perceptions by school processes	• What programs or processes different students like best, or the impact different programs or processes have on student attitudes
• Student learning by school processes by perceptions	• The relationship between the processes students prefer and learning results
Four-way Intersections	
• Demographics by student learning by perceptions by school processes	• What processes or programs have the greatest impact on subgroups of students' learning, according to student perceptions, and as measured by student learning results

Focusing the Data

Data analysis should not be about just gathering data. It is very easy to get *analysis paralysis* by spending time pulling data together and not spending time using the data. School-level data analyses should be about helping schools understand if they are achieving their guiding principles and meeting the needs of all students—and, if not, why not?

The guiding principles include the vision, created from the mission/purpose of the school and built from the values and beliefs of the school community, and standards—what we expect students to know and be able to do. Data analysis must focus on these guiding principles.

A focused data analysis process will enhance the continuous improvement process and provide comprehensive information about how the school is doing in relationship to its guiding principles.

A good way to avoid analysis paralysis is to consider using key questions that focus on the guiding principles, using the answers to these questions to guide your analyses.

The key questions used in this book are described in Chapter 3. The data we gather and analyze target the guiding principles of the school to achieve focused improvement. If this was not the case, the process could lead to nothing more than random acts of improvement, as shown in Figure 2.3.

> *Data analysis should not be about just gathering data. It is very easy to get "analysis paralysis" by spending time pulling data together and not spending time using the data.*

Figure 2.3
Focusing the Data

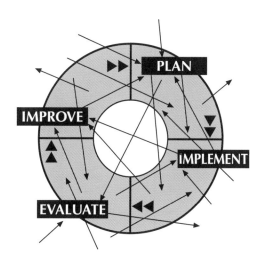

Random Acts of Improvement

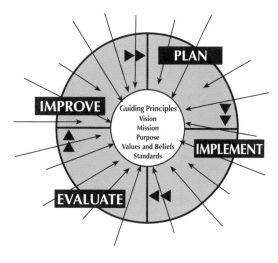

Focused Improvement

These analyses flow comfortably from questions that staff and administrators naturally ask to learn if the purpose is being met. The good news is that, by looking at trends of the intersected four measures, schools will have the same information required of program evaluations and needs analyses. These intersections can tell schools just about everything they would want to know, and the intersections are easy for everyone to understand.

Study Questions for What Data Are Important?

As mentioned previously, the study questions at the end of the chapters are intended to guide your thinking about your own data analysis and/or to analyze the example school's results. (Ch2Qs.pdf) Take some time to consider these or other questions to get the maximum benefit from this publication.

Consider how you might identify intersections in your school's data and what those intersections could tell you. Use the spaces below to write at least one question you can answer about your school with these intersections, and what data you need to answer these questions. (Examples appear in the table to get you started.)

Intersections	Questions	What data do you have or need to answer the questions?
Demographics by Student Learning	*Is there a relationship between attendance and standardized test results?*	*Number of days attended and state standardized test results for each student.*
Demographics by School Processes	*Is participation in the gifted program representative of all students?*	*Gifted enrollment by gender, ethnicity, and indicators of poverty.*

Study Questions for What Data Are Important? *(Continued)*

Intersections	Questions	What data do you have or need to answer the questions?
Perceptions by Demographics	*Are all students perceiving the learning environment in the same way?*	*Student questionnaire results disaggregated by gender, by ethnicity, and/or by grade level.*
Perceptions by Student Learning	*Are the students who are getting the best grades the happiest with the learning environment?*	*Student grades by student perceptions.*
Perceptions by School Processes	*Are there differences in how students perceive the learning environment, based on whom they have as teachers?*	*Student perceptions disaggregated by teacher.*

Intersections	Questions	What data do you have or need to answer the questions?
Student Learning by School Processes	*Is there a difference in student achievement results by program participation?*	*Student achievement test results by program.*
Demographics by Perceptions by Student Learning	*What are the differences in student learning results based on whom we have as students and how they perceive the learning environment?*	*Student achievement test results disaggregated by gender and ethnicity, compared to student questionnaire results disaggregated by gender and ethnicity.*
Perceptions by Demographics by School Processes	*Are the students most satisfied with school being taught differently from students not satisfied with school, and who are they?*	*Student questionnaires disaggregated by gender, ethnicity, grade level, and program participation.*

Intersections	Questions	What data do you have or need to answer the questions?
Perceptions by Student Learning by School Processes	*What are the differences in student achievement results because of attitudes related to whom students have as teachers?*	*Student achievement results disaggregated by teacher, compared to student questionnaire results disaggregated by teacher.*
Demographics by Student Learning by School Processes	*What are the differences in student learning results based on who the students are and how they are taught algebra?*	*Student achievement algebra results, disaggregated by gender and ethnicity, and sorted by what program they are in and whom they have as a teacher.*
Student Learning by Demographics by Perceptions by School Processes	*What are the differences in the results we are getting, based on whom we have as students and how they are being taught? How would they prefer to learn?*	*Student achievement results, disaggregated by gender, ethnicity, grade level, and program, compared to student questionnaire results, disaggregated by gender, ethnicity, grade level, and program.*

Summary

Schools cannot use student achievement measures alone for continuous school improvement. Why? Because the *context* is missing! Relying on only one measure can mislead schools into thinking they are analyzing student learning in a comprehensive fashion. Just looking at student learning measures alone could, in fact, keep teachers from progressing and truly meeting the needs of students because they are not looking at the other elements that have a great impact on student learning and teaching.

If we want to get different results, we have to change the processes (e.g., instruction, system) that create the results. When we focus only on student learning measures, we see school personnel using their time figuring out how to look better on the student learning measures. We want school personnel to use their time to determine how to *do* better for *all* students. In order to do that, we must look at intersections of *demographic, perceptual, student learning,* and *school process* data, so we can understand the inter-relationships among these elements.

Just looking at student learning measures alone could, in fact, keep teachers from progressing and truly meeting the needs of students, because they are not looking at the other elements that have a great impact on student learning and teaching.

On the CD Related to this Chapter

▼ *Multiple Measures of Data* Graphic (MMgraphc.pdf)
This is Figure 2.1 in a PDF (portable document file) for printing.

▼ *Summary of Data Intersections* (IntrscTbl.pdf)
This is Figure 2.2 in a PDF for your use with staff.

▼ *Data Discovery Activity* (ACTDiscv.pdf)
The purpose of this activity is to look closely at examples of data and to discover specific information and patterns of information, both individually and as a group.

▼ *Intersections Activity* (ACTIntrs.pdf)
The purpose of this activity is to motivate school improvement teams to think about the questions they can answer when they cross different data variables. It is also designed to help teams focus their data-gathering efforts so they are not collecting everything and anything.

▼ *Creating Intersections Activity* (ACTCreat.pdf)
This activity is similar to the *Intersections Activity.* The purpose is to have participants "grow" their intersections.

▼ *Data Analysis* Presentation (DASlides.ppt)
This *Microsoft PowerPoint* presentation is an overview to use with your staffs in getting started with data analysis.

▼ Articles (Folder)
These read-only articles, by Victoria L. Bernhardt, are useful in workshops or in getting started on data with staff.

♦ *Multiple Measures* (MMeasure.pdf)
This article summarizes why, and what, data are important to continuous school improvement.

♦ *Intersections: New Routes Open when One Type of Data Crosses Another* (Intersct.pdf)
This article, published in the *Journal of Staff Development* (Winter 2000), discusses how much richer your data analyses can be when you intersect multiple data variables.

♦ *No Schools Left Behind* (NoSchls.pdf)
This article, published in *Educational Leadership* (February 2003), summarizes how to improve learning for *all* students.

▼ Study Questions Related to *What Data are Important?* (Ch2Qs.pdf)
These study questions will help you better understand the information provided in Chapter 2. This file can be printed for use with staff as they think through the data questions they want to answer and the data they will need to gather to answer the questions.

Getting Started
On Data Analysis for Continuous School Improvement

Chapter 3

> *We want to gather and analyze data that will help us understand the system that produces the results we are getting. We also want to move our school improvement efforts from random acts of improvement to focused improvement that centers on our ultimate purpose—improving learning for all students.*

How does a school get started with comprehensive data analysis work? How do you and others at your school know if what you are currently doing for students is making a difference with respect to what you expect students to know and be able to do? How do you know which strategies ought to be the focus of your school improvement efforts?

If your school is like 95% of the schools in this country, my hunch is that your school improvement committee looks at student results on the state student assessment, attempts to explain the results to the school board and to the public, and then prepares school improvement plans to get better results next year. Your school might have special externally funded grants or programs that require the collection and analysis of data. Those who are providing the funds want progress described. Questionnaires are then sent out each year and are analyzed *for the funders,* not for those who implement the programs.

At the classroom level, some teachers have adopted rubrics and performance assessment measures. They might know their students are learning, but performance assessment measures are not easy to talk about in terms of an entire class, let alone schoolwide, progress. It can be done, but it is difficult.

Unfortunately, the scenarios described above are all too familiar in schools across the United States. What is starting to emerge, however, is a connection between the analysis of data and the school improvement plan to ensure that every student is learning. We want to see data about all parts of the school gathered and analyzed on a regular basis—not just when an external force requires it. We want members of the school community to understand how to use data to accurately inform their customers and other individuals of how the school is doing. Finally, we especially want schools to analyze data to understand which strategies are not working and what to do differently to get different results.

This chapter describes a process for analyzing data to plan for continuous schoolwide improvement. Data analysis in schools may be approached in many ways, and the effectiveness of school processes may be measured in many ways. The approach taken here is a systems approach: we want to gather and analyze data that will help us understand the *system that produces the results we are getting.* We also want to move our school improvement efforts from random acts of improvement to focused improvement that centers on our ultimate purpose—improving learning for *all* students.

Analyzing Data Using a Continuous School Improvement Planning Model

Data analysis is very logical. We need to think about what we want to know and why, gather the data we have or need, and analyze the data to answer the questions that will lead to understanding not only the effectiveness of what we are doing, but also what we need to do differently to get different results.

One approach to data analysis is to analyze and use data for continuous school improvement planning. The *Multiple Measures of Data,* Figure 2.1 in Chapter 2, can be reorganized into a series of logical questions that can guide the analysis, as illustrated in the flowchart in Figure 3.1. If the data that are listed next to the questions in the boxes were gathered satisfactorily, one would be on the right track toward discovering how to continuously improve the school or district. Those questions, the data required, and discussion follow the flowchart.

Continuous School Improvement Planning via The School Portfolio

Figure 3.1 shows the logical questions one could ask to plan for continuous school improvement, the data needed to answer the questions, and where that data would be housed if a school was creating a school portfolio. (CSIPlang.pdf and CSIdscr.pdf) *The School Portfolio* is a framework for continuous school improvement (Bernhardt, 1999). Gathering evidence around the seven categories of a school portfolio results in the story of your school and becomes a self-assessment. The seven categories of a school portfolio are:

▼ Information and Analysis

▼ Student Achievement

▼ Quality Planning

▼ Professional Development

▼ Leadership

▼ Partnership Development

▼ Continuous Improvement and Evaluation

On the CD is a *Microsoft PowerPoint* slideshow overview file, *The School Portfolio Presentation,* to use with your staffs in getting started on the school portfolio. (SPSlides.ppt)

Figure 3.1

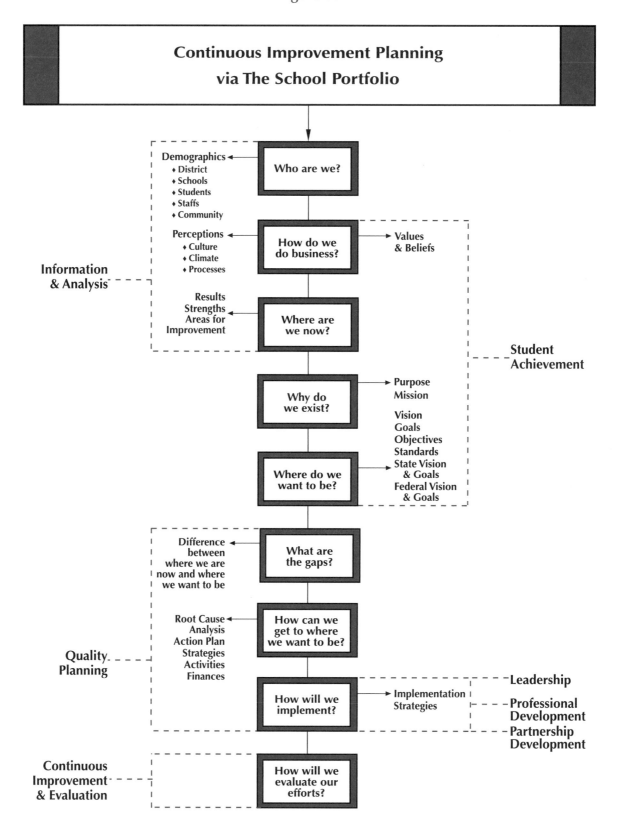

Continuous Improvement Planning
via The School Portfolio

Demographics
- District
- Schools
- Students
- Staffs
- Community

Who are we?

Perceptions
- Culture
- Climate
- Processes

How do we do business?

Values & Beliefs

Information & Analysis

Results Strengths Areas for Improvement

Where are we now?

Why do we exist?

Purpose
Mission

Vision
Goals
Objectives
Standards
State Vision & Goals
Federal Vision & Goals

Where do we want to be?

Student Achievement

Difference between where we are now and where we want to be

What are the gaps?

Root Cause Analysis
Action Plan
Strategies
Activities
Finances

How can we get to where we want to be?

Quality Planning

How will we implement?

Implementation Strategies

Leadership

Professional Development

Partnership Development

Continuous Improvement & Evaluation

How will we evaluate our efforts?

Question 1: Who are we?

Continuous school improvement planning begins by asking a question that can be answered with demographic data: *Who are we?* Specifically—

▼ *Who are the students?*

▼ *Who is the staff?*

▼ *Who is the community?*

The answers to the first questions are important in understanding the school's and district's students, staff, and community, to determine future needs. These answers are critical for continuous school improvement planning, as they establish the *context* of the classroom, school, district, and community. It is important to understand how student and community populations have changed over time, as these changes are indicators of student characteristics to plan for in the future. Staff longevity within the system and plans for retirement might lead to establishing different types of school improvement plans, as would staff experiences, certification, and levels of education. Demographic changes can also help explain results. This question is further studied in Chapter 4.

Question 2: How do we do business?

The second question, *How do we do business?*, is answered through data gathered to assess the school's culture, climate, and organizational processes. Perceptual data, school processes, and values and beliefs fall into this category. Staff values and beliefs, most often assessed through questionnaires and/or determined during visioning processes, can tell a staff what is possible to implement and if team building or specific professional development is necessary. Student and parent questionnaires can add different perspectives to the answers generated from staff data. An assessment on the *Education for the Future Continuous Improvement Continuums*[1] can provide an overview of where the staff believes the school is and where it can go, with respect to continuous school improvement. Chapter 5 reviews more on this question.

---

[1]*Note:* The *Education for the Future Continuous Improvement Continuums* (CICs) can be found in the back of this book (Appendix B) and on the accompanying CD. The CICs are a type of assessment criteria rubric made up of seven key, interrelated, and overlapping components of systemic change, representing the theoretical flow of systemic school and/or district improvement. The *Continuums* take the theory and spirit of continuous school improvement, interweave educational research, and offer practical meaning to the components that must change simultaneously and systemically. A CIC analysis appears in Chapter 5.

If you don't know
where you are going,
you could wind up
somewhere else.

Yogi Berra

Question 3: Where are we now?

The third data question, *Where are we now?*, requires a synthesis of student achievement, perceptual, demographic, and school process data to describe results and to uncover strengths and areas for improvement. We start by examining data for patterns and trends across the four multiple measures. Chapter 6 reviews the student achievement part of this question, including different types of student achievement assessments and terms associated with them.

Question 4: Why do we exist?

Question number four can be answered by determining the purpose/mission of the school. One can determine how well the school is meeting its purpose by revisiting the results collected in questions one through three. This question is answered in-depth in other resources, such as, *The School Portfolio* (Bernhardt, 1999), and *The School Portfolio Toolkit* (Bernhardt, 2002).

Question 5: Where do we want to be?

A school defines its destination through its vision, goals, and standards. The school's destination falls under the umbrella of the district's vision, goals, and standards which, in turn, are aligned with the state vision, goals, and standards. One can determine how effective the vision is being implemented through the data used to answer questions one through four. This question is answered in-depth in other resources, such as, *The School Portfolio* (Bernhardt, 1999), and *The School Portfolio Toolkit* (Bernhardt, 2002).

Question 6: What are the gaps?

Gaps are the differences between *Where are we now?* and *Where do we want to be?* Gaps are determined by synthesizing the differences in the results the school is getting with its current processes, and the results the school wants to be getting for its students. It is important to dig deeply into each gap to uncover root causes, or the gap cannot be eliminated. Gaps and root causes are studied in Chapter 7.

Question 7: How can we get to where we want to be?

The answer to *How can we get to where we want to be?* is key to unlocking how the vision will be implemented, and how gaps will be eliminated. An action plan, consisting of strategies, activities, people responsible, due dates, timelines, and resources, needs to be addressed to implement and achieve the vision and goals and to eliminate the root causes of the gaps. Chapter 8 shows how one can take the data analysis results and turn them into a continuous school improvement plan.

Question 8: How will we implement?

This question is answered in the action plan. The action plan includes how the vision will be implemented, monitored, evaluated, and improved. Action plans need to clarify how decisions will be made, identify professional development required to learn new skills and gain new knowledge, and clarify the use of partners to achieve the vision. A school's leadership structure, professional development strategies, and partnership development plan are important components of the answer to this question. Chapter 8 discusses what a plan would look like when it includes action for implementing, monitoring, evaluating, and improving the action plan.

Question 9: How will we evaluate our efforts?

Continuous Improvement and Evaluation are required to assess the alignment of all parts of the system to the vision and the results the learning organization is getting on an ongoing basis. All four data measures intersected to answer this question will assist with evaluating the continuously improving learning organization. Evaluation is a piece that needs to be built before implementation, not only at the end, to know if what a school is doing is making a real difference. How the action plan will be evaluated is a part of the plan which can be pulled out, enhanced, and monitored. This piece is described in Chapter 8.

The chapters that follow show how one school answered these questions with data as it conducted data analyses and built its continuous school improvement plan.

Study Questions for Getting Started

How will you get started with your school's continuous school improvement planning? What data do you have, or need to gather, to answer the questions discussed in this chapter? Fill in the blank cells in the tables that follow to guide your work. ⊙ (Ch3Qs.pdf) Examples appear in the table for guidance.

Questions	What data do you have or need to answer the questions?	What other data do you have or need to gather?
Who are we?	*Student enrollment by grade, by gender, by ethnicity, by free/reduced lunch status, for five years.* *Number of teachers; number of years teaching by what grade level(s) and/or subject(s) they teach; which credentials teachers hold.*	*Information about predicted community changes.* *Administrator information, such as number of years in current position, and number of years teaching.*
How do we do business?	*Perceptions: student, staff, parent, and former student questionnaires.* *Education for the Future Continuous Improvement Continuums Assessment.*	
Where are we now?	*Student achievement results.* *Process data.*	

Questions	What data do you have or need to answer the questions?	What other data do you have or need to gather?
Why do we exist?	*Mission statement.* *Purpose of the school.*	
Where do we want to be?	*Vision.* *Goals.*	
What are the gaps? What are the root causes?	*Targeted proficiency levels for each subject area.* *Number and percentage of students not proficient in each subject area.* *Characteristics of the students not meeting proficiency.* *How these students scored.* *What they know and do not know.* *How they were taught.*	

Study Questions for Getting Started *(Continued)*

Questions	What data do you have or need to answer the questions?	What other data do you have or need to gather?
How can we get to where we want to be?	*Interventions.* *Professional Development.* *Timeline.*	
How will we implement?	*Implementation strategies.* *Leadership structure.* *How we meet together to talk about the vision.*	
How will we evaluate our efforts?	*Rethinking our results data.* *Monitoring and evaluating the plan.* *Understanding the effectiveness of strategies already in place.*	

Summary

Schools that are not gathering, analyzing, and using data in purposeful ways need to transform their thinking about data and start gathering, analyzing, and using data purposefully. Comprehensive data analyses focused on the continuous improvement of the entire school will result in school improvement plans that will improve learning for all students.

Logical questions can be used to guide the gathering, analysis, and use of data. Recommended questions include:

▼ *Who are we?*

▼ *How do we do business?*

▼ *Where are we now?*

▼ *Why do we exist?*

▼ *Where do we want to be?*

▼ *What are the gaps?* and *What are the root causes?*

▼ *How can we get to where we want to be?*

▼ *How will we implement?*

▼ *How will we evaluate our efforts?*

> *Comprehensive data analyses focused on the continuous improvement of the entire learning organization will result in school improvement plans that will improve learning for all students.*

On the CD Related to this Chapter

▼ *Continuous School Improvement Planning via the School Portfolio* Graphic (CSIPlang.pdf)
This read-only file displays the questions that can be answered to create a continuous school improvement plan. The data that can answer the questions, and where the answers would appear in the school portfolio, also appear on the graphic. In the book, it is Figure 3.1.

▼ *Continuous School Improvement Planning via the School Portfolio* Description (CSIdscr.pdf)
This read-only file shows Figure 3.1, along with its description.

▼ *The School Portfolio Presentation* (SPSlides.ppt)
This *PowerPoint* presentation is an overview to use with your staffs in getting started on *The School Portfolio.*

▼ Study Questions Related to *Getting Started* (Ch3Qs.pdf)
These study questions will help you better understand the information provided in Chapter 3. This file can be printed for use with staffs as you begin continuous school improvement planning. Answering the questions will help staff determine the data needed to answer the questions discussed in this chapter.

Analyzing the Data:
Who Are We?

Chapter 4

> *Demographic data are required to answer the question, "Who are we?"*

Using the continuous school improvement planning model described in Chapter 3, our data analysis example begins with setting the context of the school by answering the question, *Who are we?* Demographic data are required to answer this question. Demographic data enable us to:

▼ *explain* and *understand* the school's context and results

▼ *disaggregate* other types of data, such as perceptual, process, and student learning data, to ensure all subgroups of students are being served

▼ *predict* and *prepare* for the students we will have in the near future

The demographic analyses for Azalea Middle School are on the pages that follow. Please note the study questions on page 57 to assist in studying the Azalea's data. (Ch4Qs.pdf) Also note that space is provided in the margins of the data pages to write your impressions about strengths, challenges, and implications for the school improvement plan as you review the data. It will help your work if you jot down your thoughts about what you are seeing in the data as you read. These first thoughts are placeholders until additional data validate the thoughts. When finished reading this chapter, think about other demographic data you wish the school would have had. At the end of the chapter, I share what I saw in the data. Graphing templates are found on the CD to help you create your school's demographic profile. (MiddDemog.xls, MiddDemog.doc, and MiddProfil.doc)

Our Example School: Azalea Middle School
Who Are We?

Azalea Middle School is a public school with grades six through eight located in Magnolia City, a metropolitan city in the South. Magnolia City is located in one of the state's most populous counties with more than 388,000 residents. Approximately 59,000 people live in 24,000 households within the city limits. Median household income is $34,435 per year. Average household income is $50,478. Of the total number of housing units in the city, 11,453 are owner-occupied and 12,929 are renter-occupied. Magnolia City is a key part of a super-regional urban corridor along an interstate highway. This area is consistently cited as one of the fastest growing urban regions in the United States. The median age of the population of this thriving city is 35.5 years. People 65 years of age and older total 44,573. According to the U.S. 2000 Census, the county's ethnic population consists of 77.7% White (n=294,324); 18.3% Black (n=69,455); 3.8% Hispanic/Latino (n=14,283); 1.4% Asian (n=5,242); and

1.5% Other (n=5,558). Magnolia City has traditionally maintained a low unemployment rate of around 4%. However, in November 2003, the unemployment rate was up to 6%. The community offers many potential resources. Several higher education institutions are within a forty-mile radius of the city. Two health care systems are located in the area. Railway transportation and the Magnolia City International Airport provide easy access. More than 240 international firms from 23 nations are located in Magnolia City, and nearly one-half of these firms have their international headquarters based in the county.

Great View School District

Azalea Middle School is part of the Great View School District, a consolidated, unified system formed in 1961 when many local school districts merged. Great View School District is widely recognized as a leader in education. The area served by the district covers 800 square miles and includes most of the county, in addition to portions of two nearby counties. Per capita income in the area served by the district is $22,081.

Great View School District currently serves 32,078 students in 45 schools: 28 elementary (K-5), 9 middle (6-8), 7 senior high (9-12), and several alternative programs. The district's current student enrollment is made up of 66% White, 27% Black, 5% Hispanic/Latino, 1% Asian, and less than one percent American Indian/Pacific Islander and Other students. The overall district enrollment has steadily increased over the past five years (Figure 4.1).

Figure 4.1

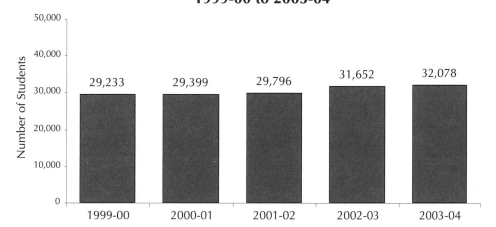

Great View School District Student Enrollment 1999-00 to 2003-04

The district enrollment by grade level for the past five years is shown in the table below (Figure 4.2).

Figure 4.2

Great View School District
Student Enrollment by Grade Level
1999-00 to 2003-04

Grade Level	1999-00 (n=29,233)	2000-01 (n=29,399)	2001-02 (n=29,796)	2002-03 (n=31,652)	2003-04 (n=32,078)
Kindergarten	2,794	2,685	2,770	2,743	2,399
Grade One	2,501	2,523	2,461	2,518	2,581
Grade Two	2,428	2,387	2,421	2,522	2,470
Grade Three	2,260	2,430	2,450	2,541	2,509
Grade Four	2,397	2,264	2,454	2,584	2,537
Grade Five	2,285	2,400	2,294	2,596	2,557
Grade Six	2,294	2,305	2,457	2,508	2,641
Grade Seven	2,260	2,286	2,291	2,565	2,543
Grade Eight	2,226	2,241	2,310	2,434	2,590
Grade Nine	2,582	2,622	2,632	2,864	3,045
Grade Ten	1,865	2,049	2,107	2,284	2,910
Grade Eleven	1,739	1,566	1,664	1,894	1,950
Grade Twelve	1,602	1,641	1,485	1,599	1,346

The School

Built in 1965, Azalea Middle School is one of 9 middle schools in the school district. The school currently houses 781 students in grades six through eight. Two administrators, 50 teachers, and 20 support personnel make up the staff. The facilities at Azalea consist of 39 classrooms, including 6 portable classrooms, a cafetorium, gymnasium, library, business computer lab, multimedia video production computer lab, art room with a kiln, drama room, and a dance studio. The school is undergoing major facilities upgrading which began in the 2003-04 school year.

Azalea Middle School is located in a quiet neighborhood within the city limits. For 35 years, the school has had a strong history of state and national awards for both excellence in education and outstanding accomplishments as it evolved from Azalea Junior High School to Azalea Middle School. Azalea combines a rigorous academic program with a strong arts education component for all students—the academically gifted, the artistically talented, the average learner, and those labeled at-risk. The comprehensive arts program provides students the opportunity to explore many art forms and to learn at least one art form well through advanced course offerings. Students can select introductory and advanced studies that include drama, dance, band, strings, choral and general music, and the visual arts. Additionally, students can select communication arts electives including computer technology, video production, creative writing, debate, world languages, journalism, and public speaking. Advanced courses require a portfolio or audition for students to be eligible for these year-long classes. Grants and Parent-Teacher Association (P.T.A.) funding provide additional monetary support for the arts program.

Great View School District has a school choice policy that allows parents to apply to enroll their children in a school other than the one to which they are assigned. Students who live in Azalea's attendance area are automatically enrolled in the school and do not need to apply for admission. Students living in the county, but outside the school's attendance area, are eligible to apply for admission. Sixty-five percent of Azalea's students are from the attendance area. The other 35% apply for admission.

Students transported by bus, from as far away as 30 miles, comprise 28.5% of the school population; walkers make up 2.5%, and the remaining 69% are transported by parent or ride in car pools. Bus students' attendance and punctuality are affected by delays and occasional failure of the bus to complete scheduled routes.

The number of applications each year indicates that interest has exceeded available seating capacity and has resulted in students' names being placed on lengthy waiting lists. New applications include students from private and public schools as well as home-schooled students. Students are admitted from the waiting list, as space becomes available up to the first day of the new school year. Additional portable classrooms were added in 2003 to accommodate approximately 60 additional students. The student body is composed of students from a wide range of socioeconomic levels as well as a variety of ethnic backgrounds. The present school population is composed of students drawn from a radius of 30 miles.

The Students

As Figure 4.3 shows, the number of students enrolled changed very little since 1999-00, until 2003-04, when the school population increased by 59 students, about 8%, from the previous year. Azalea's student enrollment is average for middle schools in the district.

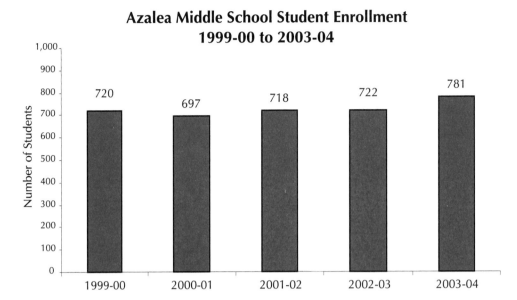

Figure 4.3

**Azalea Middle School Student Enrollment
1999-00 to 2003-04**

Azalea's population by gender shows more females than males overall, in every grade level, and for every year. Figure 4.4 shows the gender numbers and percentages, by grade level, over time.

Figure 4.4

**Azalea Middle School
Numbers and Percentages of Students Enrolled
By Grade Level and Gender, 1999-00 to 2003-04**

Grade Level	Gender	1999-00		2000-01		2001-02		2002-03		2003-04	
		Number	Percent	Number	Percent	Number	Percent	Number	Percent	Number	Percent
Grade Six	Female	135	56%	134	57%	137	54%	147	60%	149	56%
	Male	108	44%	102	43%	113	45%	100	40%	119	44%
	Total	243		236		250		247		268	
Grade Seven	Female	137	57%	137	57%	124	56%	136	55%	150	60%
	Male	103	43%	102	43%	97	44%	110	45%	102	40%
	Total	240		239		221		246		252	
Grade Eight	Female	135	57%	127	57%	142	57%	129	56%	138	53%
	Male	102	43%	95	43%	105	43%	100	44%	123	47%
	Total	237		222		247		229		261	
Overall Totals	Total Female	407	57%	398	57%	403	56%	412	57%	437	56%
	Total Male	313	43%	299	43%	315	44%	310	43%	344	44%
	Total	720		697		718		722		781	

Figure 4.5 shows that the current student population consists of 557 White (71.3%), 179 Black (22.9%), 26 Hispanic/Latino (3.3%), and 19 Asian (2.4%) students.

Figure 4.5

Azalea Middle School
Student Enrollment by Percent Ethnicity[1]
2003-04 (*N*=781)

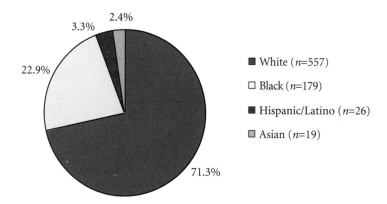

- ■ White (*n*=557)
- □ Black (*n*=179)
- ■ Hispanic/Latino (*n*=26)
- ▨ Asian (*n*=19)

[1]The ethnicity/race categories used by this school, i.e., Black, White, Hispanic/Latino, Asian,
are the federal categories used by this district and hopefully will not offend any ethnicity or race.

Over the past five years, as shown in Figure 4.6, the percentages of students by ethnicity have remained about the same. The number of White students dipped from 526 (73%) in 1999-00, to 505 (72%) in 2000-01, increased to 529 (74%) in 2001-02, dipped again to 522 (72%) in 2002-03, and increased to 557 (71%) in 2003-04. The Black student population has steadily increased from 157 students (22% of the population) from 1999-00 to 179 (23%) in 2003-04. The number of Hispanic/Latino students has also increased over time, from 11 students (2%) in 1999-00 to 26 students (3%) in 2003-04. The Asian population of students has ranged between 26 (4%) and 16 (2%) over the same time span, settling in at 19 (2%) in 2003-04.

Figure 4.6

Azalea Middle School
Percentage of Students Enrolled by Ethnicity
1999-00 to 2003-04

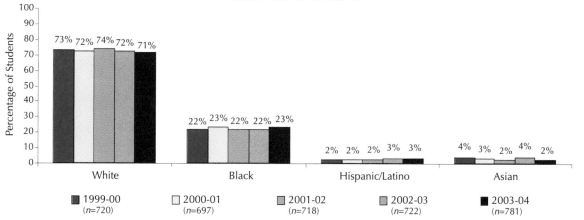

Figure 4.7 shows the number of students enrolled by ethnicity for the same time period.

Figure 4.7

Azalea Middle School Enrollment
Number of Students Enrolled by Ethnicity
1999-00 to 2003-04

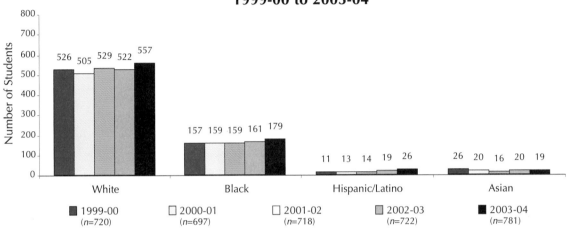

One can see the grade-level population remained fairly steady over time until 2003-04, as shown in the school enrollment by grade-level graph Figure 4.8.

Note: Looking at the same grade level over time is called *grade level analysis.*

Figure 4.8

Azalea Middle School
Student Enrollment by Grade Level
1999-00 to 2003-04

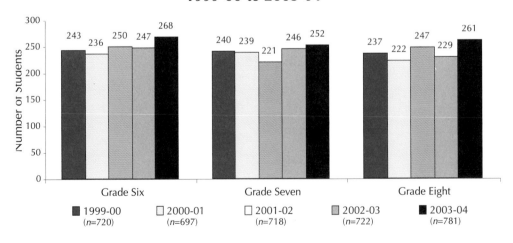

Reorganizing the data (Figure 4.9) we can see the groups of students progressing through the grades together over time. Azalea's cohorts show some fluctuation in numbers over time.

Note: Following groups of students over time is called *cohort analysis.* The numbers beneath the cohort name is the number of students that remained the same over time. This analysis is called *matched cohort analysis.* On average, approximately 75% of the sixth-grade students were still at Azalea as eighth-graders. That would mean that Azalea has a mobility rate of around 25%.

Figure 4.9

Azalea Middle School Enrollment
Student Cohorts by Grade Level
1999-00 to 2003-04

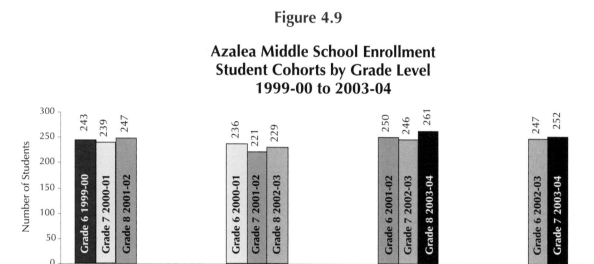

The number of English Learners (EL) by grade level and ethnicity is small and has changed very little over time. Students in the county who are English Learners can attend a designated English Language middle school until they are able to understand classes in English. As of 2003-04, there were 21 EL students at Azalea. Figure 4.10 shows the number of EL students disaggregated by grade level and ethnicity.

Figure 4.10

Azalea Middle School
English Learner (EL) Students by Grade Level and Ethnicity
2002-03 to 2003-04

Grade Level	Year	Hispanic/ Latino	Asian	Black	White	Other	Total
Grade Six	2002-03	2	3				5
	2003-04	5	3	1	3		12
Grade Seven	2002-03	1					1
	2003-04	2	2				4
Grade Eight	2002-03		2				2
	2003-04	4				1	5
	Total	15	10	1	3	1	30

From 1999-00 to 2002-03, the total percentage of students qualifying for free/reduced lunch changed very little—remaining at less than 25% of the total school population. In 2003-04, the school experienced a 5% increase in free/reduced lunch qualifiers (Figure 4.11). The number of students qualifying for free/reduced lunch varied from 159 in 2000-01 to 226 in 2003-04. There are 6 other middle schools in the district with higher free/reduced lunch counts. The average percentage of free/reduced lunch students for all middle schools in the district was 39% in 2003-04.

Figure 4.11

Azalea Middle School
Percentage of Students Qualifying for Free/Reduced Lunch
1999-00 to 2003-04

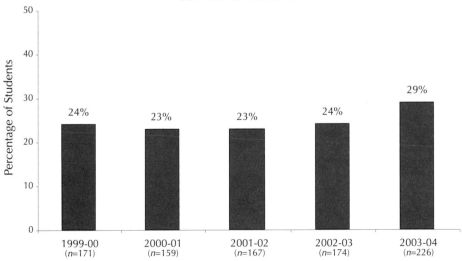

Figure 4.12 shows the number of free/reduced lunch students by grade level, ethnicity, and gender.

Figure 4.12

Azalea Middle School
Number of Free/Reduced Lunch Students by Grade Level, Ethnicity, and Gender
1999-00 to 2003-04

Grade Level	Lunch Status	Ethnicity	1999-00 (n=720)			2000-01 (n=697)			2001-02 (n=718)			2002-03 (n=722)			2003-04 (n=781)		
			Female	Male	Total	Female	Male	Total	Female	Male	Total	Female	Male	Total	Female	Male	Total
Grade Six	Free/Reduced	Asian	4	3	7	1		1	2		2	2	1	3	3		3
		Black	14	22	36	23	30	53	20	29	49	21	17	38	24	31	55
		Hispanic/Latino		1	1		1	1	4	1	5	3	3	6	4	3	7
		White	9	5	14	11	4	15	9	4	13	11	8	19	13	7	20
		Total	27	31	58	35	35	70	35	34	69	37	29	66	44	41	85
	Paid	Asian	1		1	4	3	7		2	2	1	2	3	2	2	4
		Black	7	3	10	12	3	15	8	5	13	7	7	14	2	7	9
		Hispanic/Latino			0	3		3					2	2	2	2	4
		White	100	74	174	79	61	140	94	72	166	102	60	162	99	67	166
		Total	108	77	185	98	67	165	102	79	181	110	71	181	105	78	183
Grade Seven	Free/Reduced	Asian			0	3		3	1		1	2	1	3	2	2	4
		Black	25	17	42	12	12	24	16	21	37	14	24	38	21	23	44
		Hispanic/Latino	2		2		1	1	1	1	2	4	1	5	4	1	5
		White	3	9	12	7	6	13	8	3	11	6	3	9	15	7	22
		Total	30	26	56	22	19	41	26	25	51	26	29	55	42	33	75
	Paid	Asian	4	4	8	1		1	4	2	6		1	1	3	1	4
		Black	10	9	19	6	7	13	15	6	21	8	8	16	5	5	10
		Hispanic/Latino	4		4			0	2		2	2		2		1	1
		White	89	64	153	108	76	184	77	64	141	100	72	172	100	62	162
		Total	107	77	184	115	83	198	98	72	170	110	81	191	108	69	177
Grade Eight	Free/Reduced	Asian	3	2	5		1	1	3	1	4	1	3	4	1	1	2
		Black	17	17	34	23	13	36	17	13	30	20	16	36	18	27	45
		Hispanic/Latino	3	1	4	2	1	3	1	3	4	1	1	2	3	2	5
		White	8	6	14	2	6	8	4	5	9	7	4	11	8	6	14
		Total	31	26	57	27	21	48	25	22	47	29	24	53	30	36	66
	Paid	Asian	3	2	5	3	4	7	1		1	4	2	6		1	1
		Black	8	8	16	8	9	17	4	5	9	14	5	19	10	6	16
		Hispanic/Latino			0	5		5	1		1	2		2	3	1	4
		White	93	66	159	84	61	145	111	78	189	80	69	149	94	79	173
		Total	104	76	180	100	74	174	117	83	200	100	76	176	107	87	195

Over the past five years, Azalea Middle School has served between 75 (10%) and 100 (14%) students classified as needing special education. The majority of students receiving special education assistance were classified as Learning Disabled, followed by Emotionally Disabled, and Educable Severely Handicapped. One-hundred students—less than 14% of the school enrollment—were classified as special education in 2001-02, as shown in Figure 4.13. That number decreased to 75 (10%) students in 2002-03 and increased to 96 (12%) students in 2003-04. These percentages are average for middle schools in Great View School District.

Figure 4.13

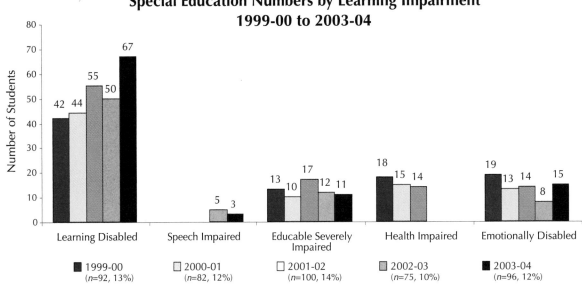

Azalea Middle School
Special Education Numbers by Learning Impairment
1999-00 to 2003-04

The table in Figure 4.14 shows the spread of special education numbers by learning impairment, grade level, ethnicity, and gender, over time. (Percentages could not be calculated because it is not known how many students had multiple descriptors.)

Figure 4.14

Azalea Middle School
Number of Special Education Students by Grade Level, Learning Impairment, Ethnicity, and Gender, 1999-00 to 2003-04

Grade Level	Learning Impairment	Ethnicity	1999-00 (n=720)			2000-01 (n=697)			2001-02 (n=718)			2002-03 (n=722)			2003-04 (n=781)		
			Female	Male	Total	Female	Male	Total	Female	Male	Total	Female	Male	Total	Female	Male	Total
Grade Six	Educable Severely Impaired	Black	3	2	5	2	3	5	3	2	5	2	1	3	1	1	2
		White			0	1	1	2	1		1			0			0
	Emotionally Disabled	Asian			0			0			0	1		1			0
		Black	1	3	4	1	2	3	3	1	4	1	1	2	2	5	7
		Hispanic/Latino			0			0	1		1			0			0
		White		1	1			0			0		1	1			0
	Health Impaired	Black		1	1		3	3	1	2	3			0			0
		White	1	4	5	1	3	4		1	1			0			0
	Learning Disabled	Asian			0			0	1		1			0			0
		Black	1	6	7	5	4	9	4	5	9		2	2	4	8	12
		Hispanic/Latino			0			0			0			0	1	1	2
		White	3	7	10		4	4	7	9	16	5	3	8	4	5	9
	Speech Impaired	White			0			0			0	2	1	3	1	2	3
		Total	**9**	**24**	**33**	**10**	**20**	**30**	**20**	**21**	**41**	**11**	**9**	**20**	**13**	**22**	**35**
Grade Seven	Educable Severely Impaired	Black	1	1	2	2		2	1	3	4	3	1	4	1	2	3
		White	1		1			0	1	1	2	1		1			0
	Emotionally Disabled	Asian			0			0			0			0	1		1
		Black		6	6		3	3	1	1	2	2		2	1		1
		White		2	2		1	1			0			0	1		1
	Health Impaired	Black	1		1		1	1	1		1			0			0
		White	3	2	5	2	2	4	1	3	4			0			0
	Learning Disabled	Asian			0			0			0	1		1			0
		Black	3	1	4	1	4	5	3	5	8	2	6	8	2	5	7
		White	2	5	7	3	9	12	1	3	4	6	8	14	5	2	7
	Speech Impaired	White			0			0			0		2	2			0
		Total	**11**	**17**	**28**	**8**	**20**	**28**	**9**	**16**	**25**	**14**	**18**	**32**	**11**	**9**	**20**
Grade Eight	Educable Severely Impaired	Black		5	5		1	1	3	2	5	1	1	2	4	1	5
		White			0			0			0	1	1	2	1		1
	Emotionally Disabled	Black		2	2		5	5		5	5	1	1	2	3	1	4
		White	1	3	4		1	1	1	1	2			0		1	1
	Health Impaired	Black	1		1			0			0			0			0
		White	1	4	5	2	1	3	3	2	5			0			0
	Learning Disabled	Asian			0			0			0			0		1	1
		Black	2	3	5	3	3	6	2	3	5	4	6	10	6	6	12
		Hispanic/Latino			0			0			0			0		1	1
		White	2	7	9	3	5	8	3	9	12	2	5	7	8	8	16
		Total	**7**	**24**	**31**	**8**	**16**	**24**	**12**	**22**	**34**	**9**	**14**	**23**	**22**	**19**	**41**

Figure 4.15 shows the number and percentage of gifted students by grade level and gender for the last four years. Figure 4.16 shows the data for gifted students by ethnicity and gender, and Figure 4.17 shows the data by free/reduced lunch. Figure 4.18 shows gifted data by all four disaggregations combined. (Gifted data were not available for 2003-04.)

Figure 4.15

Azalea Middle School
Number and Percentage of Gifted Students by Grade Level and Gender
1999-00 to 2002-03

Grade Level	1999-00 (n=277)				2000-01 (n=267)				2001-02 (n=282)				2002-03 (n=285)			
	Female		Male		Female		Male		Female		Male		Female		Male	
	Number	Percentage	Number	Percentage	Number	Percentage	Number	Percentage	Number	Percentage	Number	Percentage	Number	Percentage	Number	Percentage
Grade Six	60	62%	37	38%	51	61%	32	39%	61	66%	32	34%	69	66%	35	34%
Grade Seven	55	63%	33	38%	67	65%	36	35%	54	59%	37	41%	60	65%	33	35%
Grade Eight	63	68%	29	32%	47	58%	34	42%	63	64%	35	36%	51	58%	37	42%
Total	178		99		165		102		178		104		180		105	

Figure 4.16

Azalea Middle School
Number and Percentage of Gifted Students by Grade Level, Ethnicity, and Gender
1999-00 to 2002-03

Grade Level	Ethnicity	1999-00					2000-01					2001-02					2002-03				
		Female		Male			Female		Male			Female		Male			Female		Male		
		Number	Percentage	Number	Percentage	Total	Number	Percentage	Number	Percentage	Total	Number	Percentage	Number	Percentage	Total	Number	Percentage	Number	Percentage	Total
Grade Six	Asian					0	2	2%			2	1	1%	1	1%	2					0
	Black	2	2%			2	3	4%	1	1%	4	3	3%	3	3%	6	1	1%	1	1%	1
	Hispanic/Latino			1	1%	1					0					0			2	2%	2
	White	58	60%	36	37%	94	46	55%	31	37%	77	57	61%	28	30%	85	68	65%	32	31%	100
	Total	60		37		97	51		32		83	61		32		93	69		35		103
Grade Seven	Asian	1	1%	1	1%	2					0	2	2%	2	2%	4	1	1%			1
	Black	6	7%			6	5	5%	1	1%	6	4	4%	1	1%	5	3	3%	1	1%	4
	Hispanic/Latino	2	2%			2			1	1%	1	1	1%			1	1	1%	3	3%	4
	White	46	52%	32	36%	78	62	61%	34	33%	96	47	52%	34	38%	81	55	60%	29	32%	84
	Total	55		33		88	67		36		103	54		37		91	60		33		93
Grade Eight	Asian	2	2%			2	1	1%	2	3%	3					0	2	2%			2
	Black	4	4%	1	1%	5	5	6%	1	1%	6	4	4%			4	3	3%	2	2%	5
	Hispanic/Latino	1	1%			1	2	3%			2			1	1%	1	1	1%	2	2%	3
	White	56	61%	28	30%	84	39	49%	31	39%	70	59	61%	34	35%	93	45	52%	33	38%	78
	Total	63	68%	29	32%	92	47	58%	34	42%	81	63	64%	35	36%	98	51	58%	37	42%	88
	School Total	178	64%	99	36%	277	165	62%	102	38%	267	178	63%	104	37%	282	180	63%	105	37%	285

USING DATA TO IMPROVE STUDENT LEARNING IN MIDDLE SCHOOLS

Figure 4.17

Azalea Middle School
Number and Percentage of Gifted Students by Grade Level, Free/Reduced Lunch, and Gender, 1999-00 to 2002-03

Grade Level	Lunch Status	1999-00					2000-01					2001-02					2002-03				
		Female		Male			Female		Male			Female		Male			Female		Male		
		Number	Percentage	Number	Percentage	Total	Number	Percentage	Number	Percentage	Total	Number	Percentage	Number	Percentage	Total	Number	Percentage	Number	Percentage	Total
Grade Six	Free/Reduced	4	4%	1	1%	5	4	5%	1	1%	5	1	1%	1	1%	2	5	6%	1	1%	6
	Paid	52	57%	34	37%	86	41	55%	29	39%	70	52	63%	28	34%	80	43	56%	28	36%	71
Grade Seven	Free/Reduced	5	6%	1	1%	6	4	4%	1	1%	5	3	3%	1	1%	4	2	2%	2	2%	4
	Paid	44	54%	31	38%	75	58	60%	33	34%	91	48	55%	35	40%	83	43	59%	26	36%	69
Grade Eight	Free/Reduced	3	3%	2	2%	5	4	5%	1	1%	5	1	1%	3	3%	4			2	2%	2
	Paid	55	65%	25	29%	80	40	51%	33	42%	73	60	63%	31	33%	91	34	51%	31	46%	65
Total		163		94		257	151		98		249	165		99		264	127		90		217

Figure 4.18

Azalea Middle School
Number and Percentage of Gifted Students by Grade Level, Ethnicity, Free/Reduced Lunch Status, and Gender, 1999-00 to 2002-03

Grade Level	Ethnicity	Lunch Status	1999-00					2000-01					2001-02					2002-03				
			Female		Male			Female		Male			Female		Male			Female		Male		
			Number	Percentage	Number	Percentage	Total	Number	Percentage	Number	Percentage	Total	Number	Percentage	Number	Percentage	Total	Number	Percentage	Number	Percentage	Total
Grade Six	Asian	Free/Reduced					0	1	1%			1	1	1%			1					0
		Paid					0	1	1%			1			1	1%	1			1	1%	1
	Black	Free/Reduced					0			1	1%	1			3	3%	3	1	1%	1	1%	2
		Paid	2	2%			2	3	4%			3	3	3%			3			1	1%	1
	Hispanic/Latino	Free/Reduced			1	1%	1					0					0					0
	White	Free/Reduced	4	4%	1	1%	5	3	4%			3					0	5	5%	1	1%	6
		Paid	54	56%	35	36%	89	43	52%	31	37%	74	57	61%	28	30%	85	63	61%	31	30%	94
	Total		60		37		97	51		32		83	61		32		93	69		35		104
Grade Seven	Asian	Free/Reduced					0					0	1	1%			1	1	1%	1	1%	2
		Paid	1	1%	1	1%	2					0	1	1%	2	2%	3					0
	Black	Free/Reduced	5	7%			5	1	1%			1			1	1%	1	1	1%	3	3%	4
		Paid	1	1%			1	4	4%	1	1%	5	4	4%			4	2	2%			2
	Hispanic/Latino	Free/Reduced					0			1	1%	1					0					0
		Paid	2	3%			2					0	1	1%			1	1	1%			1
	White	Free/Reduced	1	1%	1	1%	2	4	4%	1	1%	5	2	2%			2					0
		Paid	45	67%	31	46%	76	58	57%	33	32%	91	45	49%	34	37%	79	55	59%	29	31%	84
	Total		55		33		88	67		36		103	54		37		91	60		33		93
Grade Eight	Asian	Paid	2	2%			2	1	1%	2	2%	3					0	2	2%	2	2%	4
	Black	Free/Reduced	1	1%	1	1%	2	4	5%			4	1	1%			1	1	1%	1	1%	2
		Paid	3	3%			3	1	1%	1	1%	2	3	3%			3	2	2%	1	1%	3
	Hispanic/Latino	Free/Reduced	1	1%			1					0			1	1%	1					0
		Paid					0	2	2%			2					0	1	1%			1
	White	Free/Reduced	2	2%	1	1%	3			1	1%	1			2	2%	2	1	1%	1	1%	2
		Paid	54	59%	27	29%	81	39	48%	30	37%	69	59	60%	32	33%	91	44	50%	32	36%	76
	Total		63		29		92	47		34		81	63		35		98	51		37		88

Students have the opportunity to take honors classes, enabling them to advance and enroll as sophomores in high school when leaving Azalea. Approximately 24% of the Azalea students are enrolled in high school credit courses, including:

▼ *Algebra I*

▼ *Geometry*

▼ *Spanish I*

▼ *Keyboarding*

▼ *English I*

▼ *Physical Science*

Attendance rates at Azalea Middle School have remained steady over the past five years. Azalea has an average daily student attendance rate of 95.8% and a 95.2% attendance rate for teachers.

Approximately 16 students are older than average for their grade, which implies they may have been retained at some point in their educational career.

Support systems provided for students beyond the classroom include:

▼ *Media Center*

▼ *After-school Assistance Program (ASAP)*

▼ *Teen Connection (Urban League)*

▼ *Individual Tutoring*

▼ *Group Tutoring (two-teacher teams)*

▼ *Peer Tutoring—Collaborative pairs and small groups*

▼ *Counseling (provided by the guidance counselors)*

▼ *Student Council*

▼ *Beta Club*

▼ *Junior Achievement*

All teachers at Azalea post classroom rules that are outlined in the student handbook and are consistently enforced throughout the school. Students are encouraged and expected to maintain appropriate behavior at all times to avoid disruptions in their and other students' learning.

The percentage of suspended or expelled students is low—0.8% in 2003-04—up from 0.7% in the previous year. The percentage of suspended students in the other Magnolia City middle schools is 1.3%.

The Staff

The 2003-04 staff at Azalea included: 50 regular teachers, 1 instructional coach, 1 media specialist, 5 special education teachers, and 2 guidance counselors. The majority of the teachers are female. Seven are male. Ninety-four percent are White. The other 6% are Black and Hispanic/Latino. Azalea has five National Board Certified Teachers. One-half of the teachers have advanced degrees. No teachers are teaching out of their certificated field. Figure 4.19 shows the number of teachers has remained fairly consistent since 1999-00. The increase of 3 teachers in 2003-04 is connected to the enrollment increase that year. The student to teacher ratio is approximately 16 to 1.

Figure 4.19

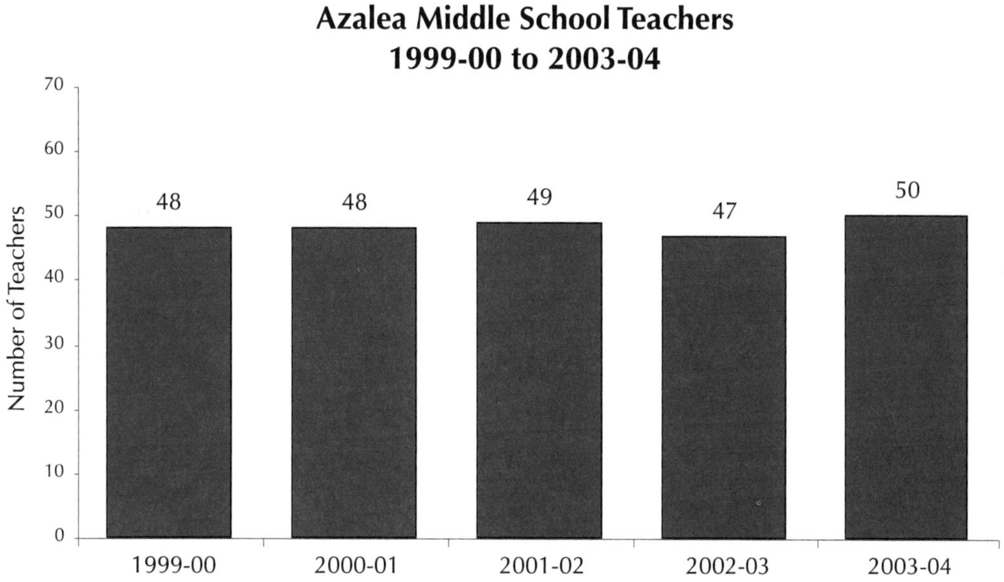

**Azalea Middle School Teachers
1999-00 to 2003-04**

There are currently five new full-time teachers and three new part-time teachers. Ninety percent of the current teaching staff has been in the school for the past ten years. The number of years of teaching experience, by grade level, is shown in the table in Figure 4.20 below.

Additional personnel include the school principal and assistant principal, secretary, instructional assistants, clerical support staff, custodial staff, library technician, campus supervisors, and food services workers. This is the third year at Azalea Middle School for the principal and the ninth year for the assistant principal. The previous principal was at the school for three years. The principal, assistant principal, and instructional coach are White females.

Figure 4.20

**Azalea Middle School Teachers
Number of Years Teaching Experience by Grade Level
2003-04**

Grade Level	0–3 Years	4–5 Years	6–8 Years	9–10 Years	11–15 Years	16–20 Years	21–25 Years	26+ Years
Grade Six					2	2	3	2
Grade Seven		1	2	2		1	2	2
Grade Eight		3		2	2		1	3
Special Education	1		3				1	
Related Arts	5		1	2	2	1	1	3
Totals	**6**	**4**	**6**	**6**	**6**	**4**	**8**	**10**

Study Questions for Who Are We?

As you review Azalea's data, use either the margins in the text, this page, or print this page from the CD-Rom to write down your early thinking. (Ch4Qs.pdf) These notes, of course, are only hunches or placeholders until all the data are analyzed. It is important to jot down your thinking as you go through the data so you can see if additional data corroborate your first impressions.

1. What are the demographic *strengths* and *challenges* for Azalea Middle School?	
Strengths	*Challenges*

2. What are some *implications* for the Azalea's school improvement plan?

3. Looking at the data presented, what other demographic data would you want to answer the question *Who are we?* for Azalea Middle School?

What I Saw in the Example: Azalea Middle School

At the end of each chapter, I add what I saw in the data, using the study questions. (Ch4Saw.pdf) When applicable, I have referenced the figure or page number that gave me my first impression of strengths and challenges.

Demographic Strengths	*Demographic Challenges*
<ul><li>Seems like a community rich in resources. (Pages 40-41)</li><li>Universities are in the area. (Page 41)</li><li>Employment and transportation look great. (Page 41)</li><li>By self-report, the district is a leader in education. (Page 41)</li><li>Azalea facilities sound good, although in need of updating. (Page 42)</li><li>Azalea is a national and state recognized school. (Page 42)</li><li>Sounds like Azalea has a great arts and academic program. (Pages 42-43)</li><li>P.T.A. sounds involved and committed. (Page 43)</li><li>There is a waiting list to get into the school, so it must have a good reputation. (Page 43)</li><li>Azalea's overall population is stable over time. (Pages 43-44)</li><li>Low, however increasing, number of English learners. (Page 47)</li><li>The number and percentage of students who qualify for free/reduced lunch stays fairly consistent—less than 25% of the student population (except 2003-04, 29%). (Figure 4.11)</li><li>The percentage of special education students is not large. (Figure 4.15)</li><li>Sounds like there is a strong gifted program at Azalea. (Page 52)</li><li>Almost a quarter of the students take high school coursework while at Azalea. (Page 54)</li><li>Student attendance rates are good. (Page 54)</li><li>A very small percentage of students are older than average for their grade. (Page 54)</li><li>Support systems are provided beyond the classroom. (Page 54)</li><li>Consistent reinforcement of discipline sounds great. (Page 54)</li><li>The percentage of suspended/expelled students is low. (Page 54)</li><li>There is an instructional coach on staff. Support staffing in general looks great. (Pages 55-56)</li><li>There are five National Board Certified Teachers on staff. (Page 55)</li><li>Staffing is spread-out by number of years of teaching, within and across grade levels. The core staff has many years of experience. (Figure 4.20)</li><li>No brand-new teachers in grades six to eight. (Figure 4.20)</li></ul>	<ul><li>The district is huge. (Page 41)</li><li>District per capita income is low. (Page 41)</li><li>District enrollment keeps increasing. (Figure 4.1)</li><li>The district appears to lose students in the highest grades. (Figure 4.2)</li><li>Kindergarten enrollment is decreasing. (Figure 4.2)</li><li>The bump-up in district enrollment in grade nine might be because of retentions, which might have implications for Azalea. (Figure 4.2)</li><li>Other students want to attend Azalea, but can't get in. (Page 43)</li><li>What if students attending Azalea are not interested in the arts?</li><li>Students are bussed from quite a distance. (Page 43)</li><li>The bus sounds unpredictable. (Page 43)</li><li>The larger percentage of females than males could be a challenge to teachers. (Page 44)</li><li>A mobility rate of 25% is pretty high for a school with only three grades. (Page 47)</li><li>There is not a lot of diversity in students or in staff. (Figure 4.5, Page 55)</li><li>There is an increase in the number of English Learner students—even though total number is still small. (Figure 4.10)</li><li>There was an increase in free/reduced lunch qualifiers in 2003-04. (Figure 4.11)</li><li>There is an increase in the number of learning disabled students. (Figure 4.13)</li><li>There are considerably more females than males identified as gifted. Over half are White and are not on free/reduced lunches. (Figures 4.15, 4.16, 4.17, and 4.18)</li><li>When compared to overall percentage of enrollment (Figure 4.6), it appears that Black students are more likely to qualify for free/reduced lunch. (Figure 4.12)</li><li>With 20% of staff having 26+ years experience, there might be several retirees in the near future. (Figure 4.20)</li><li>Does the fact that only 7 of 50 teachers are male and 44% of the students are male present a challenge?</li></ul>

Implications for Azalea's school improvement plan

♦ Possibly special education—How are students identified as and served within special education?

♦ Are the needs of all students being met? Perhaps staff might need professional development in meeting needs of students with backgrounds different from their own, particularly related to poverty, diversity, and students with disabilities?

♦ Might need a plan for recruiting new teachers in the near future, and for improving the ethnic and gender balance of staff.

♦ How is the transition from elementary to middle school for the students? Does Azalea improve their learning? Are all students prepared for high school? How do they do in high school? Is there a transition program for new ninth graders?

Other desired demographic data or information

Azalea Middle School provided an excellent summary of who they are. Other data that would be helpful in understanding the context of the school might include:

♦ How are students identified for the gifted program?

♦ What is the mobility issue? Which subgroups of students leave and why?

♦ Would like to know the differences in who lives in the neighborhood and who chooses to attend, by gender, ethnicity, and socio-economic status.

♦ Who are the kids who walk and are bussed, by socioeconomic status and ethnicity?

♦ What is the admissions policy?

♦ How are the students identified as Learning Disabled? How many have multiple designations?

♦ Retentions—How many get retained in middle school? How many have been retained in elementary school?

♦ How many of Azalea's students get retained in grade nine? Do any ultimately drop out of high school?

♦ What happens to the students when they move on into ninth grade? Do they do okay?

♦ Are there sports offerings and other extracurricular activities for those students not prone to the Arts?

♦ What about parent involvement?

♦ More discipline data need to be gathered.

USING DATA TO IMPROVE STUDENT LEARNING
IN MIDDLE SCHOOLS

> *With demographic data, we are answering the basic question, "Who are we?" The answers to the question, "Who are we?", set the context for the school, have huge implications for the direction the continuous school improvement plan will take, and can help explain how the school gets the results it is getting.*

Summary

The first data required for continuous school improvement planning are demographic data. With demographic data, we are answering the basic question, *Who are we?* The answers to the question, *Who are we?*, set the context for the school, have huge implications for the direction the continuous school improvement plan will take, and can help explain how the school gets the results it is getting. Our example school, Azalea Middle School, showed how a demographic analysis could look. The accompanying CD has tools and templates to help your school create a comprehensive demographic profile.

Typical Demographic Data to Gather to Answer the Question, *Who Are We?*

Community
▼ Location and history
▼ Economic base, population trends, and community resources (*www.census.gov* is a great resource for getting information about the community, as is your local chamber of commerce)
▼ Community involvement
▼ Business partnerships

School District
▼ Description and history
▼ Number of schools, administrators, students and teachers over time, and by grade level

School
▼ Description and history, attendance area, location
▼ Type of school, e.g., magnet, alternative, charter, private, private management
▼ Number of administrators, students and teachers over time, and by grade level
▼ Number of students electing to come to the school from out of the attendance area
▼ Grants and awards received
▼ Title 1/Schoolwide
▼ Safety/crime data
▼ *State designation as a dangerous school
▼ Uniqueness and strengths
▼ Class sizes
▼ After-school programs/summer school

- ▼ Extracurricular activities
- ▼ Advisors for extracurricular activities
  - ◆ Are they teachers on staff who receive extra pay?
  - ◆ Are they teachers in district, but at other schools, who receive extra pay?
  - ◆ Are they non-teachers paid to be advisors?
- ▼ Tutoring/peer mentoring
- ▼ Community support-services coordinated
- ▼ Counseling opportunities
- ▼ *Facilities: equipped for networked computers and handicapped
- ▼ Facilities: age, capacity, maintenance
- ▼ Availability of necessities and other supplies

Students Over Time, and by Grade Level
- ▼ Living situation/family structure/family size
- ▼ Preschool/Head Start/Even Start
- ▼ Preschool attendance
- ▼ *Number of students
- ▼ Gender of students
- ▼ *Race/ethnicity numbers and percentages
- ▼ Free/reduced lunch numbers and percentages
- ▼ *Language fluency by language
- ▼ *Migrant/immigrants by country, home languages
- ▼ *Homeless
- ▼ *Special Education by disability, gender, ethnicity, language fluency, free/reduced lunch
- ▼ *Attendance/tardies
- ▼ Mobility (where students go/come from)
- ▼ Retention rates by gender, ethnicity, language fluency, free/reduced lunch
- ▼ *Dropout rates by gender, ethnicity, free/reduced lunch, migrant, special education (where students go/what they do)
- ▼ Number of students leaving school overall by gender, ethnicity, language fluency, free/reduced lunch
- ▼ Extracurricular activity participation/clubs/service learning by gender, ethnicity, language fluency, free/reduced lunch
- ▼ Number of participants in programs, such as AP, IB, Honors, Upward Bound, Gear-up, college-prep, vocational
- ▼ Number of home schoolers associated with school, along with how they are associated with the school
- ▼ Number of students electing to come to the school from out-of-the-attendance area
- ▼ Number of bus riders and distances they ride
- ▼ Student employment

- ▼ *Discipline indicators (e.g., suspensions, referrals, types of incidences, number of students carrying weapons on school property)
- ▼ *Number of drugs on school property (offered, sold, or given illegal drugs)
- ▼ *Graduation rates by gender, ethnicity, language proficiency, free/reduced lunch, migrant, and special education (where students go/what they do)
- ▼ Number of high school students concurrently enrolled in college courses
- ▼ Number of students meeting college course entrance requirements by gender, ethnicity, language fluency, free/reduced lunch
- ▼ Number of middle students concurrently enrolled in high school courses
- ▼ Number of scholarships by gender, ethnicity, language proficiency, free/reduced lunch
- ▼ Number of students completing GEDs
- ▼ Adult education programs
- ▼ Number and percentage of students going on to college, post-graduate training, and/or employment
- ▼ Grade-point average in college
- ▼ Number of graduates ending up in college remedial classes

Staff Over Time
- ▼ *Number of teachers, administrators, instructional specialists, support staff by roles
- ▼ *Years of experience, by grade level and/or role, in this school/in teaching
- ▼ Ethnicity, gender, languages spoken
- ▼ Retirement projections
- ▼ *Types of certifications/licenses/teacher qualifications/percentage of time teaching in certified area(s)
- ▼ Grades/subjects teachers are teaching
- ▼ Degrees
- ▼ *Educational training of paraprofessionals
- ▼ Teacher-student ratios by grade level
- ▼ Teacher turnover rates
- ▼ Attendance rates
- ▼ Teacher involvement in extracurricular activities, program participation
- ▼ *Number of teachers receiving high-quality professional development
- ▼ *Percent of teachers qualified to use technology for instruction
- ▼ National Board for Professional Teaching Standards (NBPTS) teachers

Parents
- ▼ Educational levels, home language, employment, socioeconomic status
- ▼ Involvement with their child's learning
- ▼ Involvement in school activities
- ▼ Incarceration

*Required for *No Child Left Behind* (includes the numbers required to understand the disaggregated numbers required by NCLB).

On the CD Related to This Chapter

▼ Study Questions Related to *Who are we?* (Ch4Qs.pdf)

These study questions will help you better understand the information provided in Chapter 4. This file can be printed for use as you study the case study or to use with staff as you study your own demographic data.

▼ Demographic Graphing Templates (MiddDemog.xls)

All of the *Microsoft Excel* files that were used to create the demographic graphs in the Azalea Middle School example (Chapter 4) appear on the CD. Use these templates by putting your data in the data source table and changing the title/labels to reflect your data. Your graphs will build automatically. This file also explains how to use the templates.

▼ Demographic Data Table Templates (MiddDemog.doc)

All of the *Microsoft Word* files that were used to create the demographic data tables in the Azalea Middle School example (Chapter 4) appear in this file on the CD. Use these templates by putting your data in the data table and changing the title/labels to reflect your data.

▼ *School Data Profile Template* (MiddProfil.doc)

This *Microsoft Word* file provides a template for creating your own school data profile like the one for Azalea Middle School, using the graphing and table templates provided. Create your graphs in the graphing and table templates, then copy and paste them into the *School Data Profile Template.*

▼ The following profile templates for gathering and organizing data, prior to graphing, can be adjusted to add data elements you feel are important to fully complete the profile. If you just need to graph your data, use the graphing templates. These are for optional use.

◆ *School Profile* (ProfilSc.doc)

The *School Profile* is a template for gathering and organizing data about your school, prior to graphing. Please adjust the profile to add data elements you feel are important for describing the context of your school. This information is then graphed and described in narrative form. If creating a school portfolio, the data graphs and narrative will appear in *Information and Analysis.* (If you already have your data organized and just need to graph it, you might want to skip this step and use the graphing templates, described above.)

- *Community Profile* (ProfilCo.doc)

  The *Community Profile* is a template for gathering and organizing data about your community, prior to graphing. Please adjust the profile to add data elements you feel are important for describing the context of your community. It is important to describe how the community has changed over time, and how it is expected to change in the near future. This information is then graphed and written in narrative form. If creating a school portfolio, the data graphs and narrative will appear in *Information and Analysis.* (If you already have your data organized and just need to graph it, you might want to skip this step and use the graphing templates described on the previous page.)

- *Administrator Profile* (ProfilAd.doc)

  The *Administrator Profile* is a template for gathering and organizing data about your school administrators, prior to graphing. Please adjust the profile to fully describe your administrators. This information is then graphed and written in narrative form. If creating a school portfolio, the data graphs and narrative will appear in the *Information and Analysis* and *Leadership* sections. (If you already have your data organized and just need to graph it, you might want to skip this step and use the graphing templates described on the previous page.)

- *Teacher Profile* (ProfilTe.doc)

  The *Teacher Profile* is a template for gathering and organizing data about your school's teachers, prior to graphing. Please adjust the profile to fully describe your teachers. The synthesis of this information is then graphed and written in narrative form. If creating a school portfolio, the data graphs and narrative will appear in *Information and Analysis.* (If you already have your data organized and just need to graph it, you might want to skip this step and use the graphing templates described on the previous page.)

- *Staff (other than teacher) Profile* (ProfilSt.doc)

  The *Staff (Other than Teacher) Profile* is a template for gathering and organizing data about school staff who are not teachers, prior to graphing. Please adjust the profile to fully describe your non-teaching staff. The synthesis of this information is then graphed and written in narrative form. If creating a school portfolio, the data graphs and narrative will appear in *Information and Analysis.* (If you already have your data organized and just need to graph it, you might want to skip this step and use the graphing templates described on the previous page.)

▼ *History Gram Activity* (ACTHstry.pdf)

A team-building activity that will "write" the history of the school, which could help everyone see what staff has experienced since coming to the school and how many school improvement initiatives have been started over the years. It is helpful for understanding what it will take to keep this current school improvement effort going.

▼ *Questions to Guide the Analysis of Demographic Data* (QsDemogr.doc)

This *Microsoft Word* file provides a guide for interpreting your demographic data. Adjust the questions to better reflect the discussion you would like to have with your staff about the gathered demographic data.

▼ *What I Saw in the Example* (Ch4Saw.pdf)

What I Saw in the Example is a file, organized by the demographic study questions, that summarizes what the author saw in the demographic data provided by Azalea Middle School.

▼ *Demographic Data to Gather to Create the Context of the School* (DemoData.pdf)

This file defines the types of demographic data that are important to gather to create the context of the school and describe *Who are we?*

> *How a school does business can be ascertained through studying student, staff, and parent questionnaire results, and through assessing with tools that can tell how staff works together and with the larger school community.*

The second question in our continuous school improvement planning model, described in Chapter 3, is *How do we do business?* This question helps us understand organizational culture, shared assumptions, beliefs, and typical behavior. How a school does business can be ascertained through studying student, staff, and parent questionnaire results, and through assessing with tools that can tell how staff works together and with the larger school community. The answers to this question can inform a school staff of what is possible as they plan for the future, and what it will take to systemically change how they work together.

Humans cannot act any differently from what they value, believe, or perceive. Since we want all staff to act in the same way, as the vision directs, it seems wise to understand what staff are perceiving about the learning environment and what they believe will improve student learning. Staff questionnaire results can tell us about needs for professional development, team building, and motivation. Parent and student questionnaire results can point to needs that must also be considered in the continuous school improvement plan.

The example school in this book used the *Education for the Future* (EFF) student, staff, and parent questionnaires to assess how it does business. The school also used the *Education for the Future Continuous Improvement Continuums* (CICs). The CICs are powerful tools for assessing the health of a school system. (A version for the district is also found on the CD.)

As we start on *How do we do business?* with Azalea Middle School, please note the study questions on page 104 to assist in studying the Azalea data. (Ch5Qs.pdf) There is space in the margins on the data pages to write your impressions as you review the data. At the end of the chapter, I share what I saw in the data. (Ch5Saw.pdf) For reviewing your own data, you might want to use a comparison table to look across student, staff, and parent questionnaire results. (QTable.doc) You are welcome to use this as well as the study questions.

Our Example School: Azalea Middle School
How Do We Do Business?

To get a better understanding of the learning environment at Azalea Middle School, students, staff, and parents completed *Education for the Future* perception questionnaires. Staff also completed a standards assessment questionnaire, assessed where they felt the school ranked on the *Education for the Future Continuous Improvement Continuums* (CICs), and they conducted a professional development questionnaire. Summaries of those results follow, starting with the CICs.

School Processes

Azalea Middle School Continuous Improvement Continuum
Baseline Results

In August 2003, the faculty of Azalea Middle School conducted a baseline assessment of where the school is on the *Education for the Future Continuous Improvement Continuums.* (AZbase.pdf)

These Continuums, extending from *one* to *five* horizontally, represent a continuum of expectations related to school improvement with respect to an *approach* to the Continuum, *implementation* of the approach, and the *outcome* that results from the implementation. A *one* rating, located on the left in each Continuum, represents a school that has not yet begun to improve. *Five,* located on the right in each Continuum, represents a school that is one step removed from "world class quality." The elements between *one* and *five* describe how that Continuum is hypothesized to evolve in a continuously improving school. Each Continuum moves from a *reactive* mode to a *proactive* mode—from fire fighting to prevention. The *five* in each Continuum is the target.

Vertically, we have *Approach, Implementation,* and *Outcome. Approach* is how a school plans or talks about each Continuum. *Implementation* describes how the *approach* might look when *implemented,* and the *outcome* is the "pay-off" for *implementing* the *approach.* If the hypotheses are accurate, the *outcome* will not be realized until the *approach* is actually *implemented.*

After reading a Continuum, each staff member placed a dot on the Continuum to represent where she/he thought the school was with respect to *Approach, Implementation,* and *Outcome.* Staff members discussed why they thought their school was where they rated it. Following the discussion, the staff came to consensus on a number that represented where the school was for each element, and created *Next Steps* for moving up the Continuums. The ratings and brief discussions for each *Continuous Improvement Continuum* are shown in the following report that Azalea staff crafted, using the templates and tools on this CD.

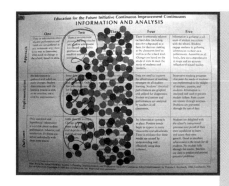

Information and Analysis

After a lively discussion about how they gather and use data, Azalea Middle School staff rated their school a 2 in *Approach,* 2 in *Implementation,* and 2 in *Outcome* with respect to *Information and Analysis.* Staff agreed that there are some data being collected, although the approach is neither systematic nor systemic.

Next Steps:

Staff agreed that the following needs to happen at the school level with respect to *Information and Analysis:*

▼ We need to understand the *Information and Analysis Continuous Improvement Continuum* better.

▼ Data must be made more accessible and used to drive decisions.

▼ Teachers need to be trained so they feel comfortable with data analysis and terms such as "root cause" and "gap analyses."

▼ We need to survey students for their perceptions.

INFORMATION AND ANALYSIS

	One	Two	Three	Four	Five
Approach	Data or information about student performance and needs are not gathered in any systematic way; there is no way to determine what needs to change at the school, based on data.	There is no systematic process, but some teacher and student information is collected and used to problem-solve and establish student learning standards.	School collects data related to student performance (e.g., attendance, achievement) and conducts surveys on student, teacher, and parent needs. The information is used to drive the strategic quality plan for school change.	There is systematic reliance on hard data (including data for subgroups) as a basis for decision making at the classroom level as well as at the school level. Changes are based on the study of data to meet the needs of students and teachers.	Information is gathered in all areas of student interaction with the school. Teachers engage students in gathering information on their own performance. Accessible to all levels, data are comprehensive in scope and an accurate reflection of school quality.
Implementation	No information is gathered with which to make changes. Student dissatisfaction with the learning process is seen as an irritation, not a need for improvement.	Some data are tracked, such as drop-out rates and enrollment. Only a few individuals are asked for feedback about areas of schooling.	School collects information on current and former students (e.g., student achievement and perceptions), analyzes and uses it in conjunction with future trends for planning. Identified areas for improvement are tracked over time.	Data are used to improve the effectiveness of teaching strategies on all student learning. Students' historical performances are graphed and utilized for diagnostics. Student evaluations and performances are analyzed by teachers in all classrooms.	Innovative teaching processes that meet the needs of students are implemented to the delight of teachers, parents, and students. Information is analyzed and used to prevent student failure. Root causes are known through analyses. Problems are prevented through the use of data.
Outcome	Only anecdotal and hypothetical information is available about student performance, behavior, and satisfaction. Problems are solved individually with short-term results.	Little data are available. Change is limited to some areas of the school and dependent upon individual teachers and their efforts.	Information collected about student and parent needs, assessment, and instructional practices is shared with the school staff and used to plan for change. Information helps staff understand pressing issues, analyze information for "root causes," and track results for improvement.	An information system is in place. Positive trends begin to appear in many classrooms and schoolwide. There is evidence that these results are caused by understanding and effectively using data collected.	Students are delighted with the school's instructional processes and proud of their own capabilities to learn and assess their own growth. Good to excellent achievement is the result for all students. No student falls through the cracks. Teachers use data to predict and prevent potential problems.

Student Achievement

Azalea Middle School staff rated their school a 3 in *Approach,* 3 in *Implementation, and* 3 in *Outcome* with respect to *Student Achievement.* Staff know the student learning standards. We need to get better with effective instruction and assessment strategies.

Next Steps:

Staff agreed that the following needs to happen at the school level with respect to *Student Achievement.* We need to—

▼ Use teams for collaboration on data and instruction.

▼ Identify and implement successful instructional strategies.

▼ Provide training in additional effective instructional strategies.

▼ Identify alternative means of assessment, other than what they are currently using.

▼ Identify ways to implement peer coaching.

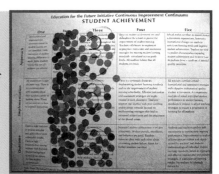

STUDENT ACHIEVEMENT

	One	Two	Three	Four	Five
Approach	Instructional and organizational processes critical to student success are not identified. Little distinction of student learning differences is made. Some teachers believe that not all students can achieve.	Some data are collected on student background and performance trends. Learning gaps are noted to direct improvement of instruction. It is known that student learning standards must be identified.	Student learning standards are identified, and a continuum of learning is created throughout the school. Student performance data are collected and compared to the standards in order to analyze how to improve learning for all students.	Data on student achievement are used throughout the school to pursue the improvement of student learning. Teachers collaborate to implement appropriate instruction and assessment strategies for meeting student learning standards articulated across grade levels. All teachers believe that all students can learn.	School makes an effort to exceed student achievement expectations. Innovative instructional changes are made to anticipate learning needs and improve student achievement. Teachers are able to predict characteristics impacting student achievement and to know how to perform from a small set of internal quality measures.
Implementation	All students are taught the same way. There is no communication with students about their academic needs or learning styles. There are no analyses of how to improve instruction.	Some effort is made to track and analyze student achievement trends on a school-wide basis. Teachers begin to understand the needs and learning gaps of students.	Teachers study effective instruction and assessment strategies to implement standards and to increase their students' learning. Student feedback and analysis of achievement data are used in conjunction with implementation support strategies.	There is a systematic focus on implementing student learning standards and on the improvement of student learning schoolwide. Effective instruction and assessment strategies are implemented in each classroom. Teachers support one another with peer coaching and/or action research focused on implementing strategies that lead to increased achievement and the attainment of the shared vision.	All teachers correlate critical instructional and assessment strategies with objective indicators of quality student achievement. A comparative analysis of actual individual student performance to student learning standards is utilized to adjust teaching strategies to ensure a progression of learning for all students.
Outcome	There is wide variation in student attitudes and achievement with undesirable results. There is high dissatisfaction among students with learning. Student background is used as an excuse for low student achievement.	There is some evidence that student achieve-ment trends are available to teachers and are being used. There is much effort, but minimal observable results in improving student achievement.	There is an increase in communication between students and teachers regarding student learning. Teachers learn about effective instructional strategies that will implement the shared vision, including student learning standards, and meet the needs of their students. They make some gains.	Increased student achievement is evident schoolwide. Student morale, attendance, and behavior are good. Teachers converse often with each other about preventing student failure. Areas for further attention are clear.	Students and teachers conduct self-assessments to continuously improve performance. Improvements in student achievement are evident and clearly caused by teachers' and students' understandings of individual student learning standards, linked to appropriate and effective instructional and assessment strategies. A continuum of learning results. No students fall through the cracks.

Quality Planning

Azalea Middle School Staff rated their school 3s in *Approach, Implementation,* and *Outcome* with respect to *Quality Planning.* We have a comprehensive plan to achieve the vision. We need to do a better job of implementing it.

Next Steps:

Staff agreed that the following needs to happen at the school level with respect to *Quality Planning:*

▼ We need better communication of the school's vision, mission, and plan.

▼ We need to continue with the school portfolio—follow through.

▼ We also need to define measurable outcomes.

QUALITY PLANNING

	One	Two	Three	Four	Five
Approach	No quality plan or process exists. Data are neither used nor considered important in planning.	The staff realize the importance of a mission, vision, and one comprehensive action plan. Teams develop goals and timelines, and dollars are allocated to begin the process.	A comprehensive school plan to achieve the vision is developed. Plan includes evaluation and continuous improvement.	One focused and integrated schoolwide plan for implementing a continuous improvement process is put into action. All school efforts are focused on the implementation of this plan that represents the achievement of the vision.	A plan for the continuous improvement of the school, with a focus on students, is put into place. There is excellent articulation and integration of all elements in the school due to quality planning. Leadership team ensures all elements are implemented by all appropriate parties.
Implementation	There is no knowledge of or direction for quality planning. Budget is allocated on an as-needed basis. Many plans exist.	School community begins continuous improvement planning efforts by laying out major steps to a shared vision, by identifying values and beliefs, the purpose of the school, a mission, vision, and student learning standards.	Implementation goals, responsibilities, due dates, and timelines are spelled out. Support structures for implementing the plan are set in place.	The quality management plan is implemented through effective procedures in all areas of the school. Everyone commits to implementing the plan aligned to the vision, mission, and values and beliefs. All share responsibility for accomplishing school goals.	Schoolwide goals, mission, vision, and student learning standards are shared and articulated throughout the school and with feeder schools. The attainment of identified student learning standards is linked to planning and implementation of effective instruction that meets students' needs. Leaders at all levels are developing expertise because planning is the norm.
Outcome	There is no evidence of comprehensive planning. Staff work is carried out in isolation. A continuum of learning for students is absent.	The school community understands the benefits of working together to implement a comprehensive continuous improvement plan.	There is evidence that the school plan is being implemented in some areas of the school. Improvements are neither systematic nor integrated schoolwide.	A schoolwide plan is known to all. Results from working toward the quality improvement goals are evident throughout the school. Planning is ongoing and inclusive of all stakeholders. Evidence of effective teaching	and learning results in significant improvement of student achievement attributed to quality planning at all levels of the school organization. Teachers and administrators understand and share the school mission and vision. Quality planning is seamless and all demonstrate evidence of accountability.

Professional Development

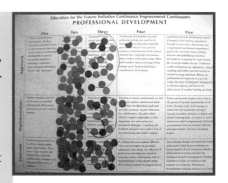

Azalea Middle School staff rated their school 3s in *Approach*, *Implementation*, and *Outcome* with respect to *Professional Development*. We need to get our professional development more aligned with the shared vision.

Next Steps:

Staff agreed that the following needs to happen at the school level with respect to *Professional Development*. We need to—

▼ Ask for staff input on professional development.

▼ Ask for teacher evaluation of professional development.

▼ Support the implementation of training.

▼ Look at a schoolwide/unified focus for staff development.

▼ Look at ways to measure the strategies they are implementing.

▼ Share information about professional development outside the school.

▼ Plan for and engage in peer coaching.

PROFESSIONAL DEVELOPMENT

	One	Two	Three	Four	Five
Approach	There is no professional development. Teachers, principals, and staff are seen as interchangeable parts that can be replaced. Professional development is external and usually equated to attending a conference alone. Hierarchy determines "haves" and "have-nots."	The "cafeteria" approach to professional development is used, whereby individual teachers choose what they want to take, without regard to an overall school plan.	The shared vision, school plan and student needs are used to target focused professional development for all employees. Staff is inserviced on relevant instructional and leadership strategies.	Professional development and data-gathering methods are used by all teachers and are directed toward the goals of the shared vision and the continuous improvement of the school. Teachers have ongoing conversations about student achievement data. Other staff members receive training in their content areas. Systems thinking is considered in all decisions.	Leadership and staff continuously improve all aspects of the learning organization through an innovative, data-driven, and comprehensive continuous improvement process that prevents student failures. Effective job-embedded professional development is ongoing for implementing the vision for student success. Traditional teacher evaluations are replaced by collegial coaching and action research focused on student learning standards. Policies set professional development as a priority budget line-item. Professional development is planned, aligned, and lead to the achievement of student learning standards.
Implementation	Teacher, principal, and staff performance is controlled and inspected. Performance evaluations are used to detect mistakes.	Teacher professional development is sporadic and unfocused, lacking an approach for implementing new procedures and processes. Some leadership training begins to take place.	Teachers are involved in year-round quality professional development. The school community is trained in shared decision making, team building concepts, effective communication strategies, and data analysis at the classroom level.	Teachers, in teams, continuously set and implement student achievement goals. Leadership considers these goals and provides necessary support structures for collaboration. Teachers utilize effective support approaches as they implement new instruction and assessment strategies. Coaching and feedback structures are in place. Use of new knowledge and skills is evident.	Teams passionately support each other in the pursuit of quality improvement at all levels. Teachers make bold changes in instruction and assessment strategies focused on student learning standards and student learning styles. A teacher as action researcher model is implemented. Staffwide conversations focus on systemic reflection and improvement. Teachers are strong leaders.
Outcome	No professional growth and no staff or student performance improvement. There exists a high turnover rate of employees, especially administrators. Attitudes and approaches filter down to students.	The effectiveness of professional development is not known or analyzed. Teachers feel helpless about making schoolwide changes.	Teachers, working in teams, feel supported and begin to feel they can make changes. Evidence shows that shared decision making works.	A collegial school is evident. Effective classroom strategies are practiced, articulated schoolwide, are reflective of professional development aimed at ensuring student achievement, and the implementation of the shared vision, that includes student learning standards.	True systemic change and improved student achievement result because teachers are knowledgeable of and implement effective, differentiated teaching strategies for individual student learning gains. Teachers' repertoire of skills are enhanced and students are achieving. Professional development is driving learning at all levels.

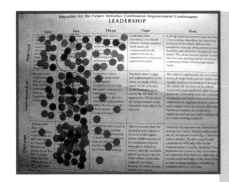

Leadership

Azalea Middle School staff rated their school a 2 in *Approach*, 2 in *Implementation*, and 2 in *Outcome* with respect to *Leadership*. We would like to truly implement shared decision making. We need to learn how to do it well and right.

Next Steps:

Staff agreed that the following needs to happen at the school level with respect to *Leadership*. We need to—

▼ Develop ways to increase teacher leadership.

▼ Investigate and move toward site-based management.

▼ Receive training to implement shared decision making.

LEADERSHIP

	One	Two	Three	Four	Five
Approach	Principal as decision maker. Decisions are reactive to state, district, and federal mandates. There is no knowledge of continuous improvement.	A shared decision-making structure is put into place and discussions begin on how to achieve a school vision. Most decisions are focused on solving problems and are reactive.	Leadership team is committed to continuous improvement. Leadership seeks inclusion of all school sectors and supports study teams by making time provisions for their work.	Leadership team represents a true shared decision making structure. Study teams are reconstructed for the implementation of a comprehensive continuous improvement plan.	A strong continuous improvement structure is set into place that allows for input from all sectors of the school, district, and community, ensuring strong communication, flexibility, and refinement of approach and beliefs. The school vision is student focused, based on data and appropriate for school/ community values, and meeting student needs.
Implementation	Principal makes all decisions, with little or no input from teachers, the community, or students. Leadership inspects for mistakes.	School values and beliefs are identified; the purpose of school is defined; a school mission and student learning standards are developed with representative input. A structure for studying approaches to achieving student learning standards is established.	Leadership team is active on study teams and integrates recommendations from the teams' research and analyses to form a comprehensive plan for continuous improvement within the context of the school mission. Everyone is kept informed.	Decisions about budget and implementation of the vision are made within teams, by the principal, by the leadership team, and by the full staff as appropriate. All decisions are communicated to the leadership team and to the full staff.	The vision is implemented and articulated across all grade levels and into feeder schools. Quality standards are reinforced throughout the school. All members of the school community understand and apply the quality standards. Leadership team has systematic interactions and involvement with district administrators, teachers, parents, community, and students about the school's direction. Necessary resources are available to implement and measure staff learning related to student learning standards.
Outcome	Decisions lack focus and consistency. There is no evidence of staff commitment to a shared vision. Students and parents do not feel they are being heard. Decision-making process is clear and known.	The mission provides a focus for all school improvement and guides the action to the vision. The school community is committed to continuous improvement. Quality leadership techniques are used sporadically.	Leadership team is seen as committed to planning and quality improvement. Critical areas for improvement are identified. Faculty feel included in shared decision making.	There is evidence that the leadership team listens to all levels of the organization. Implementation of the continuous improvement plan is linked to student learning standards and the guiding principles of the school. Leadership capacities for implementing the vision among teachers are evident.	Site-based management and shared decision making truly exists. Teachers understand and display an intimate knowledge of how the school operates. Teachers support and communicate with each other in the implementation of quality strategies. Teachers implement the vision in their classrooms and can determine how their new approach meets student needs and leads to the attainment of student learning standards. Leaders are standards-driven at all levels.

Partnership Development

Azalea Middle School staff rated their school a 2 in *Approach*, 2 in *Implementation*, and 2 in *Outcome* with respect to *Partnership Development*. Our approach to partnerships is mostly seeking money and things. We need to plan for partnerships that are win-win and tied to student learning standards.

Next Steps:

Staff agreed that the following needs to happen at the school level with respect to *Partnership Development*. We need to—

▼ Increase knowledge of school partnership development.

▼ Find ways we can help the businesses.

▼ Identify our needs and businesses' needs.

▼ Increase partnerships across student groups.

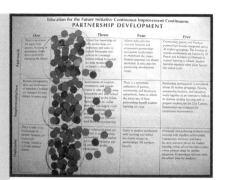

PARTNERSHIP DEVELOPMENT

	One	Two	Three	Four	Five
Approach	There is no system for input from parents, business, or community. Status quo is desired for managing the school.	Partnerships are sought, but mostly for money and things.	School has knowledge of why partnerships are important and seeks to include businesses and parents in a strategic fashion related to student learning standards for increased student achievement.	School seeks effective win-win business and community partnerships and parent involvement to implement the vision. Desired outcomes are clearly identified. A solid plan for partnership development exists.	Community, parent, and business partnerships become integrated across all student groupings. The benefits of outside involvement are known by all. Parent and business involvement in student learning is refined. Student learning *regularly* takes place beyond the school walls.
Implementation	Barriers are erected to close out involvement of outsiders. Outsiders are managed for least impact on status quo.	A team is assigned to get partners and to receive input from parents, the community, and business in the school.	Involvement of business, community, and parents begins to take place in some classrooms and after school hours related to the vision. Partners begin to realize how they can support each other in achieving school goals. School staff understand what partners need from the partnership.	There is a systematic utilization of parents, community, and businesses schoolwide. Areas in which the active use of these partnerships benefit student learning are clear.	Partnership development is articulated across all student groupings. Parents, community, business, and educators work together in an innovative fashion to increase student learning and to prepare students for the 21st Century. Partnerships are evaluated for continuous improvement.
Outcome	There is little or no involvement of parents, business, or community at-large. School is a closed, isolated system.	Much effort is given to establishing partnerships. Some spotty trends emerge, such as receiving donated equipment.	Some substantial gains are achieved in implementing partnerships. Some student achievement increases can be attributed to this involvement.	Gains in student satisfaction with learning and school are clearly related to partnerships. All partners benefit.	Previously non-achieving students enjoy learning with excellent achievement. Community, business, and home become common places for student learning, while school becomes a place where parents come for further education. Partnerships enhance what the school does for students.

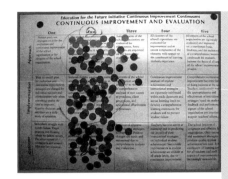

Continuous Improvement and Evaluation

Azalea Middle School staff rated their school 2s in *Approach, Implementation* and *Outcome* with respect to *Continuous Improvement and Evaluation.* We have not done a comprehensive evaluation of our programs and school.

Next Steps:

Staff agreed that the following needs to happen at the school level with respect to *Continuous Improvement and Evaluation.* We need to—

▼ Identify root causes of problems and plan improvement based on the results.

▼ Explore alternative ways to prevent student failure.

▼ Define assessment parameters.

▼ Define data to be used (e.g., classroom grades, assessments, etc.).

▼ Seek information about client perceptions.

CONTINUOUS IMPROVEMENT AND EVALUATION

	One	Two	Three	Four	Five
Approach	Neither goals nor strategies exist for the evaluation and continuous improvement of the school organization or for elements of the school organization.	The approach to continuous improvement and evaluation is problem-solving. If there are no problems, or if solutions can be made quickly, there is no need for improvement or analyses. Changes in parts of the system are not coordinated with all other parts.	Some elements of the school organization are evaluated for effectiveness. Some elements are improved on the basis of the evaluation findings.	All elements of the school's operations are evaluated for improvement and to ensure congruence of the elements with respect to the continuum of learning students experience.	All aspects of the school organization are rigorously evaluated and improved on a continuous basis. Students, and the maintenance of a comprehensive learning continuum for students, become the focus of all aspects of the school improvement process.
Implementation	With no overall plan for evaluation and continuous improvement, strategies are changed by individual teachers and administrators only when something sparks the need to improve. Reactive decisions and activities are a daily mode of operation.	Isolated changes are made in some areas of the school organization in response to problem incidents. Changes are not preceded by comprehensive analyses, such as an understanding of the root causes of problems. The effectiveness of the elements of the school organization, or changes made to the elements, is not known.	Elements of the school organization are improved on the basis of comprehensive analyses of root causes of problems, client perceptions, and operational effectiveness of processes.	Continuous improvement analyses of student achievement and instructional strategies are rigorously reinforced within each classroom and across learning levels to develop a comprehensive learning continuum for students and to prevent student failure.	Comprehensive continuous improvement becomes the way of doing business at the school. Teachers continuously improve the appropriateness and effectiveness of instructional strategies based on student feedback and performance. All aspects of the school organization are improved to support teachers' efforts.
Outcome	Individuals struggle with system failure. Finger pointing and blaming others for failure occurs. The effectiveness of strategies is not known. Mistakes are repeated.	Problems are solved only temporarily and few positive changes result. Additionally, unintended and undesirable consequences often appear in other parts of the system. Many aspects of the school are incongruent, keeping the school from reaching its vision.	Evidence of effective improvement strategies is observable. Positive changes are made and maintained due to comprehensive analyses and evaluation.	Teachers become astute at assessing and in predicting the impact of their instructional strategies on individual student achievement. Sustainable improvements in student achievement are evident at all grade levels, due to continuous improvement.	The school becomes a congruent and effective learning organization. Only instruction and assessment strategies that produce quality student achievement are used. A true continuum of learning results for all students and staff. The impact of improvements is increasingly measurable.

Perceptions

Azalea Middle School students, staff, and parents completed *Education for the Future* questionnaires. *Note:* The complete narratives of these results are located on the CD, along with the tools used to gather and assess perceptions, including questionnaires, and the *School IQ,* which includes the templates to administer the questionnaire online, and to analyze and graph results. (StuNarr.doc, AZStudntQ.pdf, StfNarr.doc, AZStaffQ.pdf, AZStndrdsQ.pdf, ParNarr.doc, AZParentQ.pdf, and the School IQ Folder) For more information about designing questionnaires, see *Data Analysis for Continuous School Improvement* (Bernhardt, 2004).

The icons in the graphs that follow show the average responses to each item by disaggregation indicated in the legend. The lines join the icons to help the reader know the distribution results for each disaggregation. The lines have no other meaning.

Note: Some of the subgroup numbers do not add up to the total number of respondents because some respondents did not identify themselves by this demographic, or identified themselves by more than one demographic.

Student Questionnaire Results

Eighty-six percent of the students in grades six through eight at Azalea Middle School responded in May 2004 to a questionnaire designed to measure how they feel about their learning environment. Students were asked to respond to items using a five-point scale: 1 = strongly disagree; 2 = disagree; 3 = neutral; 4 = agree; and, 5 = strongly agree.

Average responses to each item on the questionnaire were graphed by the totals and disaggregated by gender, grade level, and ethnicity. Some of the graphs are shown on the pages that follow. A summary of results is shown below. (StuNarr.doc)

Average Student Responses

Figure 5.1 shows average student responses to all the items in the student questionnaire were in agreement with the statements, with the exception of three items that were close to neutral (total average shown in all student graphs). These items were: *I have freedom at school, I have choices in what I learn,* and *Students are treated fairly by teachers.*

Student Responses by Gender

Student responses disaggregated by gender revealed responses very similar to each other, and clustered around the overall average. (Graph not shown.)

Student Responses by Grade Level

The questionnaire results were also disaggregated by grade level. There were 229 sixth graders (85% response rate); 215 seventh graders (85% response rate); and 217 eighth graders (83% response rate) responding. The graph (Figure 5.1) revealed some slight differences when disaggregated by grade level. Sixth graders were generally the highest in agreement, while eighth graders were generally in lowest agreement.

Figure 5.1

Azalea Middle School Student Responses By Grade Level
May 2004

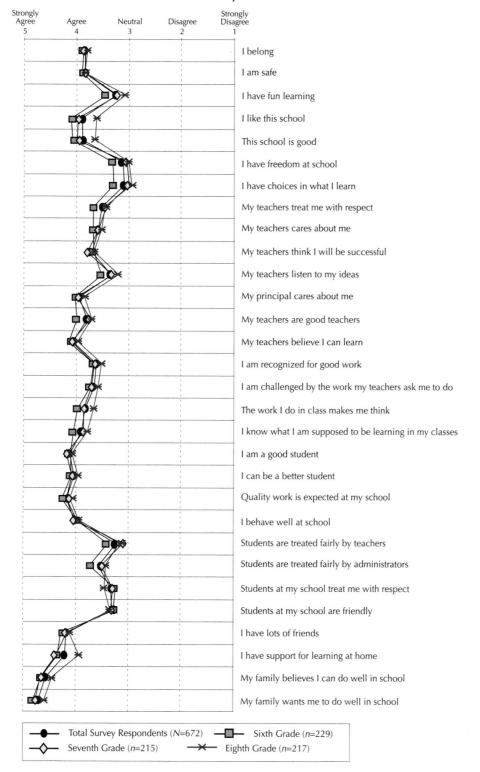

	Strongly Agree 5	Agree 4	Neutral 3	Disagree 2	Strongly Disagree 1

I belong

I am safe

I have fun learning

I like this school

This school is good

I have freedom at school

I have choices in what I learn

My teachers treat me with respect

My teachers cares about me

My teachers think I will be successful

My teachers listen to my ideas

My principal cares about me

My teachers are good teachers

My teachers believe I can learn

I am recognized for good work

I am challenged by the work my teachers ask me to do

The work I do in class makes me think

I know what I am supposed to be learning in my classes

I am a good student

I can be a better student

Quality work is expected at my school

I behave well at school

Students are treated fairly by teachers

Students are treated fairly by administrators

Students at my school treat me with respect

Students at my school are friendly

I have lots of friends

I have support for learning at home

My family believes I can do well in school

My family wants me to do well in school

Legend:
- ● Total Survey Respondents (*N*=672)
- ■ Sixth Grade (*n*=229)
- ◇ Seventh Grade (*n*=215)
- ✳ Eighth Grade (*n*=217)

Student Responses by Ethnicity

Student questionnaire data were also disaggregated by ethnicity (414 White; 122 Black; 46 Asian; 34 Hispanic/Latino; and 97 Other students responded). Responses were similar and revealed few differences (Figure 5.2) with this exception: Asian students generally responded less positively than other subgroups. While the subgroup of students marking themselves as Asian is different from enrollment numbers, we need to follow-up to find out who these students are and why they responded this way.

Student Open-ended Responses

In May 2004, Azalea Middle School students were asked to respond to two open-ended questions: *What do you like about your school?* and *What do you wish was different at your school?* The top ten responses are shown below. (*Note:* When analyzing open-ended results, one must keep in mind the number of responses that were written-in. Open-ended responses often help us understand the multiple choice responses, although caution must be exercised around small numbers of respondents. A file to help you analyze open-ended responses is on the CD.) (OEanalz.pdf)

What do you like about your school?	What do you wish was different at your school?
◆ Good teachers (145)	◆ Less strict dress code (65)
◆ This school has a very strong arts program (98)	◆ Teachers more respectful of all students (59)
◆ My friends (51)	◆ Better lunches and more food in the cafeteria (53)
◆ The class choices we have for electives (30)	◆ Bigger hallways (37)
◆ Gym (27)	◆ Cleaner bathrooms with locks on the doors (32)
◆ Nothing! (23)	◆ Less homework and fewer projects (25)
◆ Learning can be fun (14)	◆ Students would treat each other better (20)
◆ The people (14)	◆ No teaming (14)
◆ The band program (10)	◆ Be able to chew gum (8)
◆ My work is challenging (9)	◆ More freedom (7)

Figure 5.2

Azalea Middle School Student Responses By Ethnicity
May 2004

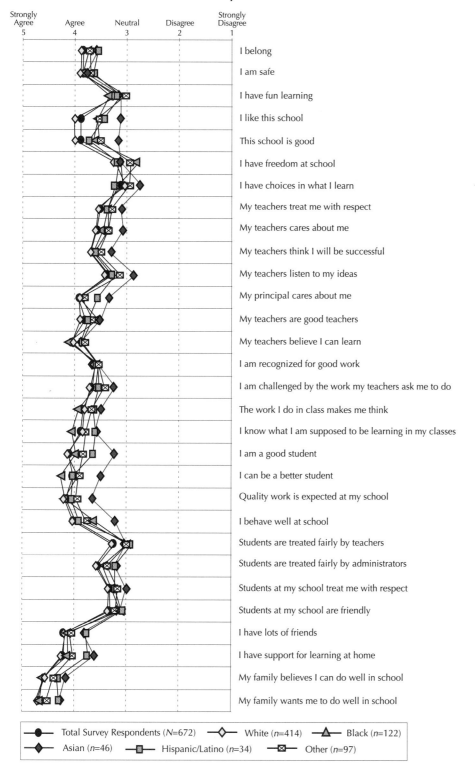

Staff Questionnaire Results

Azalea staff (n=49, 98%) responded in May 2004 to a questionnaire designed to measure their perceptions of the school environment. Members of the staff were asked to respond to items using a five-point scale: 1 = strongly disagree; 2 = disagree; 3 = neutral; 4 = agree; and 5 = strongly agree.

Average responses to the items on the questionnaire were graphed and disaggregated by the total and number of years teaching. A summary of results is shown below, while the full narrative is a file on the CD. (StfNarr.doc)

Average Staff Responses

Overall, the average responses to the staff questionnaire are in agreement with most of the statements in the questionnaire. The average for the total group is graphed in Figure 5.3.

Figure 5.3

Azalea Middle School Staff Responses
May 2004

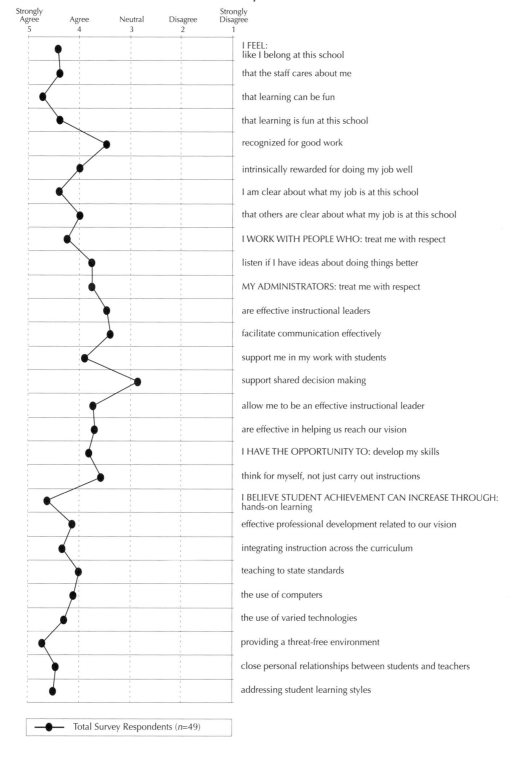

Total Survey Respondents (n=49)

Figure 5.3 (Continued)

Azalea Middle School Staff Responses
May 2004

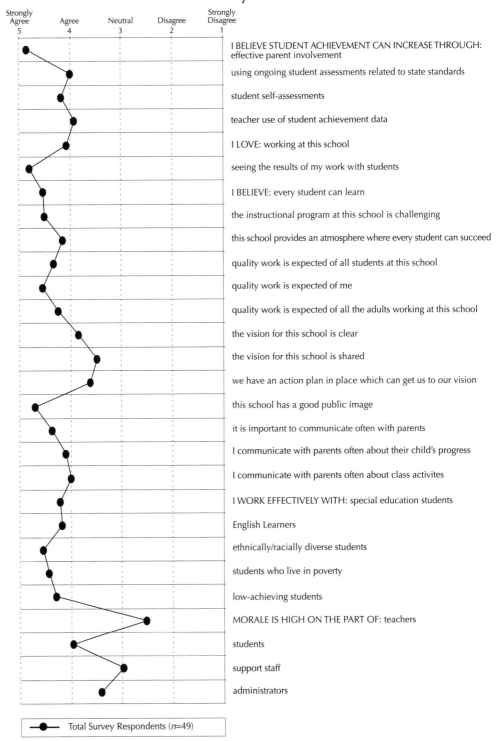

Total Survey Respondents (*n*=49)

Figure 5.3 (Continued)

Azalea Middle School Staff Responses
May 2004

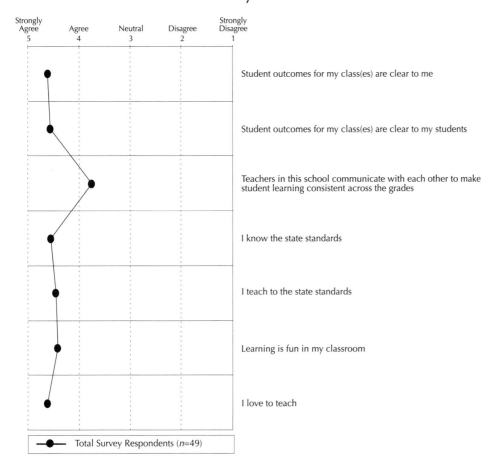

Staff Responses by Number of Years Teaching

Staff questionnaire data were also disaggregated by the number of years of teaching (one to three years, $n=5$; four to six years, $n=5$; seven to ten years, $n=8$; and eleven or more years, $n=31$). Results graphed by this demographic reveal some apparent differences in responses, although the size of the subgroups needs to be taken into consideration (Figure 5.4).

Note: The size of most of the subgroups is very small. This graph would be used for inhouse improvement only.

Figure 5.4

Azalea Middle School Staff Responses by Number of Years Teaching
May 2004

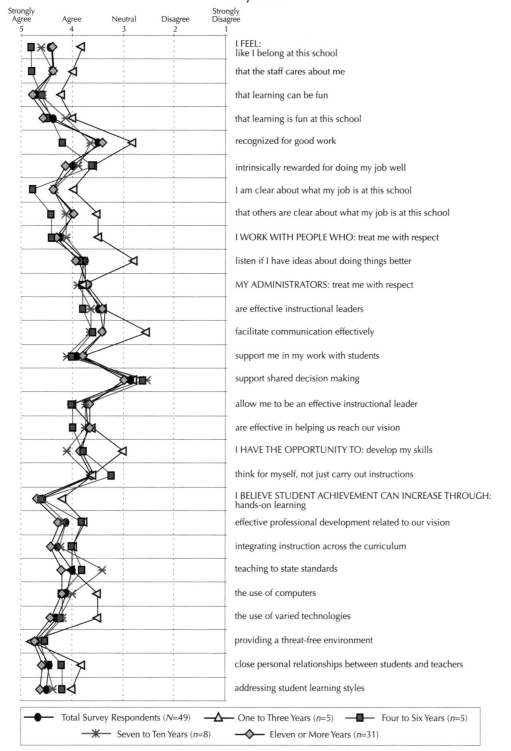

Strongly Agree	Agree	Neutral	Disagree	Strongly Disagree
5	4	3	2	1

I FEEL:
like I belong at this school

that the staff cares about me

that learning can be fun

that learning is fun at this school

recognized for good work

intrinsically rewarded for doing my job well

I am clear about what my job is at this school

that others are clear about what my job is at this school

I WORK WITH PEOPLE WHO: treat me with respect

listen if I have ideas about doing things better

MY ADMINISTRATORS: treat me with respect

are effective instructional leaders

facilitate communication effectively

support me in my work with students

support shared decision making

allow me to be an effective instructional leader

are effective in helping us reach our vision

I HAVE THE OPPORTUNITY TO: develop my skills

think for myself, not just carry out instructions

I BELIEVE STUDENT ACHIEVEMENT CAN INCREASE THROUGH:
hands-on learning

effective professional development related to our vision

integrating instruction across the curriculum

teaching to state standards

the use of computers

the use of varied technologies

providing a threat-free environment

close personal relationships between students and teachers

addressing student learning styles

●— Total Survey Respondents (*N*=49)	△— One to Three Years (*n*=5)	■— Four to Six Years (*n*=5)
✳— Seven to Ten Years (*n*=8)	◆— Eleven or More Years (*n*=31)	

Figure 5.4 (Continued)

Azalea Middle School Staff Responses by Number of Years Teaching
May 2004

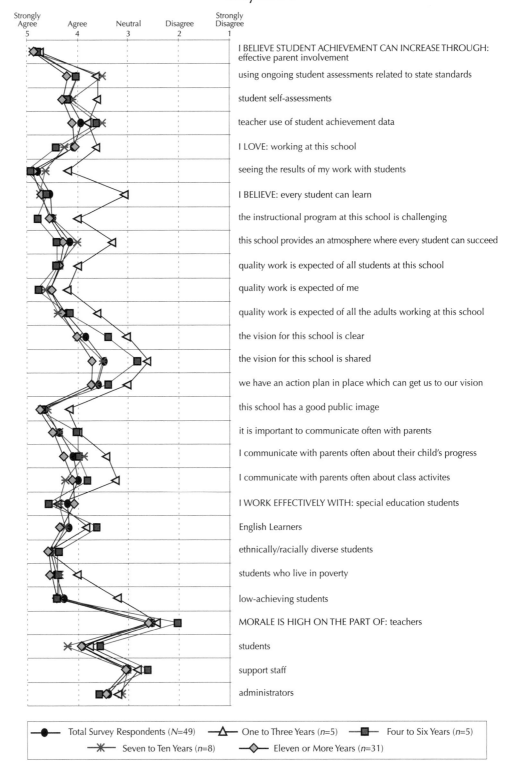

Figure 5.4 (Continued)

Azalea Middle School Staff Responses by Number of Years Teaching
May 2004

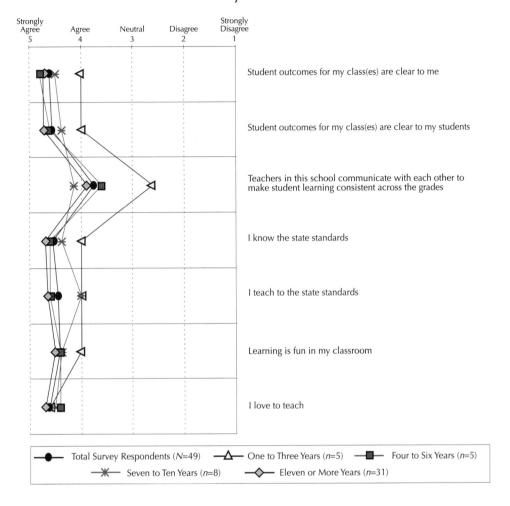

Staff Open-ended Responses

Azalea Middle School staff responded to two open-ended questions in May 2004: *What are the strengths of this school?* and *What needs to be improved?* The top ten responses are shown below.

What are the strengths of this school?	*What needs to be improved?*
• Dedicated staff (32) • Extremely talented students (10) • The Arts program (8) • The school's reputation (2) • The teachers' love for their students and their curriculum • Appropriate facilities for our unique program • The parents of the children we teach are wonderful and helpful • Majority of students are motivated to learn • Principal has a strong vision for student achievement • Student diversity	• Incorporate shared decision making so teachers have a voice (12) • An administration that will listen to our input and use our ideas (7) • Time emphasis should be on teachers' teaching (6) • We need more teacher input related to the areas we teach (4) • Teacher morale (3) • Communication among all staff members (3) • Learning-focused teaching strategies (middle school initiative in our district) (2) • Achievement of our impoverished children and slow learners (2) • Learning styles • Literacy instruction for below-grade-level readers

Parent Questionnaire Results

Parents of students attending Azalea Middle School responded in May 2004 to a questionnaire designed to measure their perceptions of the school environment (n=350; 75% response rate). Parents were asked to respond to items using a five-point scale: 1 = strongly disagree; 2 = disagree; 3 = neutral; 4 = agree; and, 5 = strongly agree.

Average responses to each item on the questionnaire were graphed and disaggregated by ethnicity, children's grade levels, number of children in the household, and number of children in the school. A summary of results is shown below. (ParNarr.doc)

Average Parent Responses

Overall, the average responses to the items in the parent questionnaire were in agreement. The item averages are shown on the graphs that follow.

Parent Responses by Ethnicity

When parent questionnaire data were disaggregated by ethnicity, 274 White, 32 Black, 18 Hispanic/Latino, 17 Asian, and 16 Other students responded (Figure 5.5). Results show that Black and "Other" parents were generally less positive in their responses. Some differences were noted, although most averages were in agreement. The lowest averages were near or just below neutral. Once again, we must take the small subgroups into consideration.

Figure 5.5

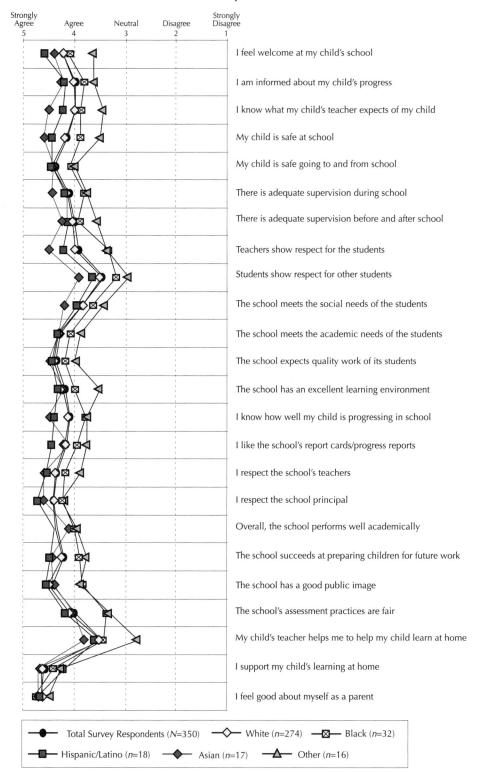

Azalea Middle School Parent Responses by Ethnicity
May 2004

Parent Responses by Children's Grade Levels

Parent questionnaire responses disaggregated by children's grade levels revealed few differences. No significant distinguishing pattern emerged when looking at the data by these subgroups. (Graph not shown here.)

Parent Responses by Number of Children in the School

Parent questionnaire data disaggregated by the number of children in the school clustered around the overall average and reveal few differences in responses. (Graph not shown here.)

Parent Responses by Number of Children in the Household

Parent questionnaire data were also disaggregated by the number of children in the household (one child, $n=62$; two children, $n=158$; three children, $n=82$; and four children, $n=24$). Results graphed by this demographic revealed some differences in responses (Figure 5.6).

Figure 5.6

Azalea Middle School Parent Responses by Number of Children in the Household, May 2004

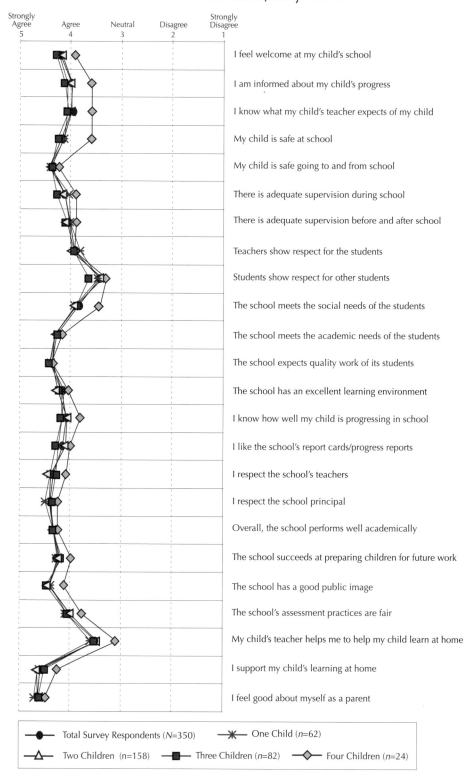

Standards Assessment

During May 2004, *Education for the Future* piloted a Standards Assessment questionnaire for middle school teachers. The questionnaire contained nine questions, asking about how well teachers know the standards, and to what degree they are implementing the standards. 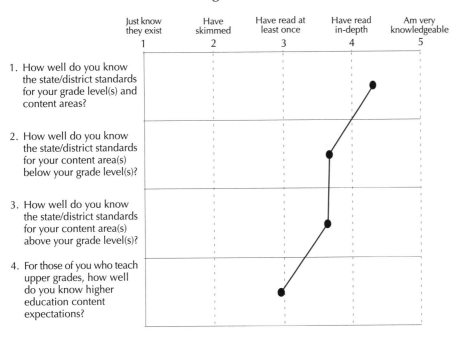 (AZStandards.pdf) A total of 36 teachers at Azalea Middle School responded (72%). A summary of the results for questions one through four are shown in two different ways—Figure 5.7 shows average responses, followed by Figure 5.8, which shows the percentage responding to each response option for the questions.

Figure 5.7

Figure 5.8

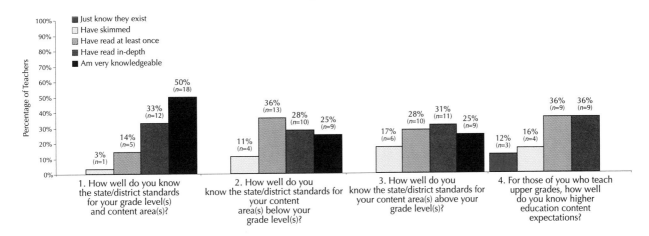

Azalea Middle School teachers were asked how well they know what it would look like, sound like, and feel like if they were teaching to the standards 100% of the time. Responses to question 5 are shown in Figure 5.9.

Figure 5.9

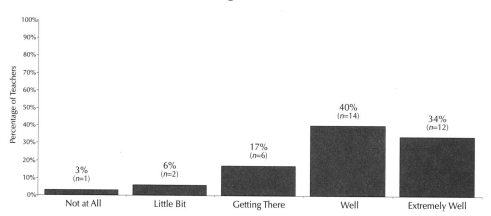

Azalea teachers were asked what would help them better know the standards. They were asked to select all statements that apply. Responses to question 6 are shown in Figure 5.10.

Figure 5.10

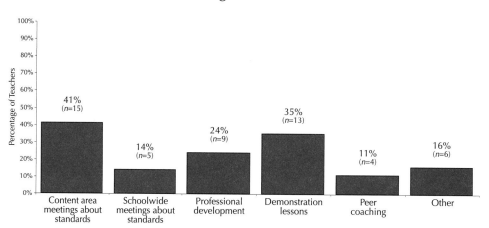

In addition to the response option statements in Figure 5.10, teachers added comments about other things that would help them better know the standards:

▼ We need more time to teach and plan—we don't have the time to get to all of the standards. (3)

▼ The instructional coaching that we are getting now does not affect all areas of instruction.

▼ Planning with other teachers in the district that teach my subject and grade level, with continued contact as the year progresses.

▼ Quality peer coaching.

▼ Professional development sessions especially for my content area— not generic sessions that cross all, or multiple disciplines (i.e., not Fine Arts, but a session for Visual Arts, Dance).

Teachers were asked which statement best describes how they use standards to design instruction. Responses to question 7 are shown in Figure 5.11.

Figure 5.11

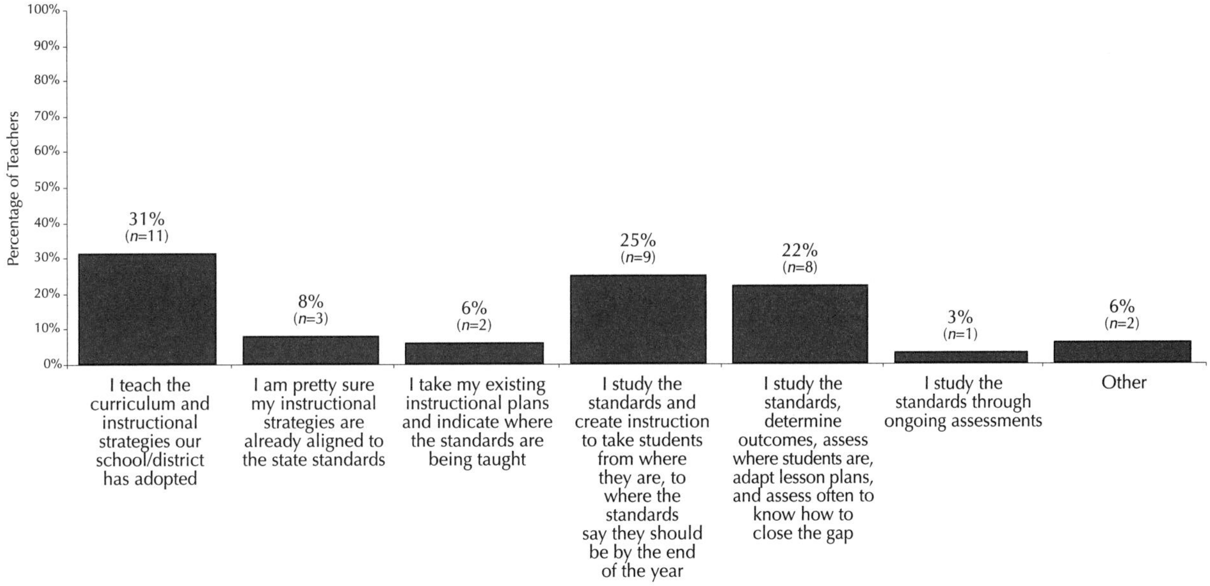

Teachers were asked what they do when students do not learn the standards. Teachers were able to select all statements that apply. Responses to question 8 are shown in Figure 5.12.

Figure 5.12

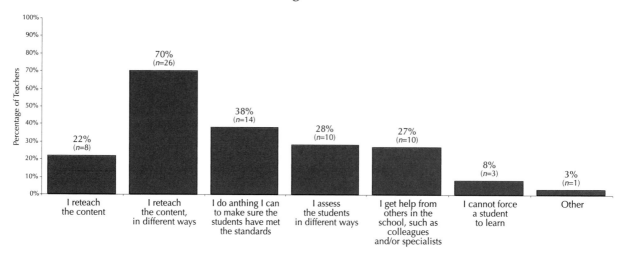

Azalea middle school teachers were asked how much support they feel from their learning organization to ensure that standards are being implemented. Question 9 results are shown in two different ways—Figure 5.13 shows average responses, followed by Figure 5.14, which shows the percentage responding to each response option.

In addition to the response option statements in Figures 5.13 and 5.14, teachers added comments about what they would like to see their learning organization do to help them ensure that all students are meeting the state/district content standards:

▼ We need specific content area meeting time with other schools/teachers in the same area. (6)

▼ Smaller classes. (3)

▼ We need to get parents of reluctant learners more involved.

▼ Less quantity, more quality.

▼ Less paperwork.

▼ Fewer meetings.

▼ I felt lost not being prepared for the new and totally different Language Arts standards.

Figure 5.13

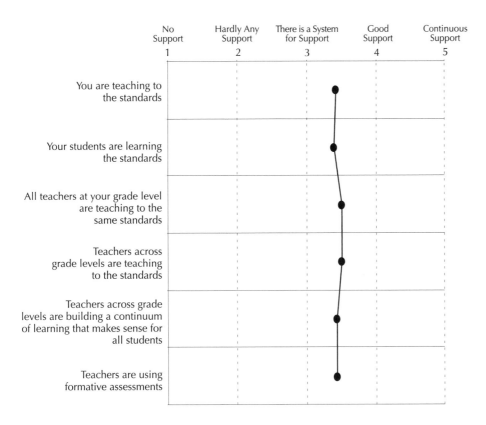

Figure 5.14

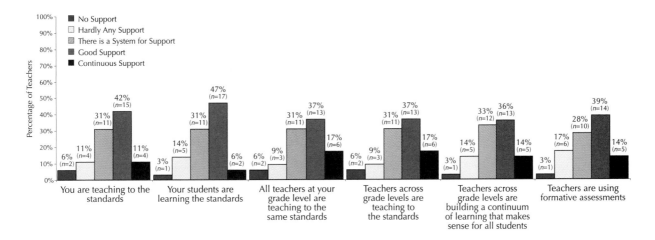

Professional Development Assessment

At the beginning of the 2003-04 year, Azalea staff rated the school 3s in *Approach, Implementation,* and *Outcome* with respect to *Professional Development.* According to this rating, the staff viewed Azalea as a school where student needs are used to target professional development. There is year-round professional development on relevant instructional and leadership strategies, many of which begin to lead in the direction of shared decision making, team building, and data analysis. However, it is apparent from the rating on the Continuum that staff viewed professional development neither as the driver of learning at all levels, nor as a tool aligned to the achievement of student learning standards. The consensus seemed to be that, though Azalea's multiple professional development opportunities may be seen as a strength, this plethora of opportunities may also be seen as a weakness, as it accentuates a lack of focus and connection. The volume of professional development opportunities does not allow for adequate feedback, continuity, and time to implement the strategies learned.

Next Steps were agreed upon that included asking staff for input on professional development and looking for a schoolwide unified focus. In creating a shared vision, two areas of focus were agreed upon—improving student achievement and improving school climate.

Professional development will continue throughout the year, and the staff will be surveyed again in 2004-05 to evaluate the effectiveness of this professional development.

Professional Development Questionnaire

In Spring 2004, Azalea Middle School staff completed a questionnaire designed to assess the frequency with which teachers implemented strategies that are a part of their vision, and their comfort with implementing the strategies. Staff were also asked about their professional development activities. Staff were asked to respond to frequency items using a five-point scale: 1 = every day; 2 = three or more times per week; 3 = once per week; 4 = monthly; and, 5 = seldom or never. The results follow.

The results of the professional development assessment indicate a few trends (Figure 5.15). According to the average responses, 67% of the staff view the professional development opportunities at Azalea as *somewhat helpful;* 14% view the professional development as *very helpful;* and 17% view it as *not helpful.* Based on the comments that were recorded on the assessment, some of the same weaknesses noted at the beginning of the year are still considered weaknesses: opportunities are too broad and unfocused, time constraints make implementation very difficult, and there is little follow-through or feedback on the professional development opportunities that could give staff the continuity necessary for the effective implementation.

Staff indicated that small group settings for professional development, such as grade-level or department, are preferred over entire faculty sessions. Other indications were that teachers' comfort levels and frequency of use of standards-based instruction as well as arts-focused instruction were high. On the other hand, the comfort level and frequency of use of learning focused strategies, differentiated instructional strategies, and technology were lower. The indication was that the staff would benefit greatly from focused professional development on a *few* areas in small group settings.

Figure 5.15

Azalea Middle School
Professional Development Assessment Results, Spring 2004

Frequency of Strategies and Instruction Implemented by Teachers	Seldom or Never		Monthly		Once per Week		Three or More Times Per Week		Everyday	
	Number	Percent	Number	Percent	Number	Percent	Number	Percent	Number	Percent
Learning-focused strategies (*n*=34)	1	3%	2	6%	12	35%	9	27%	10	29%
Differentiated instructional strategies (*n*=33)	2	6%	1	3%	7	21%	18	55%	5	15%
Standards-based instruction(*n*=33)	0	0%	0	0%	1	3%	8	24%	24	73%
Internet as tool(*n*=34)	6	18%	18	53%	4	12%	6	18%	0	0%
Arts-focused instruction(*n*=34)	3	9%	9	27%	12	35%	7	21%	3	9%
Implementation of technology tools (*n*=34)	8	24%	8	24%	9	27%	6	18%	3	9%
Comfort Level Implementing Strategies and Instruction	Not Familiar		Uncomfortable		Somewhat Comfortable		Comfortable		Very Comfortable	
Learning-focused strategies (*n*=33)	0	0%	1	3%	13	38%	13	38%	6	18%
Differentiated instructional strategies (*n*=32)	0	0%	2	6%	10	29%	14	41%	6	18%
Standards-based instruction (*n*=34)	0	0%	1	3%	4	12%	8	24%	21	62%
Internet as tool (*n*=34)	1	3%	4	12%	13	38%	9	27%	7	21%
Arts-focused instruction (*n*=34)	0	0%	1	3%	5	15%	13	38%	15	44%
Implementation of technology tools (*n*=34)	1	3%	4	12%	9	27%	13	38%	7	21%
Most Effective Setting for Professional Development	Entire Faculty		Grade Level		Department		Team			
Most effective setting (*n*=32)	3	9%	11	32%	11	32%	7	21%		
Effectiveness of Professional Development Activities	Not Effective		Effective		Very Effective					
Vertical Teaming (*n*=28)	10	29%	17	68%	1	3%				
Helpfulness of Professional Development Activities	Not Effective		Effective		Very Effective					
Peer observation (*n*=34)	13	38%	16	47%	5	15%				
Literacy strategies (*n*=34)	12	35%	13	38%	9	27%				
Overall usefulness of PD activities (*n*=34)	6	18%	23	68%	5	15%				

Other Comments

Staff were also asked to write-in comments they had about the professional development opportunities at Azalea:

▼ While once a week team time may be an *easy time* to schedule professional development, it often creates added stress to an already overwhelmed faculty spread thin to accommodate student needs, parent demands, and school/ district expectations. As mere mortals, we can only do so much!

▼ Allow teachers to attend content area professional development on teacher workdays, without having that particular day count towards our days absent from Azalea.

▼ Could the Instructional Coach assist teachers to tutor below-basic students? I have felt somewhat overwhelmed with meetings this year.

▼ In computer technology, small groups would be more helpful (1-4 people, grouped by competency level), rather than half the faculty or teams.

▼ In other training, I prefer whole faculty when it is pertinent to all. Otherwise, professional development should be limited to those for whom it is pertinent.

▼ There were too many weekly meetings. Maybe arts integration would be better done by departments some of the time so they could concentrate on a subject area. There was very little time to meet as a team some weeks because of conferences, other meetings, and class coverage.

▼ Teachers will not use strategies if we are not given time to implement them!

▼ It would be nice to have professional development on workdays— during the average day we are extremely busy! Lately, grades are due before workdays anyway!

▼ Ask teachers what would best help them instead of providing professional development that serves the purpose of someone unrelated to this school.

▼ Need arts integration workshops on how we can better do what we are already trying to do.

▼ Need to be allowed to have input that is taken into consideration, not constantly ignored.

▼ Need more content area for all concerned, not just a select few.

▼ Need flexibility to attend content area opportunities when they are available.

Study Questions for How Do We Do Business?

As you review Azalea's perceptual data, use either the margins in the text, this page, or print this page from the CD to write down your early thinking. ⊙ (Ch5Qs.pdf) These notes, of course, are only hunches or placeholders until all the data are analyzed.

1. What are the perceptual *strengths* and *challenges* for Azalea Middle School?	
Strengths	*Challenges*

2. What are some *implications* for the Azalea school improvement plan?

3. Looking at the data presented, what other perceptual data would you want to answer the question *How do we do business?* for Azalea Middle School?

What I Saw in the Example: Azalea Middle School

Using the study questions as an outline, what I saw in the data for Chapter 5 appears below. 🔘 (Ch5Saw.pdf) When applicable, I have referenced the figure or page number that gave me my first impression of strengths and challenges.

Continuous Improvement Continuums Assessment

Perceptual Strengths	*Perceptual Challenges*
◆ Staff did the assessments on the CICs to see how their system is doing. (Page 69-76) ◆ The discussion must have been powerful, as consensus seemed to go against the majority's initial impressions. ◆ Love the digital pictures to see the spread of dots across the continuums. ◆ Staff knows what they need to do, and the next steps are doable.	◆ There have been no follow-up assessments on the CICs. ◆ Need better collaboration and communication. (Pages 70-71) ◆ Staff would like more training in data analysis. (Page 70) ◆ Staff wants to survey students (which was done). (Page 70) ◆ Staff would like their school teams to collaborate on data and instruction. (Page 71) ◆ Staff would like training in effective instructional strategies and ways to implement peer coaching. (Page 71) ◆ Staff would like other ways to assess students. (Page 71) ◆ Staff needs to do a better job of communicating the school's vision, mission, and plan. (Page 72) ◆ The Azalea plan needs measurable outcomes. (Page 72) ◆ Staff need to follow-through with the school portfolio. (Page 72) ◆ Need staff input on professional development, to evaluate professional development, and support its implementation. (Page 73) ◆ Need to plan for and engage in peer coaching. (Page 73) ◆ Staff needs to implement shared decision making. (Page 74) ◆ Need to increase partnerships in meaningful ways. (Page 75) ◆ Staff needs to perform a comprehensive evaluation of programs and the school, and identify root causes. (Page 76)

Implications for Azalea's school improvement plan

◆ Need to schedule time to reassess on the CICs.
◆ Need to make data more assessable, so it can be used to drive decisions.
◆ Teachers need to be trained in data analysis, in gap analysis, and in determining root causes.
◆ Staff would like professional development in effective instructional strategies.
◆ Staff want and need alternative assessments, and to define measurable outcomes.
◆ Staff would like to implement peer coaching.
◆ Staff wants follow-through on the school portfolio.
◆ The vision, mission, and plan need to be communicated to and implemented by everyone.
◆ The school needs to seek perceptions of clients.
◆ Need to move staff toward shared decision making. Professional development in shared decision making and an increase in teacher leadership would help.
◆ Need schoolwide focus and input on professional development. Also need to implement and evaluate professional development aligned to the vision.
◆ Need a plan for partnerships after studying strategies related to student learning standards.
◆ Need to study root causes, other ways to prevent student failure, evaluate programs and processes, and the school as a whole.
◆ Define data to be used for continuous improvement and evaluation.

Other desired perceptual data or information

◆ Need another assessment on the CICs to see progress.

What I Saw in the Example: Azalea Middle School (Continued)

Questionnaire Data

Perceptual Strengths	Perceptual Challenges
Student questionnaires • Students are in agreement with most items on an average. Although three items are neutral, no real differences exist between genders, grade levels, or ethnicities. (Figures 5.1 and 5.2) • Students feel their families want them to do well and believe they can do well. (Page 79) • There are no real differences between grade levels. (Page 79) • Students like their friends. (Page 80) • One hundred forty-five students think the teachers are good. (Page 80) • Students like the arts program. (Page 80)	*Student questionnaires* • The student responses pointed to some issues about treatment of students by students and teachers, and having freedom and choices. (Figure 5.2) • Asian students rated the learning environment the lowest. Although the numbers of the Asians do not match the enrollment, this needs to be followed-up. (Figure 5.2) • Twenty-three students wrote in that there was nothing they liked about the school. (Page 80) • Sixty-five students do not like the strict dress code. (Page 80) • Fifty-nine students mentioned that teachers should be more respectful of all students. (Page 80)
Staff questionnaires • Staff did a great job of administering the questionnaires. It was identified as a need, they did it, and got good response rates. (Page 82) • Most teachers' averages were in agreement. (Figure 5.3) • Many teachers feel staff is dedicated. (Page 90) • Staff feel strongly that the school has a good public image; that student achievement can increase through effective parent involvement, hands-on learning, and providing a threat-free environment; and they love seeing the results of their work with students. (Page 90) • Teachers feel student outcomes for their classes are clear to them and their students; they know and teach to the state standards; learning is fun in their classroom; and they love to teach. (Page 85)	*Staff questionnaires* • Shared decision making seems to be an issue for teachers. (Page 90 and Figures 5.3 and 5.4) • Teachers feel morale is low on the part of teachers and support staff. (Figure 5.3) • Communication across grade levels could improve. (Page 90) • Newer (1 to 3 years experience) teachers' responses indicate that they are not being brought along as "full" staff members. (Figure 5.4) • New (1 to 3 years experience) teachers don't think all students can learn. (Figure 5.4) • It is pretty obvious that teachers with seven or fewer years of teaching experience did not participate in the vision work. (Figure 5.4)
Parent questionnaires • Parents are pretty satisfied with the school, with the exception of students respecting each other and teachers helping parents help students learn at home. (Figure 5.5)	*Parent questionnaires* • "Other" parents generally seemed the least positive. (Figure 5.5) • Parents with four children in the household seemed less positive than parents with fewer children at home, although the differences are small. (Figure 5.6) • Not all parents feel students and teachers show respect for students. (Figure 5.5) • Not all parents feel teachers help them to help their child learn at home. (Figure 5.5)

Implications for Azalea's school improvement plan

• Might need to rethink discipline policies/strategies, how everyone respects each other, and the dress code.
• Staff needs to follow-up with students who are not feeling respected.
• Professional development in shared decision making—the creation of a true shared decision-making structure might bring up the staff and administration morale.
• Staff need to revisit the vision to bring newer teachers on board.
• A new plan needs to be created to implement a vision that everyone believes in and supports.
• Staff needs to implement strategies to improve communication, collaboration, and morale.
• Staff might need to work with parents more to help them help their children learn at home.

Other desired perceptual data or information

• Parents need an opportunity to write-in open-ended responses.
• Follow-up with students saying they are not feeling respected.

Standards Assessment Data

Perceptual Strengths	*Perceptual Challenges*
• Staff assessed where they were with standards. • Eighty-three percent indicated they know their content and grade-level standards in-depth. (Page 95) • Most teachers reported that they know what it would look like, sound like, and feel like if they were teaching to the standards 100% of the time. (Page 96) • Many of the teachers seem to be aware of standards-based instruction. (Pages 97-98) • Teachers feel there is a support system for standards teaching and learning. (Page 99)	• Teachers feel that content-area meetings and demonstration lessons would help them better know the standards—not peer coaching as mentioned in the CIC assessment. (Figure 5.10) • Teachers need more time to plan and teach the standards. (Page 97) • Current instructional coaching does not include all areas of instruction. (Page 97) • There is one teacher who does not know what it would look like to be teaching to the standards; two others said they knew a little bit. (Figure 5.9) • Teachers seem to be a little less aware of education expectations that follow them than the expectations of the previous grades. (Page 95)

Implications for Azalea's school improvement plan

Need to get all teachers knowing and implementing content standards, through:
• Content-area meetings about standards.
• Demonstration lessons.
• Planning and ongoing communication with other teachers in the district who teach the same subjects and grade levels.
• Planning time by subject and grade level.
• A stronger support system for ensuring teaching to standards.
• Perhaps an instructional coach in subject areas other than those currently covered—peer coaching could help, too.

Other desired perceptual data or information

• Are there particular subject-area standards that teachers do not know? Or is it teacher-dependent?

What I Saw in the Example: Azalea Middle School (Continued)

Professional Development Assessment

Perceptual Strengths	Perceptual Challenges
• It is great that staff decided to assess the effectiveness of their professional development. • It is wonderful that staff is assessing the implementation of their vision. • One can tell from this customized questionnaire that this staff has done a lot of professional development. • Seventy-three percent of staff reported they are implementing standards-based instruction everyday; 97%, three or more times per week. (Figure 5.15) • Fifty-six percent reported they are using learning-focused strategies three or more times per week. (Figure 5.15) • Seventy percent of the staff indicated they are differentiating instruction three or more times per week. (Figure 5.15) • Staff is most comfortable implementing standards-based instruction. (Page 101 and Figure 5.15)	• The response rate did not include all instructional staff. • Almost one-half of the responding staff indicated they are implementing technology tools—monthly, seldom, or never. (Figure 5.15) • Staff seems to be least comfortable with implementing technology tools in instruction. (Page 101 and Figure 5.15) • In the open-ended responses, staff suggested improvements in how they work and learn together. (Page 103) • Only one person felt that vertical teaming was very effective. (Figure 5.15) • Perhaps having so many professional development opportunities leads to a lack of focus and connection.

Implications for Azalea's school improvement plan

• Explore the feasibility of adding more professional development days.
• Implement more grade level and department meetings focused on demonstrating different instructional strategies.
• Focus professional development opportunities on the school vision and standards.

Other desired perceptual data or information

• Why do teachers perceive vertical teaming to be less than effective?

Summary

The second question, *How do we do business?*, tells us about perceptions of the learning environment from student, staff, and parent perspectives. Multiple-choice questionnaires can give us a quick snapshot of different groups' perspectives. Open-ended responses, used with the multiple choice responses, help paint the picture of the school. Understanding how we do business can help a school know what is possible, what is appropriate, and what is needed in the continuous school improvement plan.

The *Education for the Future Continuous Improvement Continuums* are also a valuable assessment tool for understanding the system.

On the CD Related to this Chapter

▼ *Continuous Improvement Continuums* for Schools (CICs.pdf)
This read-only file contains the seven *School Portfolio Continuous Improvement Continuums* for schools. These can be printed as is and enlarged for posting individual staff opinions during staff assessments.

▼ *Continuous Improvement Continuums* for Districts (CICsDstrct.pdf)
This read-only file contains the seven *School Portfolio Continuous Improvement Continuums* for assessing the district level. These can be printed as is and enlarged for posting individual staff opinions during staff assessments.

▼ *Azalea Middle School Baseline CIC Results* (AZBase.pdf)
This read-only file is the summary of Azalea's baseline assessment on the *School Portfolio Continuous Improvement Continuums.*

▼ *Continuous Improvement Continuum* Tools Folder
These files are tools for assessing on the CICs and for writing the CIC report.

◆ *Continuous Improvement Continuums Self-Assessment Activity* (ACTCIC.pdf)
Assessing on the *Continuous Improvement Continuums* will help staffs see where their systems are right now with respect to continuous improvement and ultimately will show they are making progress over time. The discussion has major implications for the *Continuous School Improvement (CSI) Plan.*

◆ *Coming to Consensus* (Consenss.pdf)
This read-only file provides strategies for coming to consensus, useful when assessing on the *Continuous Improvement Continuums.*

> *Understanding how we do business can help a school know what is possible, what is appropriate, and what is needed in the continuous school improvement plan.*

- *Continuous Improvement Continuums Report Example* (ExReprt1.pdf)
  This read-only file shows a real school's assessment on the *School Portfolio Continuous Improvement Continuums,* as an example.

- *Continuous Improvement Continuums Report Example for Follow-up Years* (ExReprt2.pdf)
  This read-only file shows a real school's assessment on the *School Portfolio Continuous Improvement Continuums* over time, as an example.

- *Continuous Improvement Continuums Baseline Report Template* (ReptTemp.doc)
  This *Microsoft Word* file provides a template for writing your school's report of its assessment on the *School Portfolio Continuous Improvement Continuums.*

- *Continuous Improvement Continuums Graphing Templates* (CICGraph.xls)
  This *Microsoft Excel* file is a template for graphing your assessments on the seven *School Portfolio Continuous Improvement Continuums.*

▼ Study Questions Related to *How Do We Do Business?* (Ch5Qs.pdf)
These study questions will help you better understand the information provided in Chapter 5. This file can be printed for use with staffs as you answer the question, *How do we do business?,* through analyzing Azalea's perceptual data.

▼ *What I Saw in the Example* (Ch5Saw.pdf)
What I Saw in the Example is a file, organized by the perceptual study questions, that summarizes what the author saw in the perceptual data provided by Azalea Middle School.

▼ *Analysis of Questionnaire Data Table* (QTable.doc)
This *Microsoft Word* file is a tabular guide for interpreting your student, staff, and parent questionnaires, independently and interdependently. It will help you see the summary of your results and write the narrative.

▼ Full Narratives of Questionnaire Results Used in the Azalea Example:
- *Azalea Student Questionnaire Results* (StuNarr.doc)
- *Azalea Staff Questionnaire Results* (StfNarr.doc)
- *Azalea Parent Questionnaire Results* (ParNarr.doc)

▼ *Education for the Future* Perception Questionnaires Used in the Azalea Example:

◆ *Student Questionnaire* (AZStudntQ.pdf)

◆ *Staff Questionnaire* (AZStaffQ.pdf)

◆ *Staff Standards Assessment Questionnaire* (AZStndrdsQ.pdf)

◆ *Parent Questionnaire* (AZParentQ.pdf)

▼ *School IQ: School Improvement Questionnaire Solutions* is a powerful tool for analyzing *Education for the Future* questionnaires. *School IQ* reduces an otherwise technical and complicated process to one that can be navigated with pushbutton ease. There are different versions of *IQ* for each of the eleven standard *Education for the Future* questionnaires. *School IQ* includes online questionnaire templates, all eleven questionnaires in PDF format, the analysis tool, the *School IQ*, and graphing templates.

◆ Other Popular *Education for the Future* Questionnaires:
(Online templates and graphs are located with the *School IQ*)

  ✳ *Student (Kindergarten to Grade 3) Questionnaire* (StQKto3.pdf)

  ✳ *Student (Grades 1 to 6) Questionnaire* (StQ1to6.pdf)

  ✳ *Student (Grades 6 to 12) Questionnaire* (StQ6to12.pdf)

  ✳ *Student (High School) Questionnaire* (StQHS.pdf)

  ✳ *Staff Questionnaire* (StaffQ.pdf)

  ✳ *Administrator Questionnaire* (Admin.pdf)

  ✳ *Teacher Predictions of Student Responses (Grades 1 to 6) Questionnaire* (TchPr1.pdf)

  ✳ *Teacher Predictions of Student Responses (Grades 6 to 8) Questionnaire* (TchPr2.pdf)

  ✳ *Parent Questionnaire* (ParntK12.pdf)

  ✳ *High School Parent Questionnaire* (ParntHS.pdf)

  ✳ *Alumni Questionnaire* (Alumni.pdf)

▼ *How to Analyze Open-ended Responses* (OEanalz.pdf)
This read-only file discusses how to analyze responses to the open-ended questions on questionnaires.

▼ *Questions to Guide the Analysis of Perceptions Data* (PerceptQ.doc)
This *Microsoft Word* file is a tabular guide for interpreting your perceptions data. You can change the questions if you like or use the file to write in the responses. It will help you write the narrative for your results.

Chapter 6

> *Most often, the way schools determine their results is through student learning measures only.*

So, what are the results of current processes? Where are we now? The results from the demographic data collection and analysis, reviewed in Chapter 4, provide a framework for understanding student performance data. Further, the understanding of school culture developed through the analyses of beliefs, values, and perceptions contribute to a richer understanding of the environment within which student learning takes place. We must remember, however, that the overall purpose of the continuous school improvement model is to *get results:* to improve student learning.

Most often, schools determine their results through student learning measures only. More often than not, schools use a simple student learning measure, usually a state-required assessment. While this is clearly a good starting point, generating a sound understanding of how well students are learning *requires multiple measures* that are disaggregated, across demographic groups over time. Only by understanding the different type of assessment data, analyzed for detail, can we get to a real understanding of what we need to do to continuously improve our results.

Why do we measure student learning?
We measure student learning to know—

▼ if students have particular skills and knowledge

▼ if students have attained a level of proficiency/competence/mastery

▼ if instructional strategies are making a difference for all students

▼ the effectiveness of instructional strategies and curricula

▼ how to improve instructional strategies

▼ how to classify students into instructional groups

▼ that students are ready to graduate or proceed to the next level of instruction

▼ if school processes are making the intended progress

Unfortunately, student learning results are not always used in these ways. Most of the time it is because school personnel struggle with the way student learning is measured and the analyses to display the results. The purpose of this chapter is to show different ways of measuring, analyzing, and reporting student learning results.

We start with discussions of different ways to measure student learning in middle schools; then the example, Azalea Middle School, is shown. Please note the study questions on page 168 to assist in interpreting the data. 🔘 (Ch6Qs.pdf) Also note that there is space in the margins on the data pages to write your impressions as you review the data. At the end of the chapter, I have shared what I saw in the data.

How Can Middle Schools Measure Student Learning?

Middle schools use a variety of means to assess student learning. Most schools are members of districts and states that use standardized tests at some, or all, grade levels. Other common means of assessing student learning are more classroom-based, such as performance assessments, portfolio assessments, teacher-given grades, and teacher observations. Different means of assessing student learning are defined below, followed by the analyses the example school, Azalea Middle School, created with its state criterion-referenced assessment.

Standardized Tests

Standardized tests are assessments that have uniformity in content, administration, and scoring. They can be used for comparing results across students, classrooms, schools, school districts, and states. Norm-referenced, criterion-referenced, and diagnostic tests (which can be normed and criterion-referenced) are the most commonly used standardized tests. Arguments *for* and *against* standardized testing appear in Figure 6.1. (TestArgu.pdf)

Figure 6.1

Arguments For and Against Standardized Testing

Arguments For Standardized Testing

- Standardized testing can be designed to measure performance, thinking, problem solving, and communication skills.
- The process students use to solve a problem can be tested, rather than just the result.
- Standardized tests can be developed to match state standards.
- Standardized tests can help drive the curriculum standards that are supposed to be taught.
- Ways need to be developed to determine if students have the skills to succeed in society; standardized tests can ensure all students, across a state or the entire country, have essential skills.
- Employers and the public need to know if students are able to apply skills and knowledge to everyday life; standardized testing can help with that assurance.
- Standardized testing may be helping to raise the bar of expectations for students in public schools—especially the lowest performing schools.
- Many schools, districts, and states have seen achievement levels rise in recent years which they attribute to higher expectations of students because of standardized tests.
- Standardized tests provide data that show which skills students are lacking, giving educators the information necessary to tailor classes and instructional strategies to student needs.
- Standardized tests can tell how the school or student is doing in comparison to a norming group, which is supposed to represent the typical students in the country.
- With most standardized tests, one can follow the same students over time.

Arguments Against Standardized Testing

- Standardized testing often narrows student learning to what is tested; what is tested is usually only a sample of what students should know.
- Standardized tests typically focus on what is easy to measure, not the critical thinking skills students need to develop.
- Standardized tests do not always match the state standards.
- To make standardized tests align to the state standards requires expertise and can be costly.
- The quality of standardized tests is a concern.
- Standardized tests are better at measuring rote learning than evaluating thinking skills.
- Too much instructional time is used to prepare students for multiple-choice tests, to the detriment of other uses of instructional time.
- Standardized tests could be culturally biased, drawing primarily upon the experiences of one socio-economic group.
- Decisions are sometimes made about a student's promotion from grade to grade or graduation based solely on one multiple-choice test.
- It is not fair to hold students accountable on one test when the schools might not be providing students with quality teachers, curricula, and time to master concepts.
- Students are not always provided with time to master what is expected on the standardized tests.
- There is a concern with standardized tests over getting the right answers.
- Standardized tests sometimes measure only what students know, not what they understand.
- Standardized testing is expensive.
- Testing is costly in teaching time and student time.

Norm-referenced Tests

Norm-referenced tests are also standardized tests. Norm-referenced test scores create meaning through comparing the test performance of a school, group, or individual with the performance of a norming group. A norming group is a representative group of students whose results on a norm-referenced test help create the scoring scales with which others compare their performance. Norming groups' results are professed to look like the normal curve, shown in Figure 6.2 below.

Figure 6.2

The Normal Curve and Scores

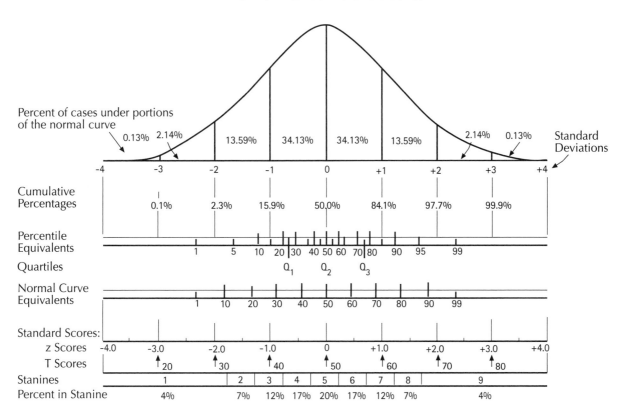

Adapted from Test Service Bulletin No. 48. Copyright © 1955 by
The Psychological Corporation. Reproduced by permission. All rights reserved.

The national percentile rank is one of the most used scales; it is also misused the most.

Normal curve equivalent scores are excellent for looking at scores over time.

The normal curve is a distribution of scores or other measures that in graphic form has a distinctive bell-shaped appearance. In a normal distribution, the measures are distributed symmetrically about the mean, or average score. Most results are near the mean and decrease in frequency the farther one departs from the mean. Stated another way—the theory of the normal curve basically says that when test publishers give a test to a representative sample of students, most students score around the mean with very few students scoring very high or very low. Using this theory, test publishers are able to create scales that are useful for schools to compare their scores with the norming group.

National Percentile Ranks. The two most commonly used and useful normed scales, or score types, are national percentile ranks and normal curve equivalents. The national percentile rank (NPR), also known as the national percentile equivalent, ranges from 1 to 99, with a midscore of 50. The NPR is one of the most used scales; it is also misused the most. The misuse of this scale stems from the fact that it is an unequal interval scale, which *prohibits* adding, subtracting, multiplying, and dividing the scores. *One should not look at gains, losses, or averages with percentile ranks.* Median scores, or the middle scores, are the most appropriate means of describing a whole school's typical performance.

Normal Curve Equivalent Scores. Normal curve equivalent (NCE) scores were created to alleviate the problem of unequal interval scales presented by percentile ranks. This equal interval scale has a mean of 50, and range of 1 to 99, just like the NPR. A standard deviation of 21.06 forces the intervals to be equal, spreading the scores away from the mean. NCEs have the same meaning across students, subtests, grade levels, classrooms, schools, and school districts. Fifty (50) is what one would expect for an average year's growth. You can look at how close your scores are to expected performance, averages, gains, losses, highest, and lowest scores. NCEs are excellent for looking at scores over time.

Grade-level Equivalent Scores. Another score type used with norm-referenced tests is grade-level equivalent. Grade-level equivalent scores result in an interesting scale that shows the grade and month of the school year for which a given score is the actual or estimated average. Its meaning is that the student obtained the same score that one would expect average x^{th} grade students in their x^{th} month to score if they took the xth grade test. Based on a ten-month school year, scores would be noted as 6.1 for sixth grade, first month, or 8.7 for eighth grade, seventh month. For example, if a sixth grader scored a 7.4 on a subtest, that does not mean that she/he should be doing seventh grade, eighth-month work. It only means that the student obtained the same score that one would expect average seventh grade students to score if they took the same sixth-grade test during the eighth month of grade six. Grade-level equivalent scores are okay for a snapshot in time, but they should not be averaged or taken literally.

Standard Scores. Standard scores, or scaled scores, refer to scores that have been *transformed* for reasons of convenience, comparability, and ease of interpretation. Ranges vary depending upon the test, and sometimes even the subtest. The best uses of standard scores are averages calculated over time allowing for the study of change. These scores are good to use for calculations because of their equal intervals and their easy conversions to other score types. The downsides are that, with the various ranges, it is difficult to look across subtests, grade levels, and years. It is often hard for the layperson to create meaning from these scores. The normal curve is needed to interpret the results with respect to other scores and people. The NCE is a standard score and probably one of the best to use because of the constant range and mean.

Anticipated Achievement/Cognitive Abilities Scores. Occasionally, norm-referenced tests provide indicators of ability, such as anticipated achievement scores, cognitive abilities, or cognitive skills indexes. The anticipated achievement score is an estimate of the average score for students of a similar age, grade, and academic aptitude. It can be computed in grade-level equivalents, normal curve equivalents, standard scores, and national percentiles. The higher the student scores on sequences, analogies, memory, and verbal reasoning tests, the higher the student is expected to score on standardized tests.

A cognitive abilities or cognitive skills index is also created from the same four tests mentioned above, and assesses the student's academic aptitude. The range of this scale is 58 to 141, with a mean of 100. Two-thirds of the scores will fall between 84 and 118. Anticipated Achievement/Cognitive Abilities scores can tell teachers if they are teaching to students' potential.

Grade-level equivalent scores are okay for a snapshot in time, but they should not be averaged or taken literally.

The best uses of standard scores are averages calculated over time allowing for the study of change.

Anticipated Achievement/ Cognitive Abilities scores can tell teachers if they are teaching to the students' potential.

Criterion-referenced assessments tell us how well students are performing on specific criteria, goals, or standards.

Diagnostic tests can help teachers know the nature of students' difficulties, but not the cause of the difficulty.

Criterion-referenced Tests

Criterion-referenced tests compare an individual's performance to a specific learning objective or performance standard and not to the performance of other test takers. Criterion-referenced assessments tell us how well students are performing on specific criteria, goals, or standards. For school level analyses, criterion-referenced tests are usually scored in terms of the number or percentage of students meeting the standard or criterion, or the number or percentage of students falling in typical descriptive categories, such as *far below basic, below basic, basic, proficient,* and *advanced.* Criterion-referenced tests can be standardized or not, and they can also have norming groups.

Diagnostic Tests

Diagnostic tests, usually standardized and normed, are given before instruction begins to help the instructor(s) understand student learning needs. Diagnostic tests can help teachers know the nature of students' difficulties, but not the cause of the difficulty. Many different score types are used with diagnostic tests.

These tests, score types, and other frequently used terms are defined in Figure 6.3, along with a description of most effective uses and cautions for use. (TestTerm.pdf)

Figure 6.3

Standardized Test Score Terms, Their Most Effective Uses, and Cautions for Their Uses			
Score	**Definition**	**Most Effective Uses**	**Cautions**
Anticipated Achievement Scores	A student's anticipated achievement score is an estimate of the average score for students of similar ages, grade levels, and academic aptitude. It is an estimate of what we would expect the student to score on an achievement test.	Anticipated achievement scores can be used to see if a student is scoring "above" or "below" an expected score, indicating whether or not she/he is being challenged enough, or if her/his needs are being met.	It is easy to think of these scores as "IQ" scores. They are just achievement indicators on a standardized test.
Cognitive Abilities or Skills Index	The cognitive skills index is an age-dependent normalized standard score based on a student's performance on a cognitive skills test with a mean of 100 and standard deviation of 16. The score indicates a student's overall cognitive ability or academic aptitude relative to students of similar age, without regard to grade level.	Cognitive skills index scores can be used to see if a student is scoring "above" or "below" an expected score, indicating whether or not she/he is being challenged enough, or if her/his needs are being met.	It is easy to think of these scores as "IQ" scores. They are just achievement indicators on a standardized test.
Criterion-referenced Tests	Tests that judge how well a test-taker does on an explicit objective relative to a predetermined performance level.	Tell us how well students are performing on specific criteria, goals, or standards.	CRTs test only what was taught, or planned to be taught. CRTs can not give a broad estimate of knowledge.
Deciles	Deciles divide a distribution into ten equal parts: 1–10; 11–20; 21–30; 31–40; 41–50; 51–60; 61–70; 71–80; 81–90; 91–99. Just about any scale can be used to show deciles.	Deciles allow schools to show how all students scored throughout the distribution. One would expect a school's distribution to resemble a normal curve. Watching the distribution move to the right, over time, could imply that all students in the distribution are making progress.	One must dig deeper to understand if all students and all groups of students are moving forward.
Diagnostic Tests	Diagnostic tests, usually standardized and normed, are given before instruction begins to help the instructor(s) understand student learning needs. Many different score types are used with diagnostic tests.	Help teachers know the nature of students' difficulties, but not the cause of the difficulty.	Make sure the diagnostic test is measuring what you want it to measure and that it can be compared to formative and summative assessments used.

Figure 6.3 (Continued)

	Standardized Test Score Terms, Their Most Effective Uses, and Cautions for Their Uses		
Score	**Definition**	**Most Effective Uses**	**Cautions**
Grade-level Equivalents	Grade-level equivalents indicate the grade and month of the school year for which a given score is the actual or estimated average. Based on a ten-month school year, scores would be noted as 6.1 for sixth grade, first month, or 8.10 for eighth grade, tenth month.	Grade-level equivalents are most effectively used as a snapshot in time. Scores are comparable across subtests.	These scores should not be taken literally. If a sixth grader scored a 8.8 on a subtest, that does not mean that she/he should be doing eighth grade, eighth-month work. It only means that the student obtained the same score that one would expect average eighth-grade students in their eighth month of school to score if they took the sixth-grade test.
Latent-trait Scale	A latent-trait scale is a scaled score obtained through one of several mathematical approaches collectively known as Latent-Trait Procedures or Item Response Theory. The particular numerical values used in the scale are arbitrary, but higher scores indicate more knowledgeable students or more difficult items.	Latent-trait scales have equal intervals allowing comparisons over time.	These are scores set up by testing professionals. Laypeople typically have difficulty understanding their meaning.
NCE (National or Local)	Normal Curve Equivalent (NCE) scores are standard scores with a mean of 50, a standard deviation of 21.06, and a range of 1 to 99. The term National would indicate that the norming group was national; local usually implies a state or district norming group.	NCEs have equal intervals so they can be used to study gains over time. The scores have the same meaning across subtests, grade levels, and years. A 50 is what one would expect in an average year's growth.	This score, just like all scores related to norm-referenced tests, cannot be taken literally. The score simply shows relative performance of a student group or of students to a norming group.
Percent Passing	Percent passing is a calculated score implying the percentage of the student group meeting and exceeding some number, usually a cut score, proficiency/mastery level, or a standard.	With standards-based accountability, it is beneficial to know the percentage of the population meeting and exceeding a standard and to compare a year's percentages with the previous year(s) to understand progress being made.	This is a very simple statistic, and its interpretation should be simple as well. Total numbers (n=) of students included in the percentage must always be noted with the percentage to assist with the understanding.

Figure 6.3 (Continued)

	Standardized Test Score Terms, Their Most Effective Uses, and Cautions for Their Uses		
Score	**Definition**	**Most Effective Uses**	**Cautions**
Percentile / Percentile Rank (PR) (National or Local)	Percentile ranks indicate the percentage of students in a norm group (e.g., national or local) whose scores fall below a given score. The range is from 1 to 99. 50th percentile ranking would mean that 50 percent of the scores in the norming group fall below a specific score. The term National would indicate that the norming group was national; local usually implies a state or district norming group.	One-year comparison to the norming group. Schools can see the relative standing of a student or group in the same grade to the norm group who took the test at a comparable time.	Percentile rank is not a score to use over time to look for gains because of unequal intervals, unless the calculations are made with equal interval scores and then converted to percentile ranks. One cannot calculate averages using NPR because of the unequal intervals. Medians are the most appropriate statistic to use.
Quartiles	There are three quartiles points—Q1, Q2, Q3 — that divide a distribution into four equal groups: Q1=25th percentile Q2=50th percentile (Median) Q3=75th percentile	Quartiles allow schools to see the distribution of scores for any grade level, for instance. Over time, schools trying to increase student achievement would want to monitor the distribution to ensure that all students are making progress.	With quartiles, one cannot tell if the scores are at the top of a quartile or the bottom. There could be "real" changes taking place within a quartile that would not be evident.
Raw Scores	Raw scores are the number of questions answered correctly on a test or subtest. A raw score is simply calculated by adding the number of questions answered correctly. The raw score is a person's observed score.	The raw score provides information about the number of questions answered correctly. To get a perspective on performance, raw scores must be used with the average score for the group and/or the total number of questions. Alone, it has no meaning.	Raw scores do not provide information related to other students taking the test or to other subtests. One needs to keep perspective by knowing the total number possible. Raw scores should never be used to make comparisons between performances on different tests unless other information about the characteristics of the tests are known and identical.
RIT Scale Scores	RIT scores, named for George Rasch who developed the theory of this type of measurement, are scaled scores that come from a series of tests created by the Northwest Evaluation Association (NWEA). The tests, which draw from an item bank, are aligned with local curriculum and state/local standards.	RIT scores provide ongoing measurement of curriculum standards and a way for students to see progress in their knowledge. The scores can also be shown as percentiles to know performance related to other students of similar ages and/or grades. You will most probably see gains each time a measurement is taken with a group of students.	RIT scores are great as long as the test was carefully designed to measure standards.

Figure 6.3 (Continued)

	Standardized Test Score Terms, Their Most Effective Uses, and Cautions for Their Uses		
Score	**Definition**	**Most Effective Uses**	**Cautions**
Scaled Scores	A scaled score is a mathematical transformation of a raw score, resulting in interval scores within a defined range. Scaled scores take item difficulty into account.	The best uses of scaled scores are averages and averages calculated over time allowing for the study of change. These scores are good to use for calculations because of equal intervals. The scores can be applied across subtests within most tests. Scaled scores facilitate conversions to other score types.	Ranges vary, depending upon the test. Watch for the minimum and maximum values. It is sometimes hard for laypeople to create meaning from these scores. The normal curve is needed to interpret the results with respect to other scores and people.
Standard Scores	Standard score is a general term referring to scores that have been "transformed" for reasons of convenience, comparability, ease of interpretation, etc., to have a predefined mean and standard deviation. z-scores and T-scores are standard scores.	The best uses of standard scores are averages and averages calculated over time, allowing for the study of change. These scores are good to use for calculations because of equal intervals. The scores can be applied across subtests on most tests. Standard scores facilitate conversions to other score types.	Ranges vary, depending upon the test. Watch for the minimum and maximum values. It is sometimes hard for laypeople to create meaning from these scores. The normal curve is needed to interpret results with respect to other scores and people.
Standards-based Assessments	Standards-based assessments measure students' progress toward mastering local, state, and/or national content standards.	The way standards-based assessments are analyzed depends upon the scales used. The most effective uses are in revealing the percentage of students achieving a standard.	One has to adhere to the cautions of whatever test or score type used. It is important to know how far from mastering the standard the students were when they did not meet the standard.
Stanines	Stanines are a nine-point standard score scale. Stanines divide the normal curve into nine equal points: 1 to 9.	Stanines, like quartiles, allow schools to see the distribution of scores for any grade level, for instance. Over time, schools trying to increase student achievement would want to monitor the distribution to ensure that all student scores are improving.	Often, the first three stanines are interpreted as "below average," the next three as "average," and the top three as "above average." This can be misleading. As with quartiles, one cannot tell if the scores are at the top of a stanine or the bottom. There could be "real" changes taking place within a stanine that would not be evident.

Figure 6.3 (Continued)

	Standardized Test Score Terms, Their Most Effective Uses, and Cautions for Their Uses		
Score	**Definition**	**Most Effective Uses**	**Cautions**
T-scores	A T-score is a standard score with a mean of 50 and a standard deviation of 10. T-scores are obtained by the following formula: $T = 10z + 50$	The most effective uses of T-scores are averages and averages calculated over time. T-scores are good to use for calculations because of their equal intervals. T-scores can be applied across subtests on most tests because of the forced mean and standard deviation.	T-scores are rarely used because of the lack of understanding on the part of most test users.
z-scores	A z-score is a standard score with a mean of zero and a standard deviation of one. z-scores are obtained by the following formula: $z = \dfrac{\text{raw score } (x) - \text{mean}}{\text{standard deviation (sd)}}$	z-scores can tell one how many standard deviations a score is away from the mean. z-scores are most useful, perhaps, as the first step in computing other types of standard scores.	z-scores are rarely used by the lay public because of the difficulty in understanding the score.

> *The term "performance assessment" refers to assessments that measure skills, knowledge, and ability directly—such as through "performance."*

Performance Assessments

The term *performance assessment* refers to assessments that measure skills, knowledge, and ability directly—such as through *performance*. In other words, if you want students to learn to write, you assess their ability on a writing activity. One must find a way to score these results and make sense for individual students and groups of students. Some of the arguments for and against performance assessments are listed in Figure 6.4. (PerfArgu.pdf) (See *References* for sources.)

Figure 6.4

Arguments For and Against Performance Assessments

Arguments For Performance Assessments

- Performance assessments can be designed to measure performance, thinking, problem solving, and communication skills.
- Performance assessments can be used to measure the process students use to solve problems.
- Performance assessments can be developed to match state standards.
- Many schools, districts, and states have seen achievement levels rise in recent years, which they attribute to higher expectations of students and what they can do, attributed to the use of performance assessments.
- Performance assessments provide data that show what students are lacking, giving educators the information necessary to tailor classes and instructional strategies to student needs.
- Students can learn during a performance task.
- Some teachers believe that when students participate in developing a rubric for evaluating their performance, they come to appreciate high-quality work.
- Performance assessments provide opportunities for students to reflect on their own work.
- Performance assessments can allow students to work until standards are met—to ensure quality work from all students.
- Performance assessments can help the teacher improve instructional strategies.
- Performance assessments allow students to perform in the learning style that suits them best.

Arguments Against Performance Assessments

- Designing good performance assessments that accurately measure performance, thinking, problem solving, and communication skills is difficult.
- Designing good performance assessments that accurately measure performance, thinking, problem solving, and communication skills is very costly.
- Some performance tasks require long periods of time to complete, such as graduation or end-of-course exhibitions.
- To be effective, skills and performances being assessed should be taught in the same way they are measured.
- The quality of performance assessments is a concern.
- It is not fair to hold students accountable on one test when the schools might not be providing students with quality teachers, curricula, and time to master concepts.
- Scoring criteria requires analyzing performance into its components, such as breaking out the craft of writing into developmental elements.
- Many scoring criteria are no different from giving grades or norm-referenced scoring.
- Good scoring criteria could take a long time to develop.
- It is very difficult to design performance assessments that can be compared across grade levels in other than descriptive terms.

Teachers use number or letter grades to judge the quality of a student's performance on a task, unit, or during a period of time.

Grades

Teachers use number or letter grades to judge the quality of a student's performance on a task, unit, or during a period of time. Grades are most often given as A, B, C, D, F, with pluses and minuses given by some teachers for the first four to distinguish among students. Grades mean different things to different teachers. Needless to say, grades can be subjective. "It appears that teachers consider grading to be a private activity, thus 'guarding practices with the same passion with which one might guard an unedited diary' (Kain, 1996, p. 569)" (O'Connor, 2000, p. 11). Some of the arguments for and against teacher grading are shown in Figure 6.5. (GradeArg.pdf)

Figure 6.5

Arguments For and Against Teacher Grading

Arguments For Teacher Grading

- Grades can be designed to reflect performance, thinking, problem solving, and communication skills.
- Teachers can grade the process students use to solve a problem, rather than just the result.
- Grades can communicate to students, parents, and administrators the student's level of performance.
- Grading can allow teachers to be very flexible in their approaches to assessing student performance.
- Grades can match teaching.
- Grades can be given for team work and not just individual work.
- Grades can be effective if students are aware of expectations.
- Grades can cover multiple standards.
- Certain teacher-developed tests can be graded quickly.
- Most people believe they know what grades mean.

Arguments Against Teacher Grading

- It is difficult to convert activities, such as performance, thinking, and problem solving, into numbers or letters and have them hold true for all students in a class.
- Grading can be very subjective.
- Grading can be distorted by effort, extra credit, attendance, behavior, etc.
- To be beneficial, students must trust the grader and the grading process, have time to practice and complete an assessment, and have choices in how they are assessed—all of which make it time-consuming for teachers to do this type of assessment well.
- To be beneficial, grading assessments must be meaningful and promote learning.
- Grades must include a variety of assessment techniques to get to all areas of student understanding and performance.
- Often parents, students, and teachers focus on grades and not on learning.
- Grading is not reflective of instructional strategies.
- Grades are not always motivators; in fact, they can demoralize students on the low end, and on the high end.
- Grades tell little about student strengths and areas for improvement.
- Grading can mean many different things within a grade level, across grade levels by teacher, subject area, and school.
- Some teachers' highest priorities with grading are to use techniques where the grades can be calculated quickly.
- Grading is not always compatible with all instructional strategies.
- Grades often are given for more than achievement.
- Grading is not essential for learning.

Descriptive statistics summarize the basic characteristics of a particular distribution, without making any inferences about population parameters.

Analyzing the Results, Descriptively

Descriptive statistics (i.e., mean, median, percent correct) can give schools very powerful information. It is imperative that the appropriate analyses be used for the specific score type. Figure 6.6 summarizes terms of analyses, their definitions, their most effective uses, and cautions for their uses in analyzing student achievement scores descriptively. (SAterms1.pdf) Descriptive statistics are used in the examples in this chapter largely because they can show a school how its students are doing, and because anyone can do the calculations.

Descriptive statistics summarize the basic characteristics of a particular group of students, without making any inferences about any larger group that may include the one from which the scores are taken. Graphing the information can also be considered descriptive.

Figure 6.6

Terms Related to Analyzing Student Achievement Results, Descriptively, Their Most Effective Uses, and Cautions for Their Uses			
Term	**Definition**	**Most Effective Uses**	**Cautions**
Disaggregate	Disaggregation is breaking a total score into groups for purposes of seeing how subgroups performed. One disaggregates data to make sure all subgroups of students are learning.	Disaggregating student achievement scores by gender, ethnicity, backgrounds, etc., can show how different subgroups performed.	Disaggregations are for helping schools understand how to meet the needs of all students, not to say, "This group always does worse than the other group and always will." We must exercise caution in reporting disaggregations with small numbers in a subgroup.
Gain	Gain scores are the change or difference between two administrations of the same test. Gain scores are calculated by subtracting the previous score from the most recent score. One can have negative gains, which are actually losses.	One calculates gains to understand improvements in learning for groups of students and for individual students.	Gain scores should not be calculated using unequal interval scores, such as percentiles. The quality of gain score results is dependent upon the quality of the assessment instrument; the less reliable the assessment tool, the less meaningful the results. One needs to make sure the comparisons are appropriate, e.g., same students, same score types.
Maximum	A maximum is the highest score achieved, or the highest possible score on a test.	Maximum possible scores and highest received scores are important for understanding the relative performance of any group or individual, especially when using scaled or standard scores.	A maximum can tell either the highest score possible or the highest score received by a test-taker. One needs to understand which maximum is being used in the analysis. It is best to use both.
Mean	A mean is the average score in a set of scores. One calculates the mean, or average, by summing all the scores and dividing by the total number of scores.	A mean can be calculated to provide an overall average for the group, and/or student, taking a specific test. One can use any equal interval score to get a mean.	Means should not be used with unequal interval scores, such as percentile ranks. Means are more sensitive to extreme results when the size of the group is small.
Median	A median is the score that splits a distribution in half: 50 percent of the scores fall above and 50 percent of the scores fall below the median. If the number of scores is odd, the median is the middle score. If the number of scores is even, one must add the two middle scores and divide by two to calculate the median.	Medians are the way to get a midpoint for scores with unequal intervals, such as percentile ranks. The median splits all scores into two equal parts. Medians are not sensitive to outliers, like means are.	Medians are relative. Medians are most effectively interpreted when reported with the possible and actual maximum and minimum.
Minimum	A minimum is the lowest score achieved, or the lowest possible score on the test.	Minimum possible scores and lowest received scores are important for understanding the relative performance of any group or individual.	A minimum tells either the lowest score possible or the lowest score received by a test-taker. One needs to understand which minimum is being used. It is best to use both.

Figure 6.6 (Continued)

	Terms Related to Analyzing Student Achievement Results, Descriptively, Their Most Effective Uses, and Cautions for Their Uses		
Term	**Definition**	**Most Effective Uses**	**Cautions**
Mode	The mode is the score that occurs most frequently in a scoring distribution.	The mode basically tells which score or scores appear most often.	There may be more than one mode. The mode ignores other scores.
Percent Correct	Percent correct is a calculated score implying the percentage of students meeting and exceeding some number, usually a cut score, or a standard.	This calculated score can quickly tell educators how well the students are doing with respect to a specific set of items. It can also tell educators how many students need additional work to become proficient.	Percent correct is a calculated statistic, based on the number of items given. When the number of items given is small, the percent correct can be deceptively high or low.
Percent Proficient *Percent Passing* *Percent Mastery*	Percent proficient, passing, or mastery represent the percentage of students who passed a particular test at a "proficient," "passing," or "mastery" level, as defined by the test creators or the test interpreters.	With standards-based accountability, it is beneficial to know the percentage of the population meeting and exceeding the standard and to compare a year's percentage with the previous year(s) to understand progress being made.	This is a very simple statistic, and its interpretation should be simple as well. Total numbers (N=) of students included in the percentage must always be noted with the percentage to assist in understanding the results. Ninety percent passing means something very different for 10 or 100 test-takers.
Range	Range is a measure of the spread between the lowest and the highest scores in a distribution. Calculate the range of scores by subtracting the lowest score from the highest score. Range is often described as end points also, such as the range of percentile ranks is 1 and 99.	Ranges tell us the width of the distribution of scores. Educators working on continuous improvement will want to watch the range, of actual scores, decrease over time.	If there are outliers present, the range can give a misleading impression of dispersion.
Raw Scores	Raw scores refer to the number of questions answered correctly on a test or subtest. A raw score is simply calculated by adding the number of questions answered correctly. The raw score is a person's observed score.	The raw score provides information only about the number of questions answered correctly. To get a perspective on performance, raw scores must be used with the average score for the group and the total number of questions. Alone, raw scores have little meaning.	Raw scores do not provide information related to other students taking the test or to other subtests or scores. One needs to keep perspective by knowing the total number possible. Raw scores should never be used to make comparisons between performances on different tests unless other information about the characteristics of the tests are known and identical.

Figure 6.6 (Continued)

Term	Definition	Most Effective Uses	Cautions
Terms Related to Analyzing Student Achievement Results, Descriptively, Their Most Effective Uses, and Cautions for Their Uses			
Relationships	Relationships refer to looking at two or more sets of analyses to understand what they mean to each other without using extensive statistical techniques.	Descriptive statistics lend themselves to looking at the relationships of different analyses to each other; for instance, student learning results disaggregated by ethnicity, compared to student questionnaire results disaggregated by ethnicity.	This type of analysis is general and the results should be considered general as well. This is not a "correlation."
Rubric	A rubric is a scoring tool that rates performance according to clearly stated levels of criteria. The scales can be numeric or descriptive, or both.	Rubrics are used to give teachers, parents, and students an idea of where they started, where they want to be with respect to growth, and where they are right now.	Students need to know what the rubrics contain or, even better, help with the development of the rubrics.
Standard Deviation	The standard deviation is a measure of variability in a set of scores. The standard deviation indicates how far away scores are from the mean. The standard deviation is the square root of the variance. Unlike the variance, the standard deviation is stated in the original units of the variable. Approximately 68 percent of the scores in a normal distribution lie between plus one and minus one standard deviation of the mean. The more scores cluster around the mean, the smaller the variance.	Tells us about the variability of scores. Standard deviations indicate how spread-out the scores are without looking at the entire distribution. A low standard deviation would indicate that the scores of a group are close together. A high standard deviation would imply that the range of scores is wide.	Often this is a confusing statistic for laypeople to understand. There are more descriptive ways to describe and show the variability of student scores, such as with a decile graph. Standard deviations only make sense with scores that are distributed normally.
Triangulation	Triangulation is a term used for combining three or more measures to get a more complete picture of student achievement.	If students are to be retained based on standards proficiency, educators must have more than one way of knowing if the students are proficient or not. Some students perform well on standardized measures and not on other measures, while others do not do well with standardized measures. Triangulation allows students to display what they know on three different measures.	It is sometimes very complicated to combine different measures to understand proficiency. When proficiency standards change, triangulation calculations will need to be revised. Therefore, all the calculations must be documented so they can be recalculated when necessary.

Analyzing the Results, Inferentially

Many school administrators and teachers have taken statistics courses that taught them that it is important to have control groups, experimental designs, and to test for significant differences. These terms fall in the category of *inferential statistics*. Inferential statistics are concerned with measuring a sample from a population, and then making estimates, or inferences, about the population from which the sample was taken. Inferential statistics help generalize the results of data analysis, when one is not using the entire population in the analysis.

The main purpose of this book is to model analyses that school personnel can perform *without* the assistance of statisticians. Descriptive analyses provide helpful and useful information and can be understood by a majority of people. When using the entire school population in your analyses, there is no need to generalize to a larger population—you have the whole population. There is no need for inferential statistics.

Inferential statistical methods, such as analyses of variance, correlations, and regression analyses, are complex and require someone who knows statistics to meet the conditions of the analyses. Since there are times when a statistician is available to perform inferential statistics, some of the terms the statistician might use with tests include those listed in Figure 6.7. (SAterms2.pdf)

A Note About "Scientifically-based Research." With the passage of the *No Child Left Behind* (NCLB) *Act of 2001,* which reauthorized the *Elementary and Secondary Education Act of 1965,* school districts and schools are required to gather, analyze, and use data to ensure adequate yearly progress. While increased accountability is just one part of NCLB, all schools must gather data and overcome the barriers to analyzing and using the data.

> *Inferential statistics help generalize the results of data analysis, when one is not using the entire population in the analysis.*

Figure 6.7

Terms Related to Analyzing Student Achievement Results, Inferentially, Their Most Effective Uses, and Cautions for Their Uses			
Term	**Definition**	**Most Effective Uses**	**Cautions**
Analysis of Variance (ANOVA)	Analysis of variance is a general term applied to the study of differences in the application of approaches, as opposed to the relationship of different levels of approaches to the result. With ANOVAs, we are testing the differences of the means of at least two different distributions.	ANOVAs can be used to determine if there is a difference in student achievement scores between one school and another, keeping all other variables equal. It cannot tell you what the differences are, per se, but one can compute confidence intervals to estimate these differences.	Very seldom are the conditions available to study differences in education in this manner. Too many complex variables get in the way, and ethics may be involved. There are well-defined procedures for conducting ANOVAs to which we must adhere.
Correlation Analyses	Correlation is a statistical analysis that helps one understand the relationship of scores in one distribution to scores in another distribution. Correlations show magnitude and direction. Magnitude indicates the degree of the relationship. Correlation coefficients have a range of -1.0 to +1.0. A correlation of around zero would indicate little relationship. Correlations of .8 and higher, or -.8 and lower would indicate a strong relationship. When the high scores in one distribution are also high in the comparing distribution, the direction is positive. When the high scores in one distribution are related to the low scores in the other distribution, the result is a negative correlational direction.	Correlations can be used to understand the relationship of different variables to each other, e.g., attendance and performance on a standardized test; .40 to .70 are considered moderate correlations. Above .70 is considered to be high correlations.	It is wise to plot the scores to understand if the relationship is linear or not. One could misinterpret results if the scores are not linear. Pearson correlation coefficient requires linear relationships. A few outliers could skew the results and oppositely skewed distributions can limit how high a Pearson coefficient can be. Also, one must remember that correlation does not suggest causation.
Regression Analyses	Regression analysis results in an equation that describes the nature of the relationship between variables. Simple regression predicts an object's value on a response variable when given its value on one predictor variable. Multiple regression predicts an object's value on a response variable when given its value on each of several predictor variables. Correlation tells you strength and direction of relationship. Regression goes one step further and allows you to predict.	A regression equation can be used to predict student achievement results, for example. Regression can determine if there is a relationship between two or more variables (such as attendance and student background) and the nature of those relationships. This analysis helps us predict and prevent student failure, and predict and ensure student successes.	One needs to truly understand the statistical assumptions that need to be in place in order to perform a regression analysis. This is not an analysis to perform through trial and error.

Figure 6.7 (Continued)

Term	Definition	Most Effective Uses	Cautions
Terms Related to Analyzing Student Achievement Results, Inferentially, Their Most Effective Uses, and Cautions for Their Uses			
Control Groups	During an experiment, the control group is studied the same as the experimental group, except that it does not receive the treatment of interest.	Control groups serve as a baseline in making comparisons with treatment groups. Control groups are necessary when the general effectiveness of a treatment is unknown.	It may not be ethical to hold back from students some method of learning that we believe would be useful.
Experimental Design	Experimental design is the detailed planning of an experiment, made beforehand, to ensure that the data collected are appropriate and obtained in a way that will lead to an objective analysis, with valid inferences.	Experimental designs can maximize the amount of information gained, given the amount of effort expended.	Sometimes it takes statistical expertise to establish an experimental design properly.
Tests of Significance	Tests of significance use samples to test claims about population parameters.	Tests of significance can estimate a population parameter, with a certain amount of confidence, from a sample.	Often laypeople do not know what *statistically significant* really means.

The term *scientifically-based research* (Title IX, General Provisions, Part A, Section 9101, Definitions) means (A) research that involves the application of rigorous, systematic, and objective procedures to obtain reliable and valid knowledge relevant to education activities and programs; and (B) includes research that:

▼ employs systematic, empirical methods that draw on observation or experiment

▼ involves rigorous data analyses that are adequate to test the stated hypotheses and justify the general conclusions drawn

▼ relies on measurements or observational methods that provide reliable and valid data across evaluators and observers, across multiple measurements and observations, and across studies by the same or different investigators

▼ is evaluated using experimental or quasi-experimental designs in which individuals, entities, programs, or activities are assigned to different conditions and with appropriate controls to evaluate the effects of the condition of interest, with a preference for random-assignment experiments, or other designs to the extent that condition controls

▼ ensures that experimental studies are presented in sufficient detail and clarity to allow for replication or, at a minimum, offer the opportunity to build systematically on their findings

▼ has been accepted by a peer-reviewed journal or approved by a panel of independent experts through a comparably rigorous, objective and scientific review

While NCLB calls for scientific and experimental procedures, such as control groups and experimental designs, in reality, they are not always possible. Over time, well-documented case studies have become accepted as powerful designs as well.

The Azalea Middle School example that follows shows a sampling of descriptive analyses the school performed using its state criterion-referenced test.

Our Example School: Azalea Middle School

What are our results?

The State Criterion-Referenced Assessment Test (SCAT) is the test used by this state for grades six, seven, and eight in English Language Arts (ELA) and Mathematics. Student results are provided in scaled score analyses and reports by proficiency levels. The definition of the proficiency levels follow:

▼ *Below Basic*

A student who performs at the *Below Basic* level on the SCAT has not met minimum expectations for student performance based on the curriculum standards approved by the State Board of Education. The student is not prepared for work at the next grade.

▼ *Basic*

Performance at the *Basic* level means a student has passed the test. A student who performs at the *Basic* level on the SCAT has met minimum expectations for student performance based on the curriculum standards approved by the State Board of Education. The student is minimally prepared for work at the next grade.

▼ *Proficient*

A student who performs at the *Proficient* level on the SCAT has met expectations for student performance based on the curriculum standards approved by the State Board of Education. The student is well prepared for work at the next grade. The *Proficient* level represents the long-term goal for student performance.

▼ *Advanced*

A student who performs at the *Advanced* level on the SCAT has exceeded expectations for student performance based on the curriculum standards approved by the State Board of Education. The student is very well prepared for work at the next grade.

How Are We Doing Compared to the District?

The first analysis of Azalea's most recent proficiency results compares Azalea's results to the district and the state. In all areas, Azalea scored higher than the district and the state, with more students *Proficient* and *Advanced* and fewer students *Below Basic* in each grade level than the other two entities (Figure 6.8).

Figure 6.8

Azalea Middle School
Compared to the District and State
SCAT Proficiency Percentages, 2002-03 to 2003-04

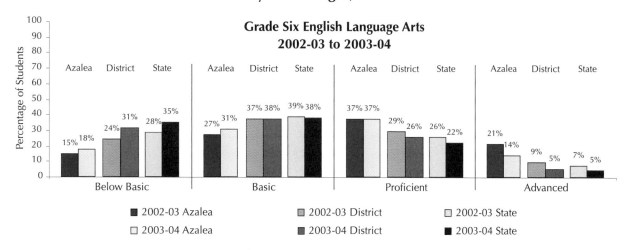

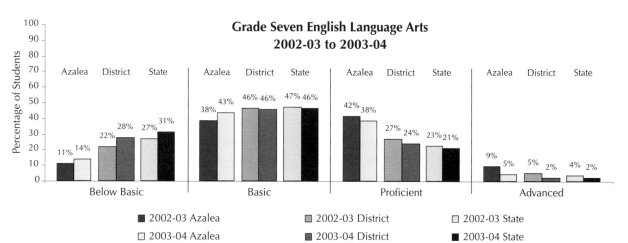

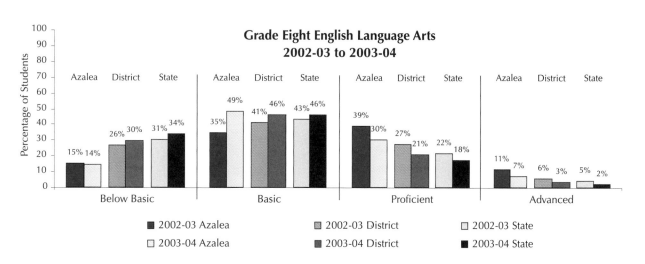

Figure 6.8 (Continued)

Azalea Middle School
Compared to the District and State
SCAT Proficiency Percentages, 2002-03 to 2003-04

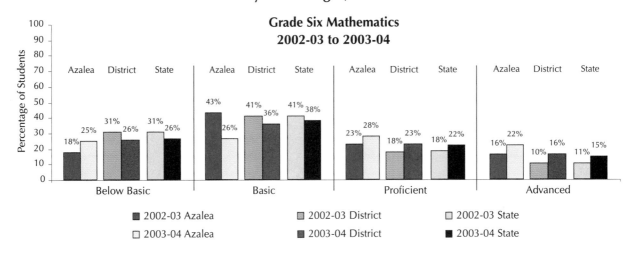

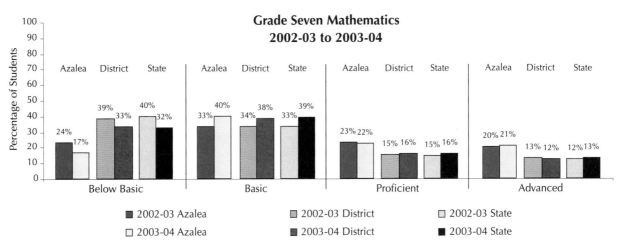

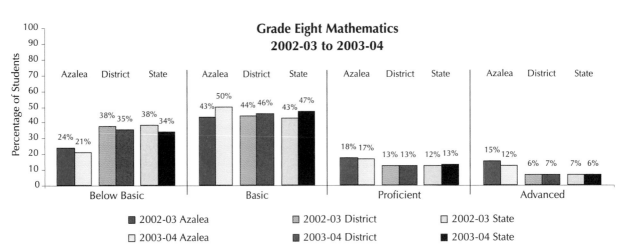

How Are We Doing for ALL Our Students?

SAT English Language Art (ELA) Scores

The next nine figures are related to English Language Arts (ELA), followed by the same displays for Mathematics.

Figure 6.9 shows the percentage of students scoring in ELA proficiency levels for grades six, seven, and eight during 1999-00 through 2003-04.

Note: This is called *trend analysis*—looking at the same grade levels over time.

Figure 6.9

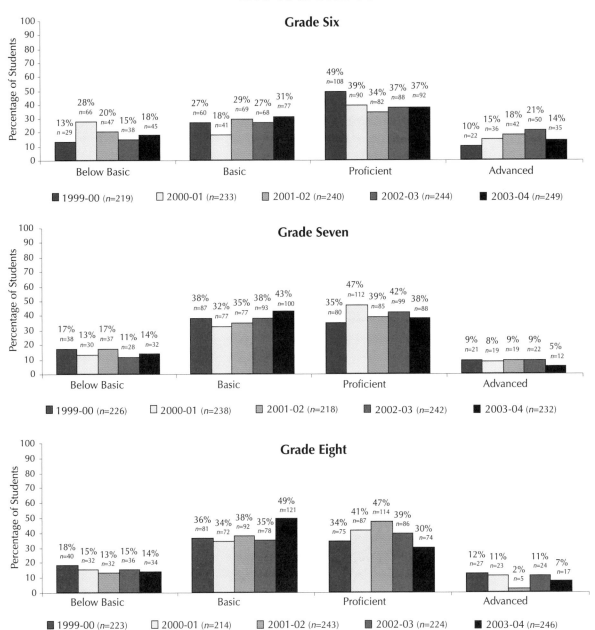

Azalea Middle School
SCAT English Language Art Proficiency Numbers and Percentages by Grade Level
1999-00 to 2003-04

Cohort analysis reorganizes the trend data to follow the same *groups* of students (unmatched) progressing through the grades, over time.

Figure 6.10 shows the percentage of Azalea students scoring in English Language Art proficiency levels by cohorts.

Figure 6.10

Azalea Middle School
SCAT English Language Art Proficiency Numbers and Percentages by Cohorts
1999-00 to 2003-04

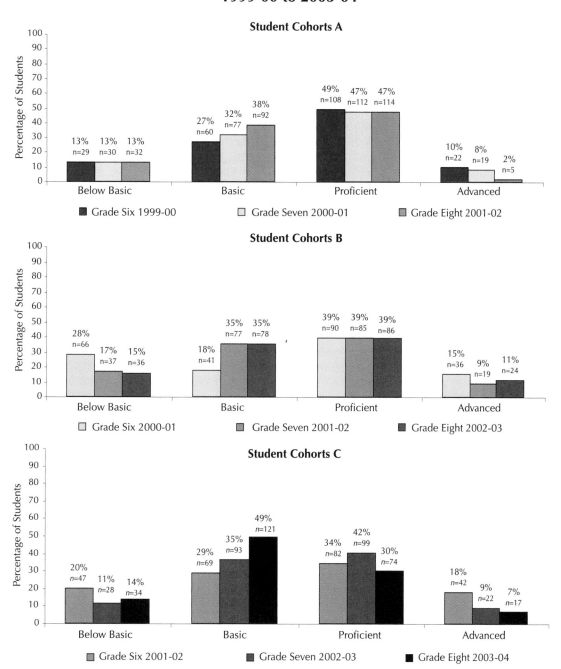

Figures 6.11 through 6.26 show proficiency breakdowns for subgroups and grade levels for the past five years. The number of students in some subgroups is very small. Caution should be taken in interpreting the results. These analyses would only be used inhouse.

(*Note:* Gifted data were not available for 2003-04.)

Figure 6.11

Azalea Middle School
SCAT ELA Proficiency Numbers and Percentages by Grade Level and Gender
1999-00 to 2003-04

Grade Level	Year	Below Basic				Basic				Proficient				Advanced			
		Female		Male		Female		Male		Female		Male		Female		Male	
		Number	Percent	Number	Percent	Number	Percent	Number	Percent	Number	Percent	Number	Percent	Number	Percent	Number	Percent
Grade Six	1999-00 (*n*=219)	10	5%	19	9%	33	15%	27	12%	71	32%	37	17%	15	7%	7	3%
	2000-01 (*n*=233)	36	15%	30	13%	19	8%	22	9%	49	21%	41	18%	28	12%	8	3%
	2001-02 (*n*=240)	22	9%	25	10%	33	14%	36	15%	47	20%	35	15%	28	12%	14	6%
	2002-03 (*n*=238)	15	6%	20	8%	37	16%	29	12%	54	23%	34	14%	38	16%	11	5%
	2003-04 (*n*=248)	22	9%	30	12%	32	13%	42	17%	58	23%	30	12%	28	11%	6	2%
Grade Seven	1999-00 (*n*=226)	16	9%	22	10%	50	23%	37	16%	51	23%	29	13%	16	7%	5	2%
	2000-01 (*n*=238)	10	4%	20	8%	37	16%	40	17%	77	32%	35	15%	13	5%	6	3%
	2001-02 (*n*=218)	15	7%	22	10%	40	18%	37	17%	50	23%	35	16%	17	8%	2	1%
	2002-03 (*n*=238)	9	4%	17	7%	49	21%	42	18%	59	25%	40	17%	15	6%	7	3%
	2003-04 (*n*=232)	18	8%	17	7%	54	23%	46	20%	60	26%	27	12%	8	3%	2	0.9%
Grade Eight	1999-00 (*n*=223)	16	7%	24	11%	43	19%	38	17%	49	22%	26	12%	24	11%	3	1%
	2000-01 (*n*=214)	15	7%	17	8%	40	19%	32	15%	51	24%	36	17%	15	7%	8	4%
	2001-02 (*n*=243)	12	5%	20	8%	49	20%	43	18%	75	31%	39	16%	4	2%	1	0%
	2002-03 (*n*=219)	16	7%	17	8%	41	19%	36	17%	49	22%	36	17%	17	8%	7	3%
	2003-04 (*n*=244)	17	7%	22	9%	52	21%	63	26%	51	21%	21	9%	12	5%	6	2%

Figure 6.12

Azalea Middle School
SCAT ELA Proficiency Numbers and Percentages
By Grade Level and Ethnicity, 1999-00 to 2003-04

Grade Level	Ethnicity	Year	Below Basic		Basic		Proficient		Advanced	
			Number	Percent	Number	Percent	Number	Percent	Number	Percent
Grade Six	Asian	1999-00	2	25%	6	75%				
		2000-01	2	25%	1	13%	5	63%		
		2001-02	1	25%			2	50%	1	25%
		2002-03	3	50%	2	33%	1	17%		
		2003-04	2	33%	3	50%	1	17%		
	Black	1999-00	17	55%	11	36%	3	10%		
		2000-01	46	70%	12	18%	7	11%	1	2%
		2001-02	28	48%	19	33%	10	17%	1	12%
		2002-03	21	45%	16	34%	10	21%		
		2003-04	33	63%	15	29%	4	8%		
	Hispanic/Latino	1999-00					1	100%		
		2000-01	1	25%	1	25%	2	50%		
		2001-02	3	75%	1	25%				
		2002-03	3	38%	5	63%				
		2003-04	3	38%	4	50%	1	13%		
	White	1999-00	10	6%	43	24%	104	58%	22	12%
		2000-01	17	11%	27	17%	76	49%	35	23%
		2001-02	15	9%	49	28%	70	40%	40	23%
		2002-03	8	5%	43	25%	77	43%	49	28%
		2003-04	14	8%	52	29%	82	45%	34	19%
Grade Seven	Asian	1999-00	1	13%	2	25%	5	63%		
		2000-01			4	100%				
		2001-02			3	43%	4	57%		
		2002-03			1	25%	3	75%		
		2003-04	3	50%	1	17%	2	33%		
	Black	1999-00	18	36%	22	44%	9	18%	1	2%
		2000-01	16	43%	15	41%	6	16%		
		2001-02	24	42%	29	51%	4	7%		
		2002-03	16	31%	25	48%	10	19%	1	2%
		2003-04	16	38%	19	45%	7	17%		
	Hispanic/Latino	1999-00	1	17%	4	67%	1	17%		
		2000-01					1	100%		
		2001-02	2	50%			2	50%		
		2002-03	3	50%	2	33%	1	17%		
		2003-04	1	17%	5	83%				
	White	1999-00	18	11%	59	36%	65	40%	20	12%
		2000-01	14	7%	58	30%	105	54%	19	10%
		2001-02	11	7%	45	30%	75	50%	19	13%
		2002-03	7	4%	63	36%	85	48%	21	12%
		2003-04	15	8%	75	42%	78	44%	10	6%

Figure 6.12 (Continued)

Azalea Middle School
SCAT ELA Proficiency Numbers and Percentages
By Grade Level and Ethnicity, 1999-00 to 2003-04

Grade Level	Ethnicity	Year	Below Basic		Basic		Proficient		Advanced	
			Number	Percent	Number	Percent	Number	Percent	Number	Percent
Grade Eight	Asian	1999-00	3	30%	4	40%	3	30%		
		2000-01	1	13%	2	25%	3	38%	2	25%
		2001-02			5	100%				
		2002-03	2	22%	2	22%	5	56%		
		2003-04			1	33%	1	33%	1	33%
	Black	1999-00	20	48%	16	38%	5	12%	1	2%
		2000-01	16	31%	26	50%	9	17%	1	2%
		2001-02	20	54%	13	35%	4	11%		
		2002-03	19	37%	26	51%	6	12%		
		2003-04	23	41%	27	48%	6	11%		
	Hispanic/Latino	1999-00	1	25%	3	75%				
		2000-01	2	29%	2	29%	3	43%		
		2001-02			2	50%	2	50%		
		2002-03			2	50%	2	50%		
		2003-04	2	33%	4	67%				
	White	1999-00	16	10%	58	35%	67	40%	26	16%
		2000-01	13	9%	42	29%	72	49%	20	14%
		2001-02	12	6%	72	37%	108	55%	5	3%
		2002-03	12	8%	45	30%	72	47%	24	16%
		2003-04	14	8%	83	47%	65	37%	16	9%

Figure 6.13

Azalea Middle School
SCAT ELA Proficiency Numbers and Percentages
By Grade Level, Ethnicity, and Gender, 1999-00 to 2003-04

Grade Level	Ethnicity	Gender	Year	Below Basic		Basic		Proficient		Advanced	
				Number	Percent	Number	Percent	Number	Percent	Number	Percent
Grade Six	Asian	Female	1999-00	1	20%	4	80%				
			2000-01	1	20%	1	20%	3	60%		
			2001-02					2	100%		
			2002-03	2	67%			1	33%		
			2003-04	2	50%	1	25%	1	25%		
		Male	1999-00	1	33%	2	67%				
			2000-01	1	33%			2	67%		
			2001-02	1	50%					1	50%
			2002-03	1	33%	2	67%				
			2003-04			2	100%				
	Black	Female	1999-00	5	31%	8	50%	3	19%		
			2000-01	23	66%	6	17%	4	11%	1	3%
			2001-02	13	50%	7	27%	4	15%	1	4%
			2002-03	8	32%	11	44%	6	24%		
			2003-04	12	57%	6	29%	3	14%		
		Male	1999-00	12	86%	3	21%				
			2000-01	23	72%	6	19%	3	9%		
			2001-02	15	45%	12	36%	6	18%		
			2002-03	13	59%	5	23%	4	18%		
			2003-04	21	68%	9	29%	1	3%		
	Hispanic/Latino	Female	1999-00								
			2000-01	1	33%			2	67%		
			2001-02	2	67%	1	33%				
			2002-03	1	33%	2	67%				
			2003-04	2	40%	2	40%	1	20%		
		Male	1999-00					1	100%		
			2000-01			1	100%				
			2001-02	1	100%						
			2002-03	2	40%	3	60%				
			2003-04	1	33%	2	67%				
	White	Female	1999-00	4	4%	21	19%	68	63%	15	14%
			2000-01	11	12%	12	13%	40	44%	27	30%
			2001-02	7	7%	25	25%	41	41%	27	27%
			2002-03	4	4%	24	21%	47	42%	38	34%
			2003-04	6	5%	23	21%	53	48%	28	25%
		Male	1999-00	6	8%	22	31%	36	51%	7	10%
			2000-01	6	9%	15	23%	36	55%	8	12%
			2001-02	8	11%	24	32%	29	39%	13	17%
			2002-03	4	6%	19	30%	30	47%	11	17%
			2003-04	8	11%	29	40%	29	40%	6	8%

Figure 6.13 (Continued)

Azalea Middle School
SCAT ELA Proficiency Numbers and Percentages
By Grade Level, Ethnicity, and Gender, 1999-00 to 2003-04

Grade Level	Ethnicity	Gender	Year	Below Basic		Basic		Proficient		Advanced	
				Number	Percent	Number	Percent	Number	Percent	Number	Percent
Grade Seven	Asian	Female	1999-00	1	25%	1	25%	2	50%		
			2000-01			4	100%				
			2001-02			2	40%	3	60%		
			2002-03					2	100%		
			2003-04	2	50%			2	50%		
		Male	1999-00			1	25%	3	75%		
			2000-01								
			2001-02			1	50%	1	50%		
			2002-03			1	50%	1	50%		
			2003-04	1	50%	1	50%				
	Black	Female	1999-00	10	30%	14	4%	8	24%	1	3%
			2000-01	6	33%	7	39%	5	28%		
			2001-02	8	27%	18	60%	4	13%		
			2002-03	5	23%	14	64%	3	14%		
			2003-04	6	32%	9	47%	4	21%		
		Male	1999-00	8	44%	8	44%	1	6%		
			2000-01	10	53%	8	42%	1	5%		
			2001-02	16	59%	11	41%				
			2002-03	11	37%	11	37%	7	23%	1	3%
			2003-04	10	43%	10	43%	3	13%		
	Hispanic/Latino	Female	1999-00	1	17%	4	67%	1	17%		
			2000-01								
			2001-02	1	33%			2	67%		
			2002-03	2	40%	2	40%	1	20%		
			2003-04	1	25%	3	75%				
		Male	1999-00								
			2000-01					1	100%		
			2001-02	1	100%						
			2002-03	1	100%						
			2003-04			2	100%				
	White	Female	1999-00	4	4%	31	34%	40	44%	15	17%
			2000-01	4	3%	26	23%	72	63%	13	11%
			2001-02	6	7%	20	24%	41	49%	17	20%
			2002-03	2	2%	33	32%	53	52%	15	15%
			2003-04	9	8%	42	37%	54	48%	8	7%
		Male	1999-00	14	20%	28	39%	25	35%	5	7%
			2000-01	10	12%	32	40%	33	41%	6	7%
			2001-02	5	7%	25	37%	34	51%	2	3%
			2002-03	5	7%	30	41%	32	44%	6	8%
			2003-04	6	9%	33	51%	24	37%	2	3%

Figure 6.13 (Continued)

Azalea Middle School
SCAT ELA Proficiency Numbers and Percentages
By Grade Level, Ethnicity, and Gender, 1999-00 to 2003-04

Grade Level	Ethnicity	Gender	Year	Below Basic		Basic		Proficient		Advanced	
				Number	Percent	Number	Percent	Number	Percent	Number	Percent
Grade Eight	Asian	Female	1999-00	2	33%	2	33%	2	33%		
			2000-01			1	33%	1	33%	1	33%
			2001-02			4	100%				
			2002-03			2	40%	3	60%		
			2003-04					1	100%		
		Male	1999-00	1	25%	2	50%	1	25%		
			2000-01	1	20%	1	20%	2	40%	1	2%
			2001-02			1	100%				
			2002-03	2	50%			2	50%		
			2003-04			1	50%			1	50%
	Black	Female	1999-00	11	44%	8	32%	5	20%	1	4%
			2000-01	10	33%	13	43%	7	23%		
			2001-02	10	53%	6	32%	4	21%		
			2002-03	10	32%	16	52%	5	16%		
			2003-04	11	42%	12	46%	3	12%		
		Male	1999-00	9	53%	8	47%				
			2000-01	6	29%	13	62%	2	10%	1	5%
			2001-02	10	63%	7	44%				
			2002-03	9	45%	10	50%	1	5%		
			2003-04	12	40%	15	50%	3	10%		
	Hispanic/Latino	Female	1999-00	1	33%	2	67%				
			2000-01	1	17%	2	33%	3	50%		
			2001-02			1	50%	1	50%		
			2002-03			1	33%	2	67%		
			2003-04	1	25%	3	75%				
		Male	1999-00			1	100%				
			2000-01	1	100%						
			2001-02			1	33%	1	33%		
			2002-03			1	100%				
			2003-04	1	50%	1	50%				
	White	Female	1999-00	2	2%	31	32%	42	43%	23	23%
			2000-01	4	5%	24	29%	40	48%	14	17%
			2001-02	2	2%	38	33%	70	61%	4	4%
			2002-03	6	7%	22	26%	39	46%	17	20%
			2003-0	5	5%	37	37%	47	47%	11	11%
		Male	1999-00	14	20%	27	39%	25	36%	3	4%
			2000-01	9	14%	18	27%	32	48%	6	9%
			2001-02	10	12%	34	41%	38	46%	1	1%
			2002-03	6	9%	23	33%	33	47%	7	10%
			2003-04	9	12%	46	60%	18	23%	5	6%

Figure 6.14

Azalea Middle School
SCAT ELA Proficiency Numbers and Percentages
By Grade Level and Free/Reduced Lunch Status, 1999-00 to 2003-04

Grade Level	Lunch Status	Year	Below Basic		Basic		Proficient		Advanced	
			Number	Percent	Number	Percent	Number	Percent	Number	Percent
Grade Six	Free/Reduced	1999-00 (n=42)	17	40%	17	40%	7	17%	1	2%
		2000-01 (n=68)	43	63%	13	19%	10	15%	2	3%
		2001-02 (n=62)	27	44%	21	34%	14	23%		
		2002-03 (n=64)	27	42%	21	33%	13	20%	3	5%
		2003-04 (n=74)	40	54%	22	30%	12	16%		
	Paid	1999-00 (n=177)	12	7%	43	24%	101	57%	21	12%
		2000-01 (n=165)	23	14%	28	17%	80	49%	34	21%
		2001-02 (n=178)	20	11%	48	27%	68	38%	42	24%
		2002-03 (n=180)	11	6%	47	26%	75	42%	47	26%
		2003-04 (n=174)	12	7%	52	30%	76	44%	34	20%
Grade Seven	Free/Reduced	1999-00 (n=46)	18	39%	18	39%	9	20%	1	2%
		2000-01 (n=40)	14	35%	19	48%	7	18%		
		2001-02 (n=49)	21	43%	23	47%	5	10%		
		2002-03 (n=55)	16	29%	27	49%	11	20%	1	2%
		2003-04 (n=63)	23	37%	30	48%	10	16%		
	Paid	1999-00 (n=180)	20	11%	69	38%	71	39%	20	11%
		2000-01 (n=198)	16	8%	58	29%	105	53%	19	10%
		2001-02 (n=169)	16	10%	54	32%	80	47%	19	11%
		2002-03 (n=187)	12	6%	66	35%	88	47%	21	11%
		2003-04 (n=169)	12	7%	70	41%	77	46%	10	6%
Grade Eight	Free/Reduced	1999-00 (n=49)	20	41%	21	43%	5	10%	3	6%
		2000-01 (n=44)	17	39%	17	39%	9	20%	1	2%
		2001-02 (n=44)	21	48%	16	36%	7	16%		
		2002-03 (n=49)	23	47%	19	39%	7	14%		
		2003-04 (n=56)	18	32%	33	59%	4	7%	1	2%
	Paid	1999-00 (n=174)	20	12%	60	35%	70	40%	24	14%
		2000-01 (n=170)	15	9%	55	32%	78	46%	22	13%
		2001-02 (n=199)	11	6%	76	38%	107	54%	5	3%
		2002-03 (n=175)	13	7%	59	34%	79	45%	24	14%
		2003-04 (n=188)	21	11%	82	44%	68	36%	17	9%

Figure 6.15

Azalea Middle School
SCAT ELA Proficiency Numbers and Percentages
By Grade Level and Learning Impairment, 1999-00 to 2003-04

Grade Level	Learning Impairment	Year	Below Basic		Basic		Proficient		Advanced	
			Number	Percent	Number	Percent	Number	Percent	Number	Percent
Grade Six	Educable Severely Impaired	2000-01	5	100%						
		2001-02	2	50%	2	50%				
		2002-03	2	100%						
		2003-04			1	50%	1	50%		
	Emotionally Disabled	2000-01	2	100%						
		2001-02	3	100%						
		2002-03	3	100%						
		2003-04	5	100%						
	Health Impaired	1999-00	5	100%						
		2000-01	3	43%	4	57%				
		2001-02	2	50%	1	25%	1	25%		
	Learning Disabilities	1999-00	2	29%	3	43%	2	29%		
		2000-01	10	77%	1	8%	2	15%		
		2001-02	13	54%	9	38%	2	8%		
		2002-03	4	44%	1	11%	3	33%	1	11%
		2003-04	18	78%	5	22%				
	No Disability	1999-00	22	11%	57	28%	106	51%	22	11%
		2000-01	46	22%	36	17%	88	43%	36	17%
		2001-02	27	13%	57	28%	79	39%	42	20%
		2002-03	26	12%	64	29%	84	38%	47	21%
		2003-04	29	13%	66	31%	86	40%	34	16%
Grade Seven	Educable Severely Impaired	2000-01	2	100%						
		2001-02	5	83%	1	17%				
		2002-03	2	50%	2	50%				
		2003-04			1	100%				
	Emotionally Disabled	1999-00	3	100%						
		2000-01	4	100%						
		2001-02	2	100%						
		2002-03			2	100%				
		2003-04	2	100%						
	Health Impaired	1999-00	4	80%	1	20%				
		2000-01	3	60%	1	20%	1	20%		
		2001-02	1	20%	4	80%				
	Learning Disabilities	1999-00	4	44%	5	56%				
		2000-01	12	71%	5	29%				
		2001-02	8	73%	3	27%				
		2002-03	11	52%	9	43%	1	5%		
		2003-04	5	36%	6	43%	3	21%		
	No Disability	1999-00	27	13%	81	39%	80	38%	21	10%
		2000-01	9	4%	71	34%	111	53%	19	9%
		2001-02	21	11%	69	36%	85	44%	19	10%
		2002-03	11	5%	78	37%	98	47%	22	11%
		2003-04	28	13%	93	43%	84	39%	10	5%

Figure 6.15 (Continued)

Azalea Middle School
SCAT ELA Proficiency Numbers and Percentages
By Grade Level and Learning Impairment, 1999-00 to 2003-04

Grade Level	Learning Impairment	Year	Below Basic		Basic		Proficient		Advanced	
			Number	Percent	Number	Percent	Number	Percent	Number	Percent
Grade Eight	Educable Severely Impaired	2000-01	1	100%						
		2001-02	4	80%	1	20%				
		2002-03	4	100%						
		2003-04	1	17%	5	83%				
	Emotionally Disabled	1999-00	4	80%	1	20%				
		2000-01	4	67%	2	33%				
		2001-02	5	83%	1	17%				
		2002-03	2	100%						
		2003-04	3	75%	1	25%				
	Health Impaired	1999-00	4	80%	1	20%				
		2000-01	2	67%	1	33%				
		2001-02	2	40%	3	60%				
	Learning Disabilities	1999-00	7	64%	1	9%	3	27%		
		2000-01	7	50%	6	43%	1	7%		
		2001-02	9	53%	8	47%				
		2002-03	11	69%	5	31%				
		2003-04	15	58%	10	38%	1	4%		
	No Disability	1999-00	25	12%	78	39%	72	36%	27	13%
		2000-01	18	9%	63	33%	86	45%	23	12%
		2001-02	12	6%	79	38%	114	54%	5	2%
		2002-03	16	8%	70	36%	85	43%	24	12%
		2003-04	20	10%	99	48%	71	34%	18	9%

Figure 6.16

Azalea Middle School
SCAT ELA Proficiency Numbers and Percentages
By Grade Level and Gifted Designations, 1999-99 to 2002-03

Grade Level	Ability	Year	Below Basic		Basic		Proficient		Advanced	
			Number	Percent	Number	Percent	Number	Percent	Number	Percent
Grade Six	Gifted	1999-00 (*n*=97)			9	9%	68	70%	20	21%
		2000-01 (*n*=83)	1	1%	3	4%	49	59%	30	36%
		2001-02 (*n*=93)	1	1%	6	6%	46	49%	40	43%
		2002-03 (*n*=104)			8	8%	53	51%	43	41%
	Not Gifted	1999-00 (*n*=122)	29	24%	51	42%	40	33%	2	2%
		2000-01 (*n*=150)	65	43%	38	25%	41	27%	6	4%
		2001-02 (*n*=147)	46	31%	63	43%	36	24%	2	1%
		2002-03 (*n*=134)	35	26%	58	43%	35	26%	6	4%
Grade Seven	Gifted	1999-00 (*n*=88)			13	15%	54	61%	21	24%
		2000-01 (*n*=103)	1	1%	14	14%	70	68%	18	17%
		2001-02 (*n*=91)			11	12%	62	68%	18	20%
		2002-03 (*n*=91)			13	14%	57	63%	21	23%
	Not Gifted	1999-00 (*n*=138)	38	28%	74	54%	26	19%		
		2000-01 (*n*=135)	29	21%	63	47%	42	31%	1	1%
		2001-02 (*n*=127)	37	29%	66	52%	23	18%	1	1%
		2002-03 (*n*=147)	26	18%	78	53%	42	29%	1	1%
Grade Eight	Gifted	1999-00 (*n*=91)	1	1%	20	22%	45	49%	25	27%
		2000-01 (*n*=78)			6	8%	52	67%	20	26%
		2001-02 (*n*=100)			11	11%	82	82%	5	5%
		2002-03 (*n*=86)			6	7%	58	67%	22	25%
	Not Gifted	1999-00 (*n*=132)	39	30%	61	46%	30	23%	2	2%
		2000-01 (*n*=136)	32	24%	66	49%	35	26%	3	2%
		2001-02 (*n*=145)	32	22%	81	56%	32	22%		
		2002-03 (*n*=131)	33	25%	69	53%	27	21%	2	2%

Figure 6.17

Azalea Middle School
SCAT ELA Proficiency Numbers and Percentages
By Grade Level and Language Proficiency
Limited English (LEP) and English Learner (EL), 2001-02 to 2003-04

Grade Level	Language Proficiency	Year	Below Basic		Basic		Proficient		Advanced	
			Number	Percent	Number	Percent	Number	Percent	Number	Percent
Grade Six	English Proficient	2001-02 (*n*=239)	46	19%	69	29%	82	34%	42	18%
		2002-03 (*n*=233)	33	14%	63	27%	88	38%	49	21%
		2003-04 (*n*=238)	48	20%	70	29%	86	36%	34	14%
	LEP / EL	2001-02 (*n*=1)	1	100%						
		2002-03 (*n*=5)	2	40%	3	60%				
		2003-04 (*n*=10)	4	40%	4	40%	2	20%		
Grade Seven	English Proficient	2001-02 (*n*=218)	37	17%	77	35%	85	39%	19	9%
		2002-03 (*n*=237)	26	11%	90	38%	99	42%	22	9%
		2003-04 (*n*=228)	33	14%	98	43%	87	38%	10	4%
	LEP / EL	2002-03 (*n*=1)			1	100%				
		2003-04 (*n*=4)	2	50%	2	50%				
Grade Eight	English Proficient	2001-02 (*n*=243)	32	13%	92	38%	114	47%	5	2%
		2002-03 (*n*=216)	32	15%	75	35%	85	39%	24	11%
		2003-04 (*n*=241)	38	16%	114	47%	72	30%	17	7%
	LEP / EL	2002-03 (*n*=1)	1	100%						
		2003-04 (*n*=3)	1	33%	1	33%			1	33%

SCAT Mathematic Scores

Figure 6.18 shows the percentage of students scoring Mathematics proficiency levels for grades six, seven, and eight, respectively.

Figure 6.18

Azalea Middle School
SCAT Mathematics Proficiency Numbers and Percentages by Grade Level
1999-00 to 2003-04

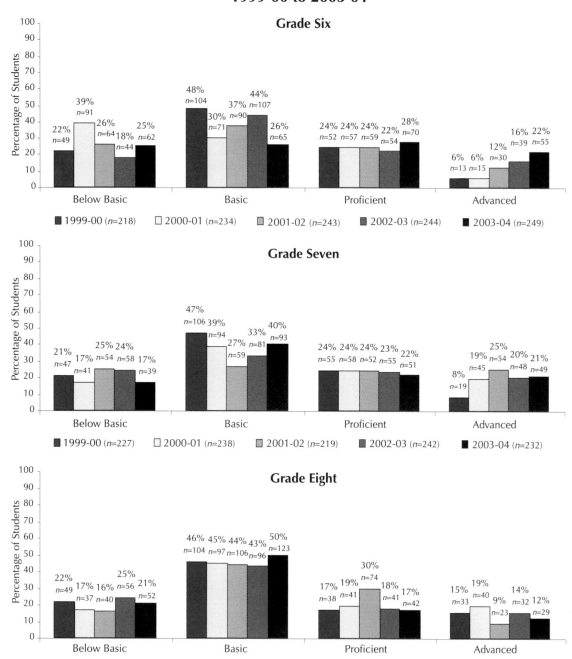

Figure 6.19 shows the percentage of student scoring in Mathematics proficiency levels by unmatched cohorts.

Figure 6.19

Azalea Middle School
SCAT Mathematics Proficiency Numbers and Percentages by Cohorts
1999-00 to 2003-04

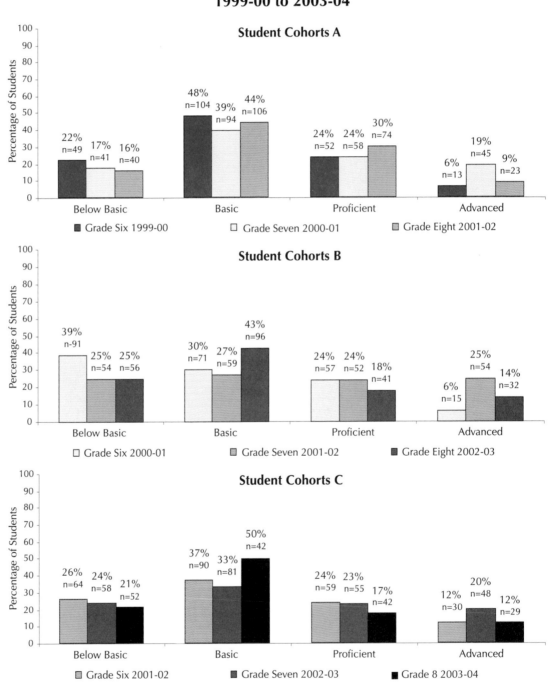

Figure 6.20

Azalea Middle School
SCAT Mathematics Proficiency Numbers and Percentages by Grade Level and Gender
1999-00 to 2003-04

Grade Level	Year	Below Basic				Basic				Proficient				Advanced			
		Female		Male		Female		Male		Female		Male		Female		Male	
		Number	Percent	Number	Percent	Number	Percent	Number	Percent	Number	Percent	Number	Percent	Number	Percent	Number	Percent
Grade Six	1999-00 (*n*=218)	26	12%	23	11%	66	30%	38	17%	32	15%	20	9%	5	2%	8	4%
	2000-01 (*n*=234)	54	23%	37	16%	45	19%	26	11%	24	10%	33	14%	10	4%	5	2%
	2001-02 (*n*=243)	36	15%	28	12%	47	19%	43	18%	39	16%	20	8%	10	4%	20	8%
	2002-03 (*n*=238)	24	10%	18	8%	67	28%	37	16%	31	13%	22	9%	22	9%	17	7%
	2003-04 (*n*=249)	33	13%	36	14%	22	9%	40	16%	33	13%	33	13%	20	8%	32	13%
Grade Seven	1999-00 (*n*=227)	26	11%	21	9%	65	29%	41	18%	34	15%	21	9%	8	4%	11	5%
	2000-01 (*n*=238)	20	8%	21	9%	55	23%	39	16%	40	17%	18	8%	22	9%	23	10%
	2001-02 (*n*=219)	29	13%	25	11%	35	16%	24	11%	29	13%	23	11%	29	13%	25	11%
	2002-03 (*n*=238)	26	11%	30	13%	47	20%	32	13%	31	13%	24	10%	28	12%	20	8%
	2003-04 (*n*=232)	18	8%	25	11%	35	15%	57	25%	19	8%	31	13%	20	9%	27	12%
Grade Eight	1999-00 (*n*=224)	26	12%	23	10%	59	26%	45	20%	27	12%	11	5%	20	9%	13	6%
	2000-00 (*n*=215)	22	10%	15	7%	56	26%	41	19%	23	11%	18	8%	21	10%	19	9%
	2001-02 (*n*=243)	22	9%	18	7%	62	26%	44	18%	45	19%	29	12%	11	5%	12	5%
	2002-03 (*n*=218)	31	14%	22	10%	52	24%	41	19%	17	8%	23	10%	23	10%	9	4%
	2003-04 (*n*=243)	29	12%	27	11%	52	21%	65	27%	16	7%	26	11%	14	6%	14	6%

Figure 6.21

Azalea Middle School
SCAT Mathematics Proficiency Numbers and Percentages
By Grade Level and Ethnicity, 1999-00 to 2003-04

Grade Level	Ethnicity	Year	Below Basic		Basic		Proficient		Advanced	
			Number	Percent	Number	Percent	Number	Percent	Number	Percent
Grade Six	Asian	1999-00	2	25%	5	63%	1	13%		
		2000-01	2	25%	2	25%	3	38%	1	13%
		2001-02	1	25%			1	25%	2	50%
		2002-03	1	17%	2	33%	2	33%	1	17%
		2003-04	4	67%	1	17%	1	17%		
	Black	1999-00	23	74%	7	23%				
		2000-01	56	85%	10	15%	1	2%		
		2001-02	36	62%	16	28%	5	9%	2	3%
		2002-03	23	49%	23	49%	1	2%		
		2003-04	41	79%	7	13%	4	8%		
	Hispanic/Latino	1999-00			1	100%				
		2000-01	3	75%	1	25%				
		2001-02	3	75%	1	25%				
		2002-03	4	50%	3	38%	1	13%		
		2003-04	2	25%	5	63%	1	13%		
	White	1999-00	24	13%	91	51%	51	28%	13	7%
		2000-01	30	19%	58	37%	53	34%	14	9%
		2001-02	24	14%	73	42%	53	30%	26	15%
		2002-03	14	8%	76	43%	49	28%	38	21%
		2003-04	22	12%	49	27%	60	33%	52	29%
Grade Seven	Asian	1999-00			2	25%	4	50%	2	25%
		2000-01			2	50%	1	25%	1	25%
		2001-02			2	29%	4	57%	1	14%
		2002-03	1	25%					3	75%
		2003-04	1	17%	3	50%	1	17%	1	17%
	Black	1999-00	21	42%	24	48%	6	12%		
		2000-01	20	54%	16	43%	1	3%		
		2001-02	37	65%	16	28%	2	4%	2	4%
		2002-03	31	60%	11	21%	8	15%	2	4%
		2003-04	20	48%	18	43%	3	7%	1	2%
	Hispanic/Latino	1999-00	2	33%	3	50%	1	17%		
		2000-01							1	100%
		2001-02	1	25%	2	50%	1	25%		
		2002-03	1	17%	5	83%				
		2003-04	2	33%	1	17%	3	50%		
	White	1999-00	24	15%	77	48%	44	27%	17	10%
		2000-01	21	11%	76	39%	56	29%	43	22%
		2001-02	16	11%	39	26%	45	30%	51	34%
		2002-03	23	13%	63	36%	47	27%	43	24%
		2003-04	20	11%	70	39%	43	24%	45	25%

Figure 6.21 (Continued)

Azalea Middle School
SCAT Mathematics Proficiency Numbers and Percentages
By Grade Level and Ethnicity, 1999-00 to 2003-04

Grade Level	Ethnicity	Year	Below Basic		Basic		Proficient		Advanced	
			Number	Percent	Number	Percent	Number	Percent	Number	Percent
Grade Eight	Asian	1999-00			7	70%	1	10%	2	20%
		2000-01	1	13%	2	25%	1	13%	4	50%
		2001-02	1	20%	3	60%			1	20%
		2002-03			5	56%	2	22%	2	22%
		2003-04	1	33%			1	33%	1	33%
	Black	1999-00	24	57%	14	33%	4	10%		
		2000-01	17	33%	27	52%	4	8%	3	6%
		2001-02	14	38%	20	54%			1	3%
		2002-03	29	57%	18	35%	3	6%	1	2%
		2003-04	33	59%	18	32%	5	9%		
	Hispanic/Latino	1999-00	1	25%	3	75%				
		2000-01	3	43%	3	43%	1	14%		
		2001-02	2	50%	2	50%	1	25%		
		2002-03	1	25%	3	75%				
		2003-04	2	33%	4	67%				
	White	1999-00	24	14%	80	48%	33	20%	31	19%
		2000-01	16	11%	65	44%	35	24%	33	22%
		2001-02	23	12%	81	41%	73	37%	21	11%
		2002-03	23	15%	67	44%	35	23%	29	19%
		2003-04	20	11%	95	53%	35	20%	27	15%

Figure 6.22

Azalea Middle School
SCAT Mathematics Proficiency Numbers and Percentages
By Grade Level, Ethnicity, and Gender, 1999-00 to 2003-04

Grade Level	Ethnicity	Gender	Year	Below Basic		Basic		Proficient		Advanced	
				Number	Percent	Number	Percent	Number	Percent	Number	Percent
Grade Six	Asian	Female	1999-00	1	20%	3	60%	1	20%		
			2000-01	1	20%	2	40%	1	20%	1	20%
			2001-02					1	50%	1	50%
			2002-03	1	33%	1	33%			1	33%
			2003-04	1	50%			1	50%		
		Male	1999-00	1	33%	2	67%				
			2000-01	1	33%			2	67%		
			2001-02	1	50%					1	50%
			2002-03			1	33%	2	67%		
			2003-04	3	75%	1	25%				
	Black	Female	1999-00	11	69%	5	31%				
			2000-01	30	86%	4	11%	1	3%		
			2001-02	18	69%	6	23%	2	8%		
			2002-03	13	48%	14	52%				
			2003-04	23	74%	4	13%	4	13%		
		Male	1999-00	12	86%	2	14%				
			2000-01	26	81%	6	19%				
			2001-02	18	55%	10	30%	3	9%	2	6%
			2002-03	12	50%	11	46%	1	4%		
			2003-04	18	86%	3	14%				
	Hispanic/Latino	Female	1999-00								
			2000-01	2	67%	1	33%				
			2001-02	2	67%	1	33%				
			2002-03	2	67%			1	33%		
			2003-04	1	33%	1	33%	1	33%		
		Male	1999-00			1	100%				
			2000-01	1	100%						
			2001-02	1	100%						
			2002-03	2	40%	3	60%				
			2003-04	1	20%	4	80%				
	White	Female	1999-00	14	13%	58	54%	31	29%	5	5%
			2000-01	21	23%	38	42%	22	24%	9	10%
			2001-02	16	16%	40	40%	36	36%	9	9%
			2002-03	9	8%	53	47%	30	27%	21	19%
			2003-04	8	11%	17	24%	27	38%	20	28%
		Male	1999-00	10	14%	33	46%	20	28%	8	11%
			2000-01	9	14%	20	31%	31	48%	5	8%
			2001-02	8	11%	33	44%	17	23%	17	23%
			2002-03	5	8%	24	36%	20	30%	17	26%
			2003-04	14	13%	32	29%	33	30%	32	29%

Figure 6.22 (Continued)

Azalea Middle School
SCAT Mathematics Proficiency Numbers and Percentages
By Grade Level, Ethnicity, and Gender, 1999-00 to 2003-04

Grade Level	Ethnicity	Gender	Year	Below Basic		Basic		Proficient		Advanced	
				Number	Percent	Number	Percent	Number	Percent	Number	Percent
Grade Seven	Asian	Female	1999-00			2	50%	1	25%	1	25%
			2000-01			2	50%	1	25%	1	25%
			2001-02			2	40%	2	40%	1	20%
			2002-03							2	100%
			2003-04			1	50%			1	50%
		Male	1999-00					3	75%	1	25%
			2000-01								
			2001-02					2	100%		
			2002-03	1	50%					1	50%
			2003-04	1	25%	2	50%	1	25%		
	Black	Female	1999-00	15	45%	12	36%	6	18%		
			2000-01	8	44%	10	56%				
			2001-02	19	63%	8	27%	1	3%	2	7%
			2002-03	13	59%	6	27%	1	5%	2	9%
			2003-04	11	48%	8	35%	3	13%	1	4%
		Male	1999-00	6	33	12	67%				
			2000-01	12	63%	6	32%	1	5%		
			2001-02	18	67%	8	30%	1	4%		
			2002-03	19	59%	6	19%	7	22%		
			2003-04	9	47%	10	53%				
	Hispanic/Latino	Female	1999-00	2	33%	3	50%	1	17%		
			2000-01								
			2001-02	1	33%	1	33%	1	33%		
			2002-03	1	20%	4	80%				
			2003-04			1	50%	1	50%		
		Male	1999-00								
			2000-01							1	100%
			2001-02			1	100%				
			2002-03			1	100%				
			2003-04	2	50%			2	50%		
	White	Female	1999-00	9	10%	48	53%	26	29%	7	8%
			2000-01	12	10%	43	37%	39	34%	21	18%
			2001-02	9	11%	24	29%	25	30%	26	31%
			2002-03	13	12%	38	36%	30	29%	24	23%
			2003-04	7	11%	25	38%	15	23%	18	28%
		Male	1999-00	15	21%	29	40%	18	25%	10	14%
			2000-01	1	1%	33	45%	17	23%	22	30%
			2001-02	7	10%	15	22%	20	30%	25	37%
			2002-03	11	15%	26	36%	17	23%	19	26%
			2003-04	13	12%	45	40%	28	25%	27	24%

Figure 6.22 (Continued)

Azalea Middle School
SCAT Mathematics Proficiency Numbers and Percentages
By Grade Level, Ethnicity, and Gender, 1999-00 to 2003-04

Grade Level	Ethnicity	Gender	Year	Below Basic		Basic		Proficient		Advanced	
				Number	Percent	Number	Percent	Number	Percent	Number	Percent
Grade Eight	Asian	Female	1999-00			4	67%			2	33%
			2000-01			1	33%	1	33%	1	33%
			2001-02	1	25%	2	50%			1	25%
			2002-03			3	60%			2	40%
			2003-04			1	100%				
		Male	1999-00			3	75%	1	25%		
			2000-01	1	20%	1	20%			3	60%
			2001-02			1	100%				
			2002-03			3	60%	2	40%		
			2003-04	1	50%					1	50%
	Black	Female	1999-00	13	52%	8	32%	4	16%		
			2000-01	10	33%	14	47%	3	10%	3	10%
			2001-02	7	37%	12	63%				
			2002-03	17	53%	13	41%	1	3%	1	3%
			2003-04	16	53%	12	40%	2	7%		
		Male	1999-00	11	65%	6	35%				
			2000-01	7	33%	13	62%	1	5%		
			2001-02	7	44%	8	50%			1	6%
			2002-03	13	62%	6	29%	2	10%		
			2003-04	17	65%	6	23%	3	12%		
	Hispanic/Latino	Female	1999-00	1	25%	2	75%				
			2000-01	3	50%	2	33%	1	17%		
			2001-02	1	50%	1	50%				
			2002-03	1	25%	2	75%				
			2003-04			2	100%				
		Male	1999-00			1	100%				
			2000-01			1	100%				
			2001-02	1	33%	1	33%	1	33%		
			2002-03			1	100%				
			2003-04	2	50%	2	50%				
	White	Female	1999-00	12	12%	45	46%	23	23%	18	18%
			2000-01	9	11%	39	47%	18	22%	17	20%
			2001-02	13	11%	47	41%	45	39%	10	9%
			2002-03	14	16%	35	41%	17	20%	20	23%
			2003-04	12	16%	38	49%	14	18%	13	17%
		Male	1999-00	12	17%	35	50%	10	14%	13	19%
			2000-01	7	11%	26	39%	17	26%	16	24%
			2001-02	10	12%	34	41%	28	34%	11	13%
			2002-03	11	15%	33	46%	19	26%	9	13%
			2003-04	8	8%	57	57%	21	21%	14	14%

Figure 6.23

Azalea Middle School
SCAT Mathematics Proficiency Numbers and Percentages
By Grade Level and Free/Reduced Lunch Status, 1999-00 to 2003-04

Grade Level	Lunch Status	Year	Below Basic		Basic		Proficient		Advanced	
			Number	Percent	Number	Percent	Number	Percent	Number	Percent
Grade Six	Free/Reduced	1999-00 (*n*=41)	22	54%	15	37%	4	10%		
		2000-01 (*n*=69)	54	78%	11	16%	2	3%	2	3%
		2001-02 (*n*=64)	38	59%	20	31%	3	5%	3	5%
		2002-03 (*n*=64)	24	38%	31	48%	7	11%	2	3%
		2003-04 (*n*=74)	53	72%	13	18%	7	9%	1	1%
	Paid	1999-00 (*n*=177)	27	15%	89	50%	48	27%	13	7%
		2000-01 (*n*=165)	37	22%	60	36%	55	33%	13	8%
		2001-02 (*n*=179)	26	15%	70	39%	56	31%	27	15%
		2002-03 (*n*=180)	20	11%	76	42%	47	26%	37	21%
		2003-04 (*n*=175)	16	9%	49	28%	59	34%	51	29%
Grade Seven	Free/Reduced	1999-00 (*n*=47)	21	45%	20	43%	6	13%		
		2000-01 (*n*=40)	18	45%	16	40%	3	8%	3	8%
		2001-02 (*n*=50)	31	62%	13	26%	3	6%	3	6%
		2002-03 (*n*=55)	28	51%	18	33%	5	9%	4	7%
		2003-04 (*n*=63)	26	41%	25	40%	11	17%	1	2%
	Paid	1999-00 (*n*=180)	26	14%	86	48%	49	27%	19	11%
		2000-01 (*n*=198)	23	12%	78	39%	55	28%	42	21%
		2001-01 (*n*=169)	23	14%	46	27%	49	29%	51	30%
		2002-03 (*n*=187)	30	16%	63	34%	50	27%	44	24%
		2003-04 (*n*=169)	17	10%	67	40%	39	23%	46	27%
Grade Eight	Free/Reduced	1999-00 (*n*=49)	20	41%	26	53%	1	2%	2	4%
		2000-01 (*n*=45)	16	36%	22	49%	5	11%	2	4%
		2001-02 (*n*=43)	18	42%	21	49%	3	7%	1	2%
		2002-03 (*n*=49)	29	59%	18	37%	2	4%		
		2003-04 (*n*=56)	30	54%	21	38%	4	7%	1	2%
	Paid	1999-00 (*n*=175)	29	17%	78	45%	37	21%	31	18%
		2000-01 (*n*=170)	21	12%	75	44%	36	21%	38	22%
		2001-02 (*n*=200)	22	11%	85	43%	71	36%	22	11%
		2002-03 (*n*=176)	27	15%	78	44%	39	22%	32	18%
		2003-04 (*n*=187)	26	14%	96	51%	38	20%	27	14%

Figure 6.24

Azalea Middle School
SCAT Mathematics Proficiency Numbers and Percentages
By Grade Level and Learning Impairment, 1999-00 to 2003-04

Grade Level	Learning Impairment	Year	Below Basic		Basic		Proficient		Advanced	
			Number	Percent	Number	Percent	Number	Percent	Number	Percent
Grade Six	Educable Severely Impaired	2000-01	6	50%					6	50%
		2001-02	5	100%						
		2002-03	1	50%	1	50%				
		2003-04	2	100%						
	Emotionally Disabled	2000-01	2	50%					2	50%
		2001-02	2	67%	1	33%				
		2002-03	3	100%						
		2003-04	5	100%						
	Health Impaired	1999-00	5	45%					6	55%
		2000-01	5	33%	2	13%			8	53%
		2001-02	4	100%						
	Learning Disabilities	1999-00	2	12%	4	24%	1	6%	10	59%
		2000-01	10	34%	2	7%	1	3%	16	55%
		2001-02	14	56%	10	40%	1	4%		
		2002-03	4	44%	4	44%	1	11%		
		2003-04	19	83%	2	9%	1	4%	1	4%
	No Disability	1999-00	22	11%	57	28%	106	51%	22	11%
		2000-01	46	22%	36	17%	88	43%	36	17%
		2001-02	27	13%	57	28%	79	39%	42	20%
		2002-03	35	15%	66	28%	84	36%	48	21%
		2003-04	43	20%	58	27%	64	30%	51	24%
Grade Seven	Educable Severely Impaired	2000-01	2	100%						
		2001-02	6	100%						
		2002-03	5	100%						
		2003-04			1	100%				
	Emotionally Disabled	1999-00	2	33%	1	17%	3	50%		
		2000-01	4	100%						
		2001-02	2	100%						
		2002-03	1	50%	1	50%				
		2003-04	2	100%						
	Health Impaired	1999-00	5	50%			5	50%		
		2000-01	5	100%						
		2001-02	3	60%	2	40%				
	Learning Disabilities	1999-00	4	22%	5	28%	9	50%		
		2000-01	11	65%	5	29%	1	6%		
		2001-02	10	83%	2	17%				
		2002-03	15	68%	7	32%				
		2003-04	8	57%	4	29%	2	14%		
	No Disability	1999-00	27	13%	81	39%	80	38%	21	10%
		2000-01	9	4%	71	34%	111	53%	19	9%
		2001-02	21	11%	69	36%	85	44%	19	10%
		2002-03	11	5%	80	38%	98	46%	22	10%
		2003-04	33	15%	87	40%	48	22%	47	22%

Figure 6.24 (Continued)

Azalea Middle School
SCAT Mathematics Proficiency Numbers and Percentages
By Grade Level and Learning Impairment, 1999-00 to 2003-04

Grade Level	Learning Impairment	Year	Below Basic		Basic		Proficient		Advanced	
			Number	Percent	Number	Percent	Number	Percent	Number	Percent
Grade Eight	Educable Severely Impaired	2001-02	1	33%	2	67%				
		2002-03	4	100%						
		2003-04	5	83%	1	17%				
	Emotionally Disabled	1999-00	4	80%	1	20%				
		2000-01	4	67%	2	33%				
		2001-02	6	100%						
		2002-03	2	100%						
		2003-04	4	100%						
	Health Impaired	1999-00	4	80%	1	20%				
		2000-01	3	100%						
		2001-02	4	80%	1	20%				
	Learning Disabilities	1999-00	7	64%	3	27%	1	9%		
		2000-01	9	64%	3	21%	2	14%		
		2001-02	14	82%	3	18%				
		2002-03	13	76%	4	24%				
		2003-04	16	62%	9	35%	1	4%		
	No Disability	1999-00	25	12%	78	39%	72	36%	27	13%
		2000-01	18	9%	63	33%	86	45%	23	12%
		2001-02	12	6%	79	38%	114	54%	5	2%
		2002-03	18	9%	73	36%	86	43%	24	12%
		2003-04	31	15%	107	52%	41	20%	28	14%

Figure 6.25

Azalea Middle School
SCAT Mathematics Proficiency Numbers and Percentages
By Grade Level and Gifted Designations, 1999-00 to 2002-03

Grade Level	Ability	Year	Below Basic		Basic		Proficient		Advanced	
			Number	Percent	Number	Percent	Number	Percent	Number	Percent
Grade Six	Gifted	1999-00 (*n*=97)			38	39%	46	47%	13	13%
		2000-01 (*n*=83)	1	1%	26	31%	42	51%	14	17%
		2001-02 (*n*=93)	1	1%	21	23%	44	47%	27	29%
		2002-03 (*n*=104))	1	1%	29	28%	39	38%	35	34%
	Not Gifted	1999-00 (*n*=121)	49	41%	66	55%	6	5%		
		2000-01 (*n*=151)	90	60%	45	30%	15	10%	1	1%
		2001-02 (*n*=150)	63	42%	69	46%	15	10%	3	2%
		2002-03 (*n*=134)	41	31%	75	56%	14	10%	4	3%
Grade Seven	Gifted	1999-00 (*n*=88)			24	27%	46	52%	18	20%
		2000-01 (*n*=103)			24	23%	39	38%	40	39%
		2001-02 (*n*=91)	1	1%	12	13%	32	35%	46	51%
		2002-03 (*n*=91)	2	2%	15	16%	33	36%	41	45%
	Not Gifted	1999-00 (*n*=139)	47	34%	82	59%	9	6%	1	1%
		2000-01 (*n*=135)	41	30%	70	52%	19	14%	5	4%
		2001-02 (*n*=128)	53	41%	47	37%	20	16%	8	6%
		2002-03 (*n*=147)	54	37%	64	44%	22	15%	7	5%
Grade Eight	Gifted	1999-00 (*n*=91)	1	1%	27	30%	31	34%	32	35%
		2000-01 (*n*=78)			10	13%	32	41%	36	46%
		2001-02 (*n*=98)			20	20%	59	60%	19	19%
		2002-03 (*n*=87)			23	26%	33	38%	31	36%
	Not Gifted	1999-00 (*n*=133)	48	36%	77	58%	7	5%	1	1%
		2000-01 (*n*=137)	37	27%	87	64%	9	7%	4	3%
		2001-02 (*n*=145)	40	28%	86	59%	15	10%	4	3%
		2002-03 (*n*=131)	53	40%	70	53%	7	5%	1	1%

Figure 6.26

Azalea Middle School
SCAT Mathematics Proficiency Numbers and Percentages
By Grade Level and Language Proficiency
Limited English (LEP) and English Learner (EL), 2001-02 to 2003-04

Grade Level	Language Proficiency	Year	Below Basic		Basic		Proficient		Advanced	
			Number	Percent	Number	Percent	Number	Percent	Number	Percent
Grade Six	English Proficient	2001-02 (*n*=242)	63	26%	90	37%	59	24%	30	12%
		2002-03 (*n*=233)	41	18%	101	43%	52	22%	39	17%
		2003-04 (*n*=239))	64	27%	58	24%	65	27%	52	22%
	LEP / EL	2001-02 (*n*=1)	1	100%						
		2002-03 (*n*=5)	1	20%	3	60%	1	20%		
		2003-04 (*n*=10)	5	50%	4	40%	1	10%		
Grade Seven	English Proficient	2001-02 (*n*=219)	54	25%	59	27%	52	24%	54	25%
		2002-03 (*n*=237)	56	24%	78	33%	55	23%	48	20%
		2003-04 (*n*=228)	42	18%	90	39%	49	21%	47	21%
	LEP / EL	2002-03 (*n*=1)			1	100%				
		2003-04 (*n*=4)	1	25%	2	50%	1	25%		
Grade Eight	English Proficient	2001-02 (*n*=243)	40	16%	106	44%	74	30%	23	9%
		2002-03 (*n*=217)	53	24%	92	42%	40	18%	32	15%
		2003-04 (*n*=240)	55	23%	116	48%	41	17%	28	12%
	LEP / EL	2002-03 (*n*=1)			1	100%				
		2003-04 (*n*=2)	1	50%	1	50%				

Study Questions for Where Are We Now?

As you review Azalea's data, use either the margins in the text, this page, or print this page from the CD to write down your early thinking. These notes, of course, are only hunches or placeholders until all the data are analyzed. (Ch6Qs.pdf)

1. What are the student learning *strengths* and *challenges* for Azalea Middle School?	
Strengths	*Challenges*

2. What are some *implications* for the Azalea school improvement plan?

3. Looking at the data presented, what other student learning data would you want to answer the question *Where are we now?* for Azalea Middle School?

What I Saw in the Example: Azalea Middle School

Using the study questions as an outline, what I saw in the data for Chapter 6 appears below. When applicable, I have referenced the figure or page number that gave me my first impression of strengths and challenges. 🔵 (Ch6Saw.pdf)

Student Learning Strengths	*Student Learning Challenges*
◆ Azalea performed better than the district and the state in English Language Arts and Mathematics in each grade in 2002-03 and 2003-04. (Figure 6.8)	◆ The number of students *Proficient* and *Advanced* in ELA decreased in 2003-04, except for sixth-grade proficient.
◆ There was an increase in *Advanced* in Mathematics in 2003-04 in grades six and seven from the previous year. (Figure 6.18)	◆ Cohorts are not really improving in either ELA or Mathematics. (Figures 6.10 and 6.19)
◆ Azalea seems to have a large gifted program. No gifted students scored below *Basic* in ELA. (Figure 6.16)	◆ Is there a gender issue in ELA? Females seem to score a lot higher than males. (Figure 6.11)
◆ There were some increases in Mathematics—more advanced students at grade six each year. (Figure 6.18)	◆ Are Black and Hispanic/Latino students' learning needs being met? Only White students typically score in the *Advanced* category.
◆ More free/reduced lunch students scored *Advanced* in Mathematics than in English Language Arts. (Figures 6.14 and 6.23)	◆ It appears that free/reduced lunch and English learner student learning needs are not being met.
	◆ There are variations in special education performance by grade level. (Figures 6.15 and 6.24)
	◆ One would expect fewer gifted students scoring in *Basic*.
	◆ There was a decrease in the number of students *Proficient* and *Advanced* in Mathematics at grade eight. (Figure 6.18)
	◆ Only White students scored *Advanced* in Mathematics in 2003-04 in grade six.
	◆ LEP and EL student scores were pretty low in ELA and Mathematics.

Implications for Azalea's school improvement plan

◆ Might need to look at getting boys more interested in ELA.
◆ Staff might need training in how to meet the needs of Black and Hispanic/Latino students, students who live in poverty, students who are limited English proficient, and students with disabilities.
◆ Across grade levels, Mathematics scores need to improve.

Other desired student learning data or information

Azalea Middle School provided an excellent summary of *where are we now*. Other data that would be helpful in understanding the results the school is getting might include:

◆ Are the *Below Basic* students the same students over time?
◆ What about student achievement results by teacher?
◆ How did these students score in elementary school and how do they perform in high school?

Analyzing required

norm-referenced and/or

criterion-referenced tests

and disaggregating by

grade level, gender,

ethnicity, and

lunch status is an

excellent way to begin

answering the question,

"How are we doing?"

Summary

Answering the question, *Where are we now?*, takes the data analysis work into the student learning realm. Analyzing required norm-referenced and/or criterion-referenced tests and disaggregating by grade level, gender, ethnicity, free/reduced lunch status, and special education is an excellent way to begin answering the question, *How are we doing?* Looking across measures can be useful and informative—another way to think about what students know and are able to do, giving us a glimpse at *how* students learn.

As one looks at the trends, she/he can begin to see discrepancies and areas for further and deeper analyses, which we follow in the next chapter. The study questions can help guide one to these next levels.

On the CD Related to this Chapter

▼ Study Questions Related to *Where Are We Now?* (Ch6Qs.pdf)

These study questions will help you understand the information provided in Chapter 6. This file can be printed for use with staff as you begin to explore your own student learning results.

▼ *Arguments For and Against Standardized Testing* (TestArgu.pdf)

This table summarizes the most common arguments for and against the use of standardized testing.

▼ *Standardized Test Score Terms, Their Most Effective Uses, and Cautions for Their Uses* (TestTerm.pdf)

This table shows the different standardized testing terms, their effective uses, and cautions for their uses.

▼ *Arguments For and Against Performance Assessments* (PerfArgu.pdf)

This table shows the most common arguments for and against the use of performance assessments.

▼ *Arguments For and Against Teacher Grading* (GradeArg.pdf)

This table shows the most common arguments for and against the use of teacher grading.

▼ *Terms Related to Analyzing Student Achievement Results, Descriptively, Their Most Effective Uses, and Cautions for Their Uses* (SAterms1.pdf)

This table shows the different terms related to analyzing student achievement results, descriptively, their effective uses, and cautions for their uses.

▼ *Terms Related to Analyzing Student Achievement Results, Inferentially, Their Most Effective Uses, and Cautions for Their Uses* (SAterms2.pdf)

This table shows the different terms related to analyzing student achievement results, inferentially, their effective uses, and cautions for their uses.

▼ *What I Saw in the Example* (Ch6Saw.pdf)

What I Saw in the Example is a file, organized by the student learning study questions, that summarizes what the author saw in the student learning data provided by Azalea Middle School.

▼ Student Achievement Graphing Templates (MiddSA.xls)

All of the *Microsoft Excel* files that were used to create the student achievement graphs in the Azalea example (Chapter 6) appear on the CD. Use these templates by putting your data in the source data table and changing the title/labels to reflect your data. The graphs will build automatically. This file also explains how to use the templates.

▼ Student Achievement Data Table Templates (MiddSA.doc)
  All of the *Microsoft Word* files that were used to create the student achievement data tables in the Azalea example (Chapter 6) appear on the CD. Use these templates by putting your data in the data table and changing the title/labels to reflect your data.

▼ *Questions to Guide the Analysis of Student Achievement Data* (QsStachv.doc)
  This *Microsoft Word* file consists of questions to guide the interpretation of your student learning data. You can write your responses into this file.

Gaps are the differences between "where the school wants to be" and "where the school is right now."

A vision is what the school would look like, sound like, and feel like when it is carrying out its purpose and mission.

Goals are the outcomes of the vision. Goals are stated in broad, general, abstract, and measurable terms.

Gaps are the differences between *where the school wants to be* and *where the school is right now*. *Where the school wants to be* can be defined through the school's vision and goals.

A *vision* is what the school would look like, sound like, and feel like when it is carrying out its purpose and mission. To be effective in getting all staff members implementing the same concepts, a vision must be spelled-out in specific terms that everyone can understand in the same way. (*The School Portfolio Toolkit: A Planning, Implementation, and Evaluation Guide for Continuous School Improvement* [Bernhardt, 2002], Chapter 5, beginning on page 97.)

Goals are the outcomes of the vision. Goals are stated in broad, general, abstract, and non-measurable terms. *Objectives* are goals that are redrafted in terms that are clearly tangible. *Objectives* are much more narrow and specific and require data to create so they can be measured. Schools often want to attempt many goals, and very few get implemented. There should be only two to three school goals that reflect the results the school wants to achieve by implementing the vision. (ACTGoals.pdf and ACTGap.pdf)

Where the school is right now are the results—specifically what the data say about strengths, challenges, and areas for improvement. To uncover *gaps*, one merely subtracts the results from the ideal (e.g., we want all students to be proficient; only 68% are proficient in math; therefore, our gap is 32%). To understand how to "decrease" the gap, one must review the data and dig deeper. Just looking at one level of analysis could be misleading. One must dig deeper to uncover those students not meeting the standards and where they rank on the scoring scale. The reason for digging deeper is that a large gap may not seem as large as a smaller gap when one discovers that the students in the area with the largest gap scored only one or two points away from mastery, while the students not mastering the subtest with the smallest gap could be on the very bottom of the distribution—a long way from mastery.

Once school personnel see the gaps, they typically want to start implementing solutions *without discovering the root causes*.

Root causes are real reasons that "problems" or "challenges" exist. Schools must uncover the root causes of their undesirable results to alleviate the problem or to get desirable results that will last over time. (ACTRoot.pdf) If they do not understand the root causes, schools could be treating a symptom and never get to the real reason for the results, leading to the same or similar results the next year. Gap and root cause analyses completed for Azalea Middle School are on the pages that follow. Several activities/processes for working with staff to uncover root causes are on the CD. (ACTCause.pdf and ACTCycle.pdf)

Please note the study questions on page 192 to assist in studying the data.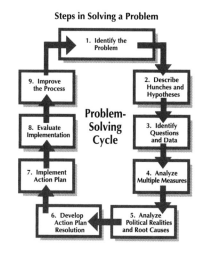
(Ch7Qs.pdf) Also note that there is space in the margins on the data pages to write your impressions as you review the data. At the end of the chapter, I have shared what I saw in the data.

Our Example School: Azalea Middle School

Azalea Middle School teachers decided to use a problem-solving cycle to "flush out" root causes for their students scoring *Below Basic* on the SCAT. (ACTCycle.pdf) Teachers very much wanted to learn what they could about moving these students to *Proficiency*. In the past teachers merely looked at SCAT scores and remediated the students falling behind. This time, they wanted to use data before jumping prematurely to unthought-out solutions. Teachers first stated the "problem" as objectively as they could. They then brainstormed 20 sincere reasons they think this problem exists, withholding any judgments, while encouraging all ideas.

Problem:

Too many students are scoring *Below Basic* on the SCAT.

Brainstormed Reasons:

1. These are students who live in poverty.

2. Most of these students do not have parental support.

3. The students are disengaged in school.

4. The test is terrible. Many students have learning disabilities.

5. These students did not do well in elementary school.

6. They don't know how to read.

7. They don't like to read.

8. Boys just score lower than girls in English Language Arts.

9. Girls just score lower than boys in Mathematics.

10. Students of diversity are not scoring as well as White students.

11. Special education students have low expectations.

12. It's not cool to achieve.

13. These students don't behave well.

14. Parents need to help more.

15. Teachers don't do enough for the low-achieving students.

16. Teachers need to work together better.

17. Teachers and administrators need to implement consistent strategies for these students.

> *Where the school is right now are the results—specifically what the data say about strengths, challenges, and areas for improvement.*

> *Root causes are real reasons that "problems" or "challenges" exist.*

18. Expectations of teachers are low for these students.

19. Not all students are treated like they can learn.

20. Teachers need skills to work with students with backgrounds different from their own.

Staff realized they started by looking externally. Ultimately they turned their thinking inward to what they know is closest to the root cause. They felt their 20th reason was probably very close to the root cause.

Following the brainstorming, staff determined the questions they needed to answer with data, before they can "solve" their problem, which included:

1. *What are the results? How many of our students are proficient?*

2. *Who are the students not achieving?*

3. *Are the same students scoring "Below Basic" in English Language Arts and Mathematics?*

4. *How did these students score on the SCAT?*

5. *What do they know? What do they not know?*

6. *How were they taught?*

7. *What do our data analyses tell us about the root causes?*

Question 1: What are the results? How many of our students are proficient?

Figures 7.1 and 7.2 show the numbers and percentages of students who scored at *Basic, Proficient,* or *Advanced* levels combined, defined as "proficient" in this state. While showing the percentage of "proficient" students by NCLB student groups, the shaded cells in the figures represent the largest gaps (50% and below of that student group). These tables could also show the gaps—that is, the numbers and percentages of students not proficient. If created in that sense, the question staff would have been answering would be *What are the gaps?*

Figure 7.1

Azalea Middle School
Summary of English/Language Arts (ELA) SCAT
Number and Percentage Proficient, 1999-00 to 2003-04

Azalea Middle School Grades 6–8			ELA Proficiency							
			Grade 6		Grade 7		Grade 8		School	
			Number	Percent	Number	Percent	Number	Percent	Number	Percent
Overall	All Students	1999-00	219	87%	226	83%	223	82%	668	84%
		2000-01	233	72%	238	87%	214	85%	685	81%
		2001-02	240	80%	218	83%	243	87%	701	83%
		2002-03	244	84%	242	88%	224	84%	710	86%
		2003-04	249	82%	232	86%	246	86%	727	85%
By Gender	Female	1999-00	129	92%	133	88%	132	88%	394	89%
		2000-01	132	73%	137	93%	121	88%	390	84%
		2001-02	130	83%	122	88%	140	91%	392	88%
		2002-03	144	90%	132	93%	123	87%	399	90%
		2003-04	140	84%	140	87%	132	87%	412	86%
	Male	1999-00	90	79%	93	76%	91	74%	274	76%
		2000-01	101	70%	101	80%	93	82%	295	77%
		2001-02	110	77%	96	77%	103	81%	309	78%
		2002-03	94	84%	106	84%	96	82%	296	83%
		2003-04	108	72%	92	82%	112	80%	312	78%
By Ethnicity	Asian	1999-00	8	75%	8	88%	10	70%	26	77%
		2000-01	8	75%	4	100%	8	88%	20	85%
		2001-02	4	75%	7	100%	5	100%	16	94%
		2002-03	6	67%	4	100%	9	78%	19	79%
		2003-04	6	67%	6	**50%**	3	100%	15	67%
	Black	1999-00	31	**45%**	50	64%	42	52%	123	55%
		2000-01	66	**30%**	37	57%	52	69%	155	**50%**
		2001-02	58	52%	57	58%	37	**46%**	152	53%
		2002-03	47	55%	52	69%	51	63%	150	63%
		2003-04	52	**37%**	42	62%	56	59%	150	52%
	Hispanic/Latino	1999-00	1	100%	6	83%	4	75%	11	82%
		2000-01	4	75%	1	100%	7	71%	12	75%
		2001-02	4	**25%**	4	**50%**	4	100%	12	58%
		2002-03	8	63%	6	**50%**	4	100%	18	67%
		2003-04	8	63%	6	83%	6	67%	20	70%
	White	1999-00	179	94%	162	89%	167	90%	508	91%
		2000-01	155	89%	196	93%	147	91%	498	91%
		2001-02	174	91%	150	93%	197	94%	521	93%
		2002-03	177	95%	176	96%	153	92%	506	95%
		2003-04	182	92%	178	92%	178	92%	538	92%

(Note: n=the number of students taking the test in that student group and grade level. Also note that Ns are small for some student groups, which means these analyses will be used very carefully and only inhouse.)

Figure 7.1 (Continued)

Azalea Middle School
Summary of English/Language Arts (ELA) SCAT
Number and Percentage Proficient, 1999-00 to 2003-04

Azalea Middle School Grades 6–8			ELA Proficiency							
			Grade 6		Grade 7		Grade 8		School	
			Number	Percent	Number	Percent	Number	Percent	Number	Percent
By Socio-Economic Status	Free/Reduced	1999-00	42	60%	46	61%	49	59%	137	60%
		2000-01	68	37%	40	65%	44	61%	152	51%
		2001-02	62	56%	49	57%	44	52%	155	55%
		2002-03	64	58%	55	71%	49	53%	168	61%
		2003-04	74	46%	63	63%	56	68%	193	58%
	Non Free/Reduced	1999-00	177	93%	180	89%	174	89%	531	90%
		2000-01	165	86%	198	92%	170	91%	533	90%
		2001-02	178	89%	169	91%	199	94%	535	93%
		2002-03	180	94%	187	94%	175	93%	542	93%
		2003-04	174	93%	169	93%	188	89%	531	92%
By Special Education Disability	Special Education Identified	1999-00	12	42%	17	35%	21	29%	50	34%
		2000-01	27	44%	30	23%	24	42%	81	36%
		2001-02	35	43%	24	33%	33	39%	92	39%
		2002-03	14	36%	27	52%	22	23%	63	38%
		2003-04	30	23%	17	59%	36	47%	83	41%
	No Disability	1999-00	207	89%	209	87%	202	88%	618	88%
		2000-01	206	78%	210	96%	190	91%	606	88%
		2001-02	205	87%	194	89%	210	94%	609	90%
		2002-03	221	88%	209	95%	195	92%	625	92%
		2003-04	215	87%	215	87%	208	90%	638	88%
By Gifted Abilities	Gifted	1999-00	97	100%	88	100%	91	99%	276	99%
		2000-01	83	99%	103	99%	78	100%	264	99%
		2001-02	93	99%	91	100%	100	100%	284	99%
		2002-03	104	100%	91	100%	87	100%	282	100%
	Not Gifted	1999-00	122	76%	138	72%	132	70%	392	73%
		2000-01	150	57%	135	79%	136	76%	421	70%
		2001-02	147	69%	127	71%	145	78%	419	73%
		2002-03	134	74%	147	82%	131	75%	412	77%
By Language Proficiency	Fluent English	2001-02	239	81%	218	83%	243	87%	700	84%
		2002-03	233	86%	237	89%	216	85%	686	87%
		2003-04	238	80%	228	86%	241	84%	707	83%
	EL / LEP	2002-03	5	60%	1	100%	1	0%	7	57%
		2003-04	10	60%	4	50%	3	67%	17	59%

(Note: n=the number of students taking the test in that student group and grade level. Also note that Ns are small for some student groups, which means these analyses will be used very carefully and only inhouse.)

Figure 7.2

Azalea Middle School
Summary of Mathematics SCAT
Number and Percentage Proficient, 1999-00 to 2003-04

Azalea Middle School Grades 6–8			Math Proficiency							
			Grade 6		Grade 7		Grade 8		School	
			Number	Percent	Number	Percent	Number	Percent	Number	Percent
Overall	All Students	1999-00	218	78%	227	79%	224	78%	669	78%
		2000-01	234	61%	238	83%	215	83%	687	76%
		2001-02	243	74%	219	75%	243	84%	705	78%
		2002-03	244	82%	242	76%	225	75%	711	78%
		2003-04	249	75%	232	83%	232	78%	713	79%
By Gender	Female	1999-00	129	80%	133	80%	132	80%	394	80%
		2000-01	133	59%	137	85%	122	82%	392	76%
		2001-02	132	73%	122	76%	140	84%	394	78%
		2002-03	144	83%	132	80%	123	75%	399	80%
		2003-04	108	69%	92	80%	111	74%	311	74%
	Male	1999-00	89	74%	94	78%	92	75%	275	76%
		2000-01	101	63%	101	79%	93	84%	295	75%
		2001-02	111	75%	97	74%	103	83%	311	77%
		2002-03	94	81%	106	72%	95	77%	295	76%
		2003-04	141	74%	140	82%	132	80%	413	79%
By Ethnicity	Asian	1999-00	8	75%	8	100%	10	100%	26	92%
		2000-01	8	75%	4	100%	8	88%	20	85%
		2001-02	4	75%	7	100%	4	75%	15	87%
		2002-03	6	83%	1	**0%**	9	100%	16	88%
		2003-04	6	**33%**	6	83%	3	67%	15	60%
	Black	1999-00	30	**23%**	51	59%	42	**43%**	123	45%
		2000-01	67	84%	37	**46%**	51	67%	155	69%
		2001-02	59	**39%**	57	**35%**	35	60%	151	**42%**
		2002-03	47	51%	52	**40%**	51	**43%**	150	**45%**
		2003-04	52	**21%**	42	52%	56	**41%**	150	**37%**
	Hispanic/Latino	1999-00	1	100%	6	67%	4	75%	11	73%
		2000-01	4	**25%**	1	100%	7	57%	12	**50%**
		2001-02	4	**25%**	4	75%	5	60%	13	54%
		2002-03	8	**50%**	6	83%	4	75%	18	67%
		2003-04	8	75%	6	**50%**	6	67%	20	65%
	White	1999-00	179	87%	162	85%	168	86%	509	86%
		2000-01	155	81%	196	89%	149	89%	500	87%
		2001-02	176	86%	151	89%	198	88%	502	92%
		2002-03	177	92%	176	87%	154	85%	507	88%
		2003-04	183	88%	178	89%	177	89%	538	88%

(*Note: n*=the number of students taking the test in that student group and grade level. Also note that Ns are small for some student groups, which means these analyses will be used very carefully and only inhouse.)

Figure 7.2 (Continued)

Azalea Middle School
Summary of Mathematics SCAT
Number and Percentage Proficient, 1999-00 to 2003-04

Azalea Middle School Grades 6–8			Math Proficiency							
			Grade 6		Grade 7		Grade 8		School	
			Number	Percent	Number	Percent	Number	Percent	Number	Percent
By Socio-Economic Status	Free/Reduced	1999-00	41	46%	47	55%	49	59%	137	54%
		2000-01	69	22%	40	55%	45	64%	154	43%
		2001-02	64	41%	50	38%	43	58%	157	45%
		2002-03	64	63%	55	49%	49	41%	168	68%
		2003-04	74	28%	63	59%	56	46%	193	44%
	Non Free/Reduced	1999-00	177	85%	180	86%	175	83%	532	85%
		2000-01	165	78%	198	88%	170	88%	533	85%
		2001-02	179	85%	169	86%	200	89%	548	87%
		2002-03	180	89%	187	84%	176	85%	543	86%
		2003-04	175	91%	169	90%	187	86%	531	89%
By Special Education Disability	Special Education Identified	1999-00	28	61%	34	68%	21	29%	83	55%
		2000-01	60	62%	28	21%	23	30%	111	45%
		2001-02	37	32%	25	16%	31	19%	93	24%
		2002-03	14	43%	29	28%	23	17%	66	27%
		2003-04	30	13%	17	41%	36	31%	83	27%
	No Disability	1999-00	207	89%	209	87%	202	88%	618	88%
		2000-01	206	78%	210	96%	190	91%	606	88%
		2001-02	205	87%	194	89%	210	94%	609	90%
		2002-03	233	85%	211	95%	201	91%	645	90%
		2003-04	216	80%	215	85%	207	85%	638	83%
By Gifted Abilities	Gifted	1999-00	97	100%	88	100%	91	99%	276	99%
		2000-01	83	99%	103	100%	78	100%	264	99%
		2001-02	93	99%	91	99%	98	100%	282	99%
		2002-03	104	99%	91	98%	87	100%	282	99%
	Not Gifted	1999-00	121	60%	139	66%	133	64%	393	63%
		2000-01	151	40%	135	70%	137	73%	423	60%
		2001-02	150	58%	128	59%	145	72%	423	63%
		2002-03	134	69%	147	63%	131	60%	412	64%
By Language Proficiency	Fluent English	2001-02	242	74%	219	75%	243	84%	704	78%
		2002-03	233	82%	237	76%	217	76%	687	78%
		2003-04	239	73%	228	82%	240	77%	707	77%
	EL / LEP	2002-03	5	80%	1	100%	1	100%	7	86%
		2003-04	10	50%	4	75%	2	50%	16	56%

(Note: n=the number of students taking the test in that student group and grade level. Also note that Ns are small for some student groups, which means these analyses will be used very carefully and only inhouse.)

Question 2: Who are the students not achieving?

The student groups (disaggregations) show that the students who are the farthest from *Proficiency* are mostly Black, Asian, and Hispanic/Latinos, qualifiers for free/reduced lunch, those identified as needing special education services, and English learners. The summary of numbers and percentages of students scoring below *Basic*, by grade level, follow for ELA in Figure 7.3, and Math in Figure 7.4. The student groups with over 50% are highlighted.

Figure 7.3

Azalea Middle School
Summary of Students Scoring Below Basic on English Language Arts
1999-00 to 2003-04

Student Groups	1999-00		2000-01		2001-02		2002-03		2003-04	
	Number	Percent	Number	Percent	Number	Percent	Number	Percent	Number	Percent
Female	42	11%	61	16%	49	12%	40	10%	57	14%
Male	65	24%	67	23%	67	22%	49	12%	69	22%
Asian	6	23%	3	15%	1	6%	4	21%	5	33%
Black	55	45%	78	**50%**	72	47%	56	37%	72	**48%**
Hispanic/Latino	2	18%	3	25%	5	42%	6	33%	6	30%
White	44	9%	44	9%	38	7%	27	5%	43	8%
Free/Reduced Lunch	55	40%	74	49%	69	45%	66	39%	81	**42%**
Paid Lunch	52	10%	54	10%	36	7%	36	7%	45	8%
Special Education Identified	33	**66%**	52	**64%**	56	**61%**	39	**62%**	49	**59%**
Not Identified for Special Education	74	12%	73	12%	60	10%	53	8%	77	12%
Not Gifted	106	27%	126	30%	115	27%	64	16%		
Fluent English					115	16%	91	13%	119	17%
EL / LEP					1	**100%**	3	43%	7	**41%**

Figure 7.4

Azalea Middle School
Summary of Students Scoring Below Basic on Mathematics
1999-00 to 2003-04

Student Groups	1999-00		2000-01		2001-02		2002-03		2003-04	
	Number	Percent	Number	Percent	Number	Percent	Number	Percent	Number	Percent
Female	78	20%	96	24%	87	22%	81	20%	80	26%
Male	67	24%	73	25%	71	23%	70	24%	88	21%
Asian	2	8%	3	15%	2	13%	2	12%	6	40%
Black	68	**55%**	48	31%	87	**58%**	83	**55%**	94	**63%**
Hispanic/Latino	3	27%	6	**50%**	6	46%	6	33%	7	35%
White	72	14%	67	13%	40	8%	60	12%	62	12%
Free/Reduced Lunch	63	46%	88	**57%**	87	**55%**	53	32%	109	**56%**
Paid Lunch	82	15%	81	15%	71	13%	77	14%	59	11%
Special Education Identified	37	45%	61	**55%**	71	**76%**	48	**73%**	61	**73%**
Not Identified for Special Education	74	12%	73	12%	60	10%	64	10%	107	17%
Not Gifted	144	37%	168	40%	156	37%	148	36%		
Fluent English					157	22%	102	15%	161	23%
EL / LEP					1	**100%**	1	14%	7	44%

Question 3: Are they the same students scoring "Below Basic" in English Language Arts and Mathematics?

Figures 7.5 and 7.6 show the total numbers and percentages of students scoring *Below Basic* by grade level for ELA and Math over the past five years. These tables show that more students scored below proficient in Math than ELA in 2003-04, and that the highest percentage of *Below Basic* scoring tended to occur in grade six. In 2002-03, eighth grade had the highest percentage of *Below Basic* students in both subject areas.

Figure 7.5

Azalea Middle School
Numbers and Percentages of Students Scoring Below Basic English Language Arts by Grade Level, 1999-00 to 2003-04

Grade Level	1999-00		2000-01		2001-02		2002-03		2003-04	
	Number	Percent	Number	Percent	Number	Percent	Number	Percent	Number	Percent
Grade Six	29	13%	66	28%	47	20%	35	14%	52	21%
Grade Seven	38	17%	30	13%	37	17%	26	11%	35	15%
Grade Eight	40	18%	32	15%	32	13%	33	15%	39	16%
Overall Totals	107	16%	128	19%	116	17%	94	13%	126	17%

Figure 7.6

Azalea Middle School
Numbers and Percentages of Students Scoring Below Basic Mathematics by Grade Level, 1999-00 to 2003-04

Grade Level	1999-00		2000-01		2001-02		2002-03		2003-04	
	Number	Percent	Number	Percent	Number	Percent	Number	Percent	Number	Percent
Grade Six	49	22%	91	39%	64	26%	42	17%	69	28%
Grade Seven	47	21%	41	17%	54	25%	56	23%	43	19%
Grade Eight	49	22%	37	17%	40	16%	53	24%	56	24%
Overall Totals	145	22%	169	25%	158	22%	151	21%	168	24%

Figure 7.7 shows the number of students that scored *Below Basic* in both ELA and Math for the past five years. Focusing in on the most recent year, one can see that 100 of the 126 students scoring *Below Basic* in ELA also scored *Below Basic* in Math. Likewise, 100 of the 168 scoring *Below Basic* in Math also scored *Below Basic* on the ELA. The highest numbers of "double" *Below Basic* were in grade six.

Figure 7.7

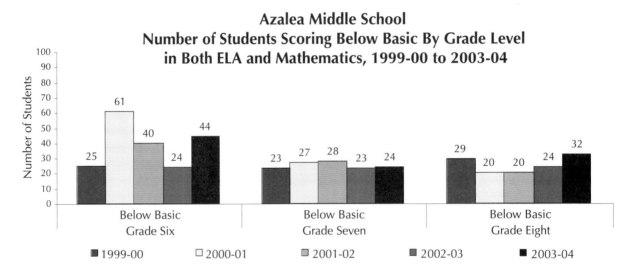

Figure 7.8 shows all the students scoring *Below Basic* on English Language Arts *and* Mathematics, disaggregated by grade level, gender, ethnicity, free/reduced lunch qualifications, and special education identification. The table shows that most of the students scoring *Below Basic* in both subjects were Black students on free/reduced lunch—some identified as special education, others not.

Figure 7.8

Azalea Middle School
Number of Students Scoring Below Basic By Grade Level, Ethnicity, Free/Reduced Lunch, and Special Education, ELA and Mathematics, 1999-00 to 2003-04

Grade Level	Ethnicity	Lunch Status	Special Education (SE) Status	1999-00		2000-01		2001-02		2002-03		2003-04	
				Female	Male	Female	Male	Female	Male	Female	Male	Female	Male
Grade Six	Asian	Free/Reduced	SE Identified							1			
			Not SE		1							2	
		Paid	SE Identified						1				
			Not SE			1	1						
	Black	Free/Reduced	SE Identified		1	4	9	4	4	1	3	4	11
			Not SE	3	8	12	10	6	5	3	5	7	8
		Paid	SE Identified				1	2	2	1			
			Not SE	2	1	6	1	1		2			
	Hispanic/Latino	Free/Reduced	SE Identified									1	1
			Not SE					2	1	1	1		
		Paid	SE Identified						1				
	White	Free/Reduced	SE Identified		1	2	2				1		1
			Not SE	1		2		1	1			2	1
		Paid	SE Identified	1	3		1	2	4	1		2	2
			Not SE	2	1	6	2	3	1	2	2	1	1
Grade Seven	Asian	Free/Reduced	SE Identified									1	
	Black	Free/Reduced	SE Identified	2	1	2	6	2	5	2	3		2
			Not SE	6	3	3	1	2	5	2	3	3	4
		Paid	SE Identified			1	1		2	1	2	1	
			Not SE	1			1	2	2		2	1	1
	Hispanic/Latino	Free/Reduced	Not SE							1		1	
		Paid	Not SE						1				
	White	Free/Reduced	SE Identified			1	1	1	2			1	1
			Not SE		2							1	2
		Paid	SE Identified	2	4	1	7		2	2	5	1	
			Not SE	1	1	2		2				2	2
Grade Eight	Asian	Free/Reduced	Not SE						1				
	Black	Free/Reduced	SE Identified	3	1	2	3	3	5	3	5	5	3
			Not SE	5	2	3		3		4	3	2	6
		Paid	SE Identified		2		2				1	1	2
			Not SE	3	2				1			1	1
	Hispanic/Latino	Free/Reduced	Not SE	1									
		Paid	Not SE			1							
	White	Free/Reduced	SE Identified	1	1		1	2		2	1	1	
		Paid	SE Identified		6	2	3		5		3	2	3
			Not SE	1	1	2			1	2		2	3
Totals	Asian	Free/Reduced	SE Identified							1		1	
			Not SE		1				1			2	
		Paid	SE Identified						1				
			Not SE			1	1						
	Black	Free/Reduced	SE Identified	5	3	8	18	9	14	6	11	9	16
			Not SE	14	13	18	11	11	10	9	11	12	18
		Paid	SE Identified		2	1	4	2	4	2	3	2	2
			Not SE	6	3	6	2	3	3	2	2	2	2
	Hispanic/Latino	Free/Reduced	SE Identified									1	1
			Not SE	1				2	1	2	1	1	
		Paid	Not SE			2		1					
	White	Free/Reduced	SE Identified	1	2	3	4	3	2	2	2	2	2
			Not SE	1	2	2		1	1			3	3
		Paid	SE Identified	3	13	3	11	2	11	3	8	5	5
			Not SE	4	3	10	2	5	2	4	2	5	6

WHAT ARE THE GAPS? AND WHAT ARE THE ROOT CAUSES OF THE GAPS?

185

Question 4: How did these students score on the SCAT?

The SCAT also provides scaled score results. Figure 7.9 shows average scaled scores for Azalea students for 2003-04. Figures 7.10 and 7.11 show the 2003-04 student scaled scores below basic on ELA and Math, disaggregated by grade level, gender, ethnicity, free/reduced lunch qualifications, special education identification, and disability model. The tables show:

▼ Overall, ELA scores were higher than Math in the *Below Basic* and *Proficient* categories.

▼ Students not identified for special education scored much higher than those identified.

Figure 7.9

Azalea Middle School
SCAT English Language Arts and Mathematics Scaled Score Results
By Grade Level, 2003-04

Subject	Grade Level	Below Basic	Basic	Proficient	Advanced
English Language Arts	Grade Six	564.2	592.7	615.2	636.3
	Grade Seven	677.6	697.0	713.0	733.9
	Grade Eight	747.2	774.7	818.6	830.1
	Totals	**652.3**	**701.2**	**708.9**	**708.3**
Mathematics	Grade Six	563.1	608.1	622.7	635.7
	Grade Seven	685.2	697.0	722.5	733.3
	Grade Eight	715.5	804.8	821.3	831.3
	Totals	**645.2**	**723.2**	**707.1**	**715.0**

Figure 7.10

Azalea Middle School
SCAT English Language Arts Scaled Score Results By Grade Level, Gender, Ethnicity, Special Education, and Disability Model, 2003-04

Grade Level	Ethnicity	Special Education (SE) Status	Disability Model	Free/Reduced Lunch		Paid Lunch	
				Female	Male	Female	Male
Grade Six	Asian	Not SE		591.0		604.0	605.0
	Black	SE Identified	Resource	365.3	505.0		301.0
			Self-contained	583.0	566.3		303.0
		Not SE		591.0	587.2	604.5	595.0
	Hispanic/Latino	SE Identified	Self-contained	566.0	576.0		
		Not SE		604.7	604.5	595.0	
	White	SE Identified	Itinerant		603.0	622.0	602.0
			Resource		372.0	575.0	386.0
			Self-contained			593.0	589.7
		Not SE		608.5	600.8	622.5	613.3
Grade Seven	Asian	SE Identified	Self-contained	686.0			
		Not SE		694.0	689.0	718.5	701.0
	Black	SE Identified	Resource	301.0	298.3		
			Self-contained		691.0	682.0	702.0
		Not SE		700.7	693.9	702.3	698.7
	Hispanic/Latino	Not SE		703.3	701.0		708.0
	White	SE Identified	Resource	668.0			
			Self-contained	700.0	677.0	704.5	707.0
		Not SE		708.2	699.2	714.8	710.4
Grade Eight	Asian	SE Identified	Resource				799.0
		Not SE		819.0	829.0		
	Black	SE Identified	Resource	296.4		281.0	283.0
			Self-contained	789.0	786.0	794.0	780.0
			Unknown		746.0		
		Not SE		800.8	800.3	804.6	797.7
	Hispanic/Latino	Not SE		803.0	803.0	799.0	791.0
	White	SE Identified	Resource	202.0			395.0
			Self-contained	788.0		800.2	796.0
		Not SE		802.5	807.5	816.0	809.7
Totals	Asian	SE Identified	Resource				799.0
			Self-contained	686.0			
		Not SE		657.2	759.0	680.3	637.0
	Black	SE Identified	Resource	319.9	416.4	281.0	292.0
			Self-contained	711.8	653.1	738.0	595.0
			Unknown		746.0		
		Not SE		675.7	704.6	745.7	697.1
	Hispanic/Latino	SE Identified	Self-contained	566.0	576.0		
		Not SE		692.6	678.3	731.0	749.5
	White	SE Identified	Itinerant		603.0	622.0	602.0
			Resource	435.0	372.0	575.0	390.5
			Self-contained	744.0	677.0	722.9	725.2
		Not SE		677.6	702.2	716.3	714.3

Figure 7.11

Azalea Middle School
SCAT Mathematics Scaled Score Results By Grade Level, Gender, Ethnicity, Special Education, and Disability Model, 2003-04

Grade Level	Ethnicity	Special Education (SE) Status	Disability Model	Free/Reduced Lunch		Paid Lunch	
				Female	Male	Female	Male
Grade Six	Asian	Not SE		592.0		563.0	610.5
	Black	SE Identified	Resource	419.7	512.5		289.0
			Self-contained	586.3	579.3		287.0
		Not SE		590.8	595.0	604.0	610.7
	Hispanic/Latino	SE Identified	Self-contained	569.0	594.0		
		Not SE		607.3	613.0	609.0	
	White	SE Identified	Itinerant		602.0	617.0	601.0
			Resource		493.0	583.0	493.0
			Self-contained			594.7	614.0
		Not SE		605.2	588.0	620.9	623.1
Grade Seven	Asian	SE Identified	Self-contained	693.0			
		Not SE		707.0	708.0	715.5	731.0
	Black	SE Identified	Resource	306.0	391.3		
			Self-contained		691.0	677.0	689.0
		Not SE		699.6	699.5	700.7	704.3
	Hispanic/Latino	Not SE		708.5	722.0		707.0
	White	SE Identified	Resource	677.0			
			Self-contained	672.0	695.0	707.0	710.0
		Not SE		711.9	709.0	718.0	719.6
Grade Eight	Asian	SE Identified	Resource				795.0
		Not SE		824.0	842.0		
	Black	SE Identified	Resource	286.8		270.0	578.0
			Self-contained	791.8	785.3	800.0	787.0
			Unknown		789.0		
		Not SE		801.5	803.2	806.4	798.0
	Hispanic/Latino	Not SE		794.5	812.0	800.5	803.0
	White	SE Identified	Resource	186.0			478.0
			Self-contained	782.0		801.0	799.2
		Not SE		810.3	800.0	814.5	815.2
Totals	Asian	SE Identified	Resource				795.0
			Self-contained	693.0			
		Not SE		661.4	775.0	664.7	650.7
	Black	SE Identified	Resource	333.2	460.6	270.0	433.5
			Self-contained	714.8	659.9	738.5	587.7
			Unknown		789.0		
		Not SE		675.2	709.8	746.3	704.3
	Hispanic/Latino	SE Identified	Self-contained	569.0	594.0		
		Not SE		693.9	690.0	736.7	755.0
	White	SE Identified	Itinerant		602.0	617.0	601.0
			Resource	431.5	493.0	583.0	485.5
			Self-contained	727.0	695.0	724.5	734.7
		Not SE		678.8	699.8	716.0	721.9

Question 5: What do they know? What do they not know?

Unfortunately, the SCAT does not tell Azalea what standards, content clusters, or even items students answered correctly or incorrectly. Azalea staff believe the scores show that students make improvement while at Azalea.

Question 6: How were they taught?

In this middle school, most students work with about seven different teachers during the week. Of the students scoring *Below Basic* and identified for special education services, 65% were in self-contained classrooms in 2003-04, and 35% received resource services. At the seventh-grade level, of the students scoring *Below Basic,* only seven were identified for special education services. Five of these students were in self-contained classrooms. Two received resource services. In eighth grade, 18 students scored Below Basic. Fourteen (78%) were in self-contained classrooms, while four received resource services. Students not identified for special education services were with regular classroom teachers. (*Note:* With data coded by teacher and programs in a data warehouse, one would be able to sort results by all school processes. We were not able to do that for Azalea.)

Implications for the school improvement plan, derived from comprehensive data analyses of strengths and challenges, will end up consistent with what gaps and root cause analyses tell one.

WHAT ARE THE GAPS? AND WHAT ARE THE ROOT CAUSES OF THE GAPS?

189

Question 7: What do our data analyses tell us about the root causes?

Studying the gap data and pulling together the implications for the school improvement plan derived from the data shown in Chapters 4 through 7, staff saw consistencies in the analyses. To close the achievement gaps, staff wanted to see the following strategies and activities addressed in the Azalea school improvement plan.

Implications for the school improvement plan, derived from comprehensive data analyses of strengths and challenges, ended up consistent with the gap and root cause analyses. Below is a summary of the implications for the school improvement plan from Chapters 4 through 7.

Demographics:

▼ Determine how students are identified as and served within special education.

▼ Determine strategies to meet the needs of *all* students, including those living in poverty, with disabilities, and of ethnicities and genders different from the teachers.

▼ Create a plan for recruiting new teachers in the near future, and improving the ethnic and gender balance of staff.

▼ How is the transition from elementary to middle school for the students? Does Azalea improve their learning? Are all students prepared for high school? How do they do in high school?

Continuous Improvement Continuums:

▼ Schedule time to reassess on the *Continuous Improvement Continuums.*

▼ Make data more accessible, so it can be used to drive decisions.

▼ Train teachers in data analysis, in gap analysis, and in determining root causes.

▼ Staff would like professional development in effective instructional strategies.

▼ Staff want and need alternative assessments, and to define measurable outcomes.

▼ Staff would like to implement peer coaching.

▼ Staff wants follow-through on the school portfolio.

▼ The vision, mission, and plan need to be communicated to, and implemented by, everyone.

▼ The school needs to seek perceptions of clients.

▼ Need to move staff toward shared decision making. Professional development in shared decision making and an increase in teacher leadership would help.

▼ Need schoolwide focus and input on professional development. Also need to implement and evaluate professional development aligned to the vision.

▼ Need a plan for partnerships after studying strategies related to student learning standards.

▼ Need to study root causes, other ways to prevent student failure, evaluate programs and processes, and the school as a whole.

▼ Define data to be used for continuous improvement and evaluation.

Questionnaires:

▼ Might need to rethink discipline policies/strategies, how everyone respects each other, and the dress code.

▼ Staff needs to follow-up on students who are not feeling respected.

▼ Professional development in shared decision making—the creation of a true shared decision-making structure might bring up the staff and administration morale.

▼ Staff need to revisit the vision to bring newer teachers on board.

▼ A new plan needs to be created to implement a vision that everyone believes in and supports.

▼ Staff needs to implement strategies to improve communication, collaboration, and morale.

▼ Staff might need to work with parents more to help them help their children learn at home.

Standards Assessment:

Need to get all teachers knowing and implementing content standards, through:

▼ Content-area meetings about standards.

▼ Demonstration lessons.

▼ Planning and ongoing communication with other teachers in the district who teach the same subjects and grade levels.

▼ Planning time by subject and grade level.

▼ A stronger support system for ensuring teaching to standards.

▼ Perhaps an instructional coach in subject areas other than those currently covered—peer coaching could help, too.

Professional Development Assessment:

▼ Explore the feasibility of adding more professional development days.

▼ Implement more grade level and department meetings focused on demonstrating different instructional strategies.

▼ Focus professional development opportunities on the school vision and standards.

Student Learning:

▼ Might need to look at getting boys more interested in ELA.

▼ Staff might need training in how to meet the needs of Black and Hispanic/Latino students, students who live in poverty, students who are limited English proficient, and students with disabilities.

▼ Across grade levels, Mathematics scores need to improve.

What Are the Root Causes of Azalea's Gaps?

After analyzing Azalea's data, the gaps, and digging deeper to discover root causes, staff came up with the idea that there are many contributing causes. What emerged at the forefront of their thinking was the fact that they needed a strong vision that would unite all staff to collaborate on creating a continuum of learning that makes sense for *all* students. Staff also saw that they need powerful professional development to help them know how to help *all* students learn, and strategies to ensure the implementation of these learnings.

Azalea staff used their next staff inservice day to begin work on their vision. The vision and the plan to implement that vision appear in Chapter 8.

Study Questions for What Are the Gaps? and What Are the Root Causes of the Gaps?

As you review Azalea's data, use either the margins in the text, this page, or print this page from the CD to write down your early thinking. (Ch7Qs.pdf) These notes, of course, are only hunches or placeholders until all the data are analyzed and verified with the staff.

1. What are Azalea's *gaps*?

2. Do you feel that the *root causes* of their student learning results were uncovered? If the answer is *no*, what other analyses would you perform?

What I Saw in the Example: Azalea Middle School

Using the study questions as an outline, what I saw in the data for Chapter 7 appears below. When applicable, I have referenced the figure or page number that gave me my first impression of strengths and challenges. (Ch7Saw.pdf)

What are the gaps?

In 2003-04, in English Language Arts, the largest gaps (pages 177-178) included:
- Sixth graders who were Black, qualifiers for free/reduced lunch, and identified as special education.
- Seventh graders who were Asian, and learning English.
- Eighth graders identified as special education.

In 2003-04, in Mathematics, the largest gaps (pages 179-180) included:
- Sixth grade Asian and Black students, qualifiers for free/reduced lunch, identified as special education, and English learners.
- Seventh grade Hispanic students, and students identified as special education.
- Eighth grade Black students, qualifiers for free/reduced lunch, identified for special education, and English learners.

What are the root causes of the gaps?

The analyses indicate that the programs and processes used to reach all students must improve. The analyses point to a lack of vision and consistency to have an impact on all students. With a clear and shared vision, staff can replace random acts of improvement with focused acts of improvement. Professional development to meet the needs of *all* students will provide teachers with the skills and support to implement new strategies. Structures and strategies to help teachers work together to close the gaps will also help.

Summary

Gap analyses are critical for answering the question, *What are the gaps?* Gap analyses help schools see the difference between where they are (current results) and where they want to be (vision and goals). To be effective, gap analyses must dig layers deep into the data to truly understand the results and to begin to uncover root causes.

Root causes, as used in this continuous school improvement planning model, refer to the deep underlying reasons for the occurrence of a specific situation, the gap. While a symptom may become evident from a needs assessment or gap analysis—the symptom (low student scores) is not the cause. To find a root cause, one often has to ask *Why?* at least five levels down to uncover the root cause of the symptom. One will know if she/he found the root cause when she/he can answer *no* to the following questions:

▼ Would the problem have occurred if the cause had not been present?

▼ Will the problem reoccur if the cause is corrected? (Preuss, 2003)

If the answers to these questions are *maybe,* you are probably looking at contributing causes, not one root cause. Most problems within schools are caused by systems rather than people. Improvement of the system will result in reduction or removal of the problem. Teams that include school programs and processes in their analyses tend not to jump to solutions or conclusions as quickly as those who do not. At some point, when searching for the root cause, one must realize that the "problem" is really a result. What we are trying to do with these analyses is to uncover how we get our results. These very same processes can be used to uncover how we get our successes.

Root causes are not easy to uncover, but the information that is uncovered is well worth the effort.

Azalea staff used a quick but analytical brainstorming approach—the problem-solving cycle—to study why so many students are scoring *Below Basic.* The next chapter will show what they did with their information to create changes in next year's results.

> *Gap analyses help schools see the difference between where they are (current results) and where they want to be (vision and goals).*

> *To find a root cause, one often has to ask "Why?" at least five levels down to uncover the root cause of the symptom.*

On the CD Related to this Chapter

▼ *Goal Setting Activity* (ACTGoals.pdf)

By setting goals, a school can clarify its end targets for the school's vision. This activity will help a school set goals for the future.

▼ *Gap Analysis and Objectives Activity* (ACTGap.pdf)

The purpose of this activity is to look closely at differences between current results and where the school wants to be in the future. It is this gap that gets translated into objectives that guide the development of the action plan.

▼ *Root Cause Analysis Activity* (ACTRoot.pdf)

Root causes are the real causes of our educational problems. We need to find out what they are so we can eliminate the true cause and not just address the symptom. This activity asks staff teams to review and analyze data and ask probing questions to uncover the root cause(s).

▼ *Cause and Effect Analysis Activity* (ACTCause.pdf)

This activity will help teams determine the relationships and complexities between an effect or problem and all the possible causes.

▼ *Problem-Solving Cycle Activity* (ACTCycle.pdf)

The purpose of the *Problem-Solving Cycle Activity* is to get all staff involved in thinking through a problem before jumping to solutions. This activity can also result in a comprehensive data analysis design.

▼ Study Questions Related to the Gaps and the Root Causes of the Gaps (Ch7Qs.pdf)

These study questions will help you better understand the information provided in Chapter 7. This file can be printed for use with staffs as you analyze their data to determine the gaps and the root causes of the gaps.

▼ *What I Saw in the Example* (Ch7Saw.pdf)

What I Saw in the Example is a file, organized by the student learning study questions, that summarizes what the author saw in the student learning data provided by Azalea Middle School.

▼ *Gap Analyses Data Table Templates* (MiddGaps.doc)

All of the *Microsoft Word* files that were used to create the gap analyses data tables in the Azalea example (Chapter 7) appear on the CD. Use these templates by putting your data in the data table and changing the title/labels to reflect your data.

▼ *No Child Left Behind* (NCLB) Templates

Table templates for analyzing student learning data for NCLB are provided on the CD.

◆ *NCLB Language Scores Template* (LangTbl.doc)

This *Microsoft Word* file is a table template to use in capturing your NCLB Language scores analysis.

◆ *NCLB Reading Scores Template* (ReadTbl.doc)

This *Microsoft Word* file is a table template to use in capturing your NCLB Reading scores analysis.

◆ *NCLB Math Scores Template* (MathTbl.doc)

This *Microsoft Word* file is a table template to use in capturing your NCLB Math scores analysis.

◆ *NCLB Student Achievement Reading Results Template* (ProfLaEl.doc)

This *Microsoft Word* file is a table template to use in summarizing your NCLB disaggregated student achievement Reading proficiency results.

◆ *NCLB Student Achievement Math Results Template* (ProfMaEl.doc)

This *Microsoft Word* file is a table template to use in summarizing your NCLB disaggregated student achievement Math proficiency results.

▼ Group Process Tools and Activities.

The files include read-only documents, examples, templates, tools, activities, and strategy recommendations. Many of the group process tools and activities can be used throughout the analysis of data.

◆ *Affinity Diagram Activity* (ACTAfnty.pdf)

The affinity diagram encourages honest reflection on the real underlying root causes of a problem and its solutions, and encourages people to agree on the factors. This activity assists teams in discussing and resolving problems, using a nonjudgmental process.

◆ *Fishbowl Activity* (ACTFish.pdf)

This activity can be used for dynamic group involvement. The most common configuration is an inner ring, which is the discussion group, surrounded by an outer ring, which is the observation group. Just as people observe the fish in the fishbowl, the outer ring observes the inner ring.

◆ *Forcefield Analysis Activity* (ACTForce.pdf)

The *Forcefield Analysis Activity* helps staffs think about the ideal state for the school and the driving and restraining forces regarding that ideal state.

◆ *Placemat Activity* (ACTPlace.pdf)

The *Placemat Activity* was developed to invite participants to share their knowledge about the school portfolio, data, a standard, an instructional strategy, a concept, etc.

◆ *T-Chart Activity* (ACTTChrt.pdf)

A *T-Chart* is a simple tool to organize material into two columns. Use a T-Chart to compare and contrast information or to show relationships. Use it to help people see the opposite dimension of an issue.

◆ *"X" Marks the Spot Activity* (ACTXSpot.pdf)

This activity helps staff understand levels of expertise or degrees of passion about a topic.

◆ *Quadrant Diagram Activity* (ACTQuadr.pdf)

A quadrant diagram is a method to determine which solution best meets two goals at once, such as low cost and high benefit.

Action plans need to clarify how decisions will be made, identify professional development required to learn new skills and gain new knowledge, and clarify the use of partners to achieve the vision.

We know the gaps in Azalea's student achievement results, and we have a better idea of the root causes. So now, *How can we get to where we want to be?* The answer to this question is the key to unlocking how the vision will be implemented and how gaps will be eliminated. An action plan consisting of strategies, actions, person(s) responsible, due dates, timelines, and resources needs to be created to achieve the vision and goals and to eliminate the root causes of the gaps.

Action plans need to clarify how decisions will be made, identify professional development required for staffs to learn new skills and gain new knowledge, and incorporate the use of partners to achieve the vision, and spell-out how all parts of the plan will be evaluated. A school's leadership structure, professional development strategies, and partnership development plan are important components of the answer to the question, *How can we get to where we want to be?*

This chapter shows how Azalea Middle School created a school improvement plan using the data gathered and analyzed, and a vision they created to close their gaps and improve all student learning.

Our Example School: Azalea Middle School
How Can We Get to Where We Want to Be?

The Azalea Vision

The data (*Continuous Improvement Continuums*, questionnaires, and root cause analysis) showed Azalea staff that they needed to revisit their vision. The following is the vision that staff created in the spring before implementing their plan that would commence in the fall of 2004. (AZVision.pdf)

Azalea Middle School
Guiding Principles, May 2004

A system of fundamental motivating assumptions, principles, values, and tenets that leads to a tangible vision.

Values and Beliefs

The staff of Azalea Middle School believe the following:

▼ All students can learn.

▼ All disciplines of study are regarded equitably, in philosophy, policy, and programming.

▼ The curriculum should be rigorous, standards based, and enhanced by the arts and technology.

▼ Effective instruction incorporates a problem-solving, critical thinking approach to learning.

▼ All students should be actively engaged in the learning process.

▼ Varied teaching strategies should be utilized to accommodate varied learning styles.

▼ Assessments should be varied and include authentic, traditional, and non-traditional.

▼ Individuality and creative talents of students and teachers are valued.

▼ Learning experiences develop a sense of civic responsibility.

▼ The faculty show a strong commitment to student success.

▼ The learning environment should be student-centered.

▼ Relationships among students, teachers, parents, and community strengthen instruction and learning.

▼ The learning environment should be safe, nurturing, and clean.

Purpose

The purpose of Azalea Middle School is to prepare students to become lifelong learners and contributing members of society through rigorous, arts-focused, standards-based instruction.

Mission

The mission of Azalea Middle School is to prepare students to become lifelong learners and contributing members of society through rigorous, arts-focused, standards-based instruction.

A school's guiding principles will focus all staff in the same direction.

Shared Vision

Curriculum—*What we teach*

▼ Relevant cutting edge course offerings in the academics and related arts

▼ Integration of the arts across the curriculum

▼ Standards based

▼ Relevant, appropriate, and meet the needs of our students

▼ Comprehensive and sequential arts programs

▼ Academics are aligned vertically

▼ Expanded career awareness opportunities that connects students to the real world of work

Instruction—*How we teach*

▼ All students have access to instruction with technology

▼ Differentiated instruction to meet the needs of the learners in all areas

▼ Rigorous

▼ Individualized

▼ Active engagement of all students

▼ Seamless arts integration throughout the curriculum

▼ Seamless technology integration throughout the curriculum

▼ Character education as an essential part of the school culture

▼ Appropriate interdisciplinary instruction

▼ Current research-based instructional strategies used to meet the needs of all learners

Assessment—*How we evaluate learning*

▼ Up-to-date technology based assessments

▼ Portfolio Assessment

▼ Authentic Assessment

▼ Self-paced Assessment

▼ Online Assessment

▼ Standardized

▼ Traditional

▼ Performance based, i.e., plays, performances, auditions, classroom theater and plays, painting, publishing, and presentations.

▼ Variety of assessment instruments used, i.e., rubrics, checklists, organizers, and self assessments

- ▼ Multiple types of assessments will be used to guide curriculum, instruction, and school programs
- ▼ Varied assessment to accommodate learning styles and abilities
- ▼ Process as well as product emphasized

Learning Environment—*Environment used for learning*

- ▼ Renovated building with a capacity for all students to provide a clean, cheerful, stimulating, and creative learning environment
- ▼ State of the art technology
- ▼ Energetic, learner-centered environment
- ▼ Flexible class schedules
- ▼ Environment that embraces the diverse culture that our school encourages
- ▼ School supports and promotes teachers as learners

Azalea Vision Narrative

Open the door to the vision of Azalea Middle School, and you will find students in a new building that has adequate space; is safe, nurturing, stimulating; and enhanced by the arts. The learning environment will be equipped with state-of-the-art safety features and up-to-date technology, including portable technology available for all classroom and work areas. You may notice the absence of bells to accommodate flexible class schedules within teams, giving teachers control of the amount of time they spend within the academic subjects based on student learning needs, instead of a bell schedule that dictates time spent in class. This learner-centered environment will reflect an arts integration approach throughout the halls, classrooms, and open spaces. This arts integration is a part of who we are and what we do that sets us apart from the rest. Continue your walk through the arts wing, and you will see performance classrooms and an art gallery which provide Azalea's fine art teachers the required space necessary to showcase our exceptional visual and performing arts program. When you visit Azalea, you will experience a unique energy that showcases the diverse culture that our arts program embraces.

The curriculum at Azalea highlights a comprehensive and sequential arts program. The academics are aligned vertically to ensure a rigorous and successful educational journey for all adolescents in our school. Our academic and related arts course offerings are relevant, cutting-edge, and standards-based. Step inside a classroom or studio and you will enjoy seeing students actively engaged in their learning, organized in pairs, small groups, or whole class. You will see movement of teachers and students, hear discussions, summarizing, sharing, and presentations. Instruction will be differentiated to meet the learning and assessment needs of all our students, embracing their rich diversity. Students will demonstrate creative thinking and reasoning when solving problems and understand how to ask the right questions, and locate, as well as learn, new information. Teachers will use the arts and technology in seamless ways to teach the content and make learning relevant to the students and their world. All students will have access to technology and the other educational resources necessary to equip them for their future.

Small group teaming of students allows for increased communication with and among teachers. Teachers have time to plan together and set goals focused on raising student achievement. Join a team meeting and you may hear discussion revolving around interdisciplinary instruction as the teachers collaborate to make curriculum connections, plan units of study, seek out common standards and themes, and look at student work. Teacher leadership emerges as teams work together to integrate the arts, promote character education, increase the use of technology, and continue their roles as learners as well as teachers.

A wide variety of assessments of student learning will be evident throughout the school, including paper and pencil activities as well as those using technology. On any given day, you might experience a variety of performance-based assessments such as plays, auditions, classroom theater/productions, painting, publishing, and other types of presentations when you observe student learning at Azalea. Rubrics, checklists, graphic organizers, and self-assessments will be pervasive, common place, and reflect our students' learning styles. Look closer into the classrooms and you may see both student and teacher portfolios, walls proudly filled with student and teacher work, and evidence of both traditional and non-traditional assessments. It will be evident to you that the process is emphasized as well as the product.

All students at Azalea are challenged every day to understand and communicate through reading, writing, listening, and speaking across the curriculum. Continuously seeking improvement in the quality of the educational experience is the norm and not the exception from our students, teachers, and administrators as we strive to ensure our students are prepared for high school and their futures. *Challenge, create,* and *communicate* at Azalea. What a great place to be!

The School Improvement Plan

Azalea's staff determined these goals and objectives to be—

Goal 1: *Raise the academic challenge and performance of each student.*
Objectives: By 2013-14, all Azalea students will show proficiency in every tested standards-based subject as measured by the SCAT scores (No Child Left Behind Act); by the end of 2005-06, Azalea Middle School will decrease by 20% the number of students (2003-04) scoring "Below Basic" in ELA and Math as measured by SCAT; and, Azalea will maintain or improve SCAT ELA and Math scores for cohort groups.

Goal 2: *Improve student learning and achievement through the use of technology.*
Objectives: Expand and integrate the use of technology as measured by teacher self-assessments, student work, and questionnaires; increase teachers' technology proficiency as measured by the district technology self-assessment; and, use information literacy skills with appropriate technology as measured by student work.

Goal 3: *Provide a school environment supportive of learning.*
Objectives: Develop a professional learning community as measured by involvement in focused study groups and perception questionnaires; develop quality arts-focused and teaching strategies as measured by teacher self-assessments, lessons, and student work; increase parent/partnership involvement at Azalea each year as measured by questionnaires completed by parents and business partners; and, develop a safe and nurturing school environment as measured by perception questionnaires.

Staff's review of data indicated that they had a long way to go with many students. Staff looked for pathways to improvement by reviewing the research on performance improvement, the implications for school improvement that came from their data analysis study, and by committing to improvement.

Staff acknowledged that they needed—

1. *Instructional coherence*—to have all teachers teaching to the state standards and creating a continuum of learning for all students.

2. *A shared vision for school improvement*—staff was glad they took the time to revisit their vision so all staff members could and would commit to teaching consistencies and school improvement.

3. *Data-driven decision making*—at all points along the way, staff would gather data to know if they were making progress with moving all students to proficiency in all subject areas. It was no longer an option not to use data, and not to know if all students are learning as the year progresses.

Staff created a plan from the data analysis and the vision. The first draft of the Azalea School Plan is shown in Figure 8.1.  (SchlPlan.pdf)

Figure 8.1

Azalea Middle School Plan for Improvement, 2004-05

GOAL 1: *Raise the academic challenge and performance of each student.*

**BASELINE
PROFICIENCY
2003-04**

Grade Six	
English Language Arts: 82%	
Mathematics: 75%	

Grade Seven	
English Language Arts: 86%	
Mathematics: 83%	

Grade Eight	
English Language Arts: 86%	
Mathematics: 79%	

School	
English Language Arts: 85%	
Mathematics: 79%	

OBJECTIVES:
▼ By 2013-14, all Azalea students will show proficiency in every tested standards-based subject as measured by the SCAT scores (*No Child Left Behind Act*).
▼ By the end of 2005-06, Azalea Middle School will decrease by 20% the number of students (2003-04) scoring *Below Basic* in English Language Arts and Mathematics as measured by SCAT.
▼ Azalea will maintain or improve SCAT English Language Arts and Mathematics scores for cohort groups.

I. Increase student performance on the state content standards

Strategy/Action	Person Responsible	Measurement	Resources Needed	Due Date	Aug	Sept	Oct	Nov	Dec	Jan	Feb	Mar	Apr	May	Jun	Jul
Create mission and vision, based on the purpose of the school, values and beliefs of the staff, and standards.																
◆ Implement professional development days and after-school meetings.				May 2004/ Completed								X	X	X		
◆ Utilize professional development days and after-school meetings to ensure all staff understand how to implement the vision.	Principal, Portfolio Coach, Leadership			April 2005	X	X	X	X	X	X	X	X	X	X	X	X
◆ Adapt and use the self-assessment tool in *The School Portfolio Toolkit* to assist all teachers in assessing the degree to which they are implementing the vision and standards.	Principal, Portfolio Coach, Leadership	Assessment on the shared vision tool	*The School Portfolio, The School Portfolio Toolkit*	April 2005			X		X		X			X		
Support increased knowledge and alignment of content standards.																
Align the curriculum with state content standards through:																
◆ Vertical/horizontal department meetings.	Leadership, Instructional Coach, Principal	Monthly vertical/ horizontal team minutes	Team leader meeting agenda	August 2004	X	X	X	X	X	X	X	X	X	X		
◆ Vertical meetings with elementary/high schools.	Leadership, Instructional Coach, Principal	Vertical/ horizontal team minutes	Team leader meeting agenda	May 2005				X	X	X						
◆ Peer observations focused on standards.	Leadership, Instructional Coach, Principal	Peer observation forms	Peer observation forms	Ongoing	X	X	X	X	X	X	X	X	X	X		
◆ Demonstration lessons focused on standards.	Leadership, Instructional Coach, Principal	Peer observation forms	Demonstration lesson documentation	Ongoing	X	X	X	X	X	X	X	X	X	X		
◆ Weekly team meetings focused on standards.	Leadership, Instructional Coach, Principal	Team leader meeting agenda	Team leader meeting agenda	May 2005	X	X	X	X	X	X	X	X	X	X		

Figure 8.1 (Continued)

Azalea Middle School Plan for Improvement, 2004-05 (Continued)

I. Increase student performance on the state content standards (Continued)

Strategy/Action	Person Responsible	Measurement	Resources Needed	Due Date	Aug	Sept	Oct	Nov	Dec	Jan	Feb	Mar	Apr	May	Jun	Jul
Team leader meetings, monthly	Leadership, Instructional Coach, Principal	Team leader agenda/notes	Team leader meeting agenda	May 2005	X	X	X	X	X	X	X	X	X	X		
Mentor program that includes a standards/curriculum component.	Leadership, Instructional Coach, Principal	Creation and use of mentor program		October 2004			X									
Teacher lesson plans and syllabi addressing standards.	Leadership, Instructional Coach, Principal	Lesson plans	Lesson plan; syllabi	May 2005	X	X	X	X	X	X	X	X	X	X		
Align curriculum through the use of curriculum mapping.	Leadership, Instructional Coach, Principal	Curriculum maps	Curriculum mapping book, software, training	October 2004	X	X	X	X	X	X	X	X	X	X		
Standards in Practice—curriculum calibration.	Leadership, Instructional Coach, Principal	Sign-in sheets, team minutes	*Standards in Practice* information training	October 2005	X	X	X	X								
Writing process focused across the curriculum.	Leadership, Instructional Coach, Principal	Writing guidelines	District Language Arts Coordinator, Texts support, writing process across curriculum	April 2005	X	X	X	X	X	X	X	X				
State/district workshops that address the standards.	Arts Coordinator	Verification of attendance, workshop notes/handouts	State Department of Education	April 2005	X	X	X	X	X	X	X	X	X			
Modify course offerings to meet the standards.	Instructional coaches, teachers	Syllabi, course offerings		May 2005						X	X	X	X	X		
Support increased knowledge and understanding of test data to evaluate progress and inform instruction.																
Provide training to teachers to review, interpret, and analyze SCAT data for diagnostic and instructional purposes.	Data warehouse trained staff	Professional development forms, sign-in sheets	Data warehouse software training, test data loaded in warehouse—fall	November 2004			X	X								
Provide test data as soon as it is available for teachers to use for planning instruction.	Data warehouse trained staff	Data analysis for portfolio	Data warehouse software training, test data loaded in warehouse—fall	November 2004				X								
Administer *Math Plus* benchmark tests to assess student achievement quarterly.	Math teachers	*Math Plus* benchmark tests each quarter (3)	*Math Plus* benchmark	March 2005		X			X		X					

Figure 8.1 (Continued)

Azalea Middle School Plan for Improvement, 2004–05 *(Continued)*

I. Increase student performance on the state content standards *(Continued)*

Support the investigation and implementation of instructional strategies focused on closing the gap.

Strategy/Action	Person Responsible	Measurement	Resources Needed	Due Date	Aug	Sept	Oct	Nov	Dec	Jan	Feb	Mar	Apr	May	Jun	Jul
◆ Read and discuss *A Framework for Understanding Poverty,* by Ruby Pane.	Team Leaders	Team notes/minutes showing text-based seminars	Set of *Framework for Understanding Poverty* books	April 2005	X	X	X	X	X	X	X	X	X			
◆ Investigate *Standards in Practice* model as a strategy to increase achievement and test scores of all students.	Leadership Team	*Standards in Practice* presentation	*Standards in Practice* facilitator	December 2004	X	X	X	X	X							
◆ Use *Learning Focus Strategies* in each content area/classes.	Principal, Instructional Coach, Team Leaders	Lesson plans	Internet website information on successful middle schools	April 2005	X	X	X	X	X	X	X	X	X			
◆ Continue to investigate and report on instructional strategies proven successful with middle schools that have shown measurable gains on SCAT.	Leadership Team	Report given to faculty on instructional strategies that work with low-achieving students (poverty/minority)	Internet website information on successful middle schools	April 2005								X	X			
◆ Provide additional training as needed for all teachers on the components of a *Learning Focus* unit and the strategies which support increased achievement.	District Instructional Coaches	Training documentation, attendance filed, consistent expectations written for writing process/assessment	Time	April 2005									X			
◆ Develop consistent expectations for the writing process and assessment across the curriculum for all students in all classes. Review student work.	Language Arts Department Chair, Instructional Coach	LA study group formed Writing/assessment guide developed	Language Arts Coordinator, texts such as *In the Middle* by Nancy Altwell	September 2004	X	X	X									
◆ Continue to develop arts-focused strategies that raise student achievement.	Arts Coordinator	Staff training	Peace Center, Tanglewood Project, *Champ of Change*	Ongoing	X	X	X	X	X	X	X	X	X			
◆ After-school program continued two days a week for students scoring *Below Basic* on SCAT, with quarterly benchmarks to evaluate attendance, student performance in both the program and in the classroom.	Assistant Principal	ASAP program, quarterly summary submitted, attendance/grades, program evaluation	*Curriculum Assessment Reading/Math Strategies* software and other purchased materials	October 2004 Each quarter			X			X		X		X		

Figure 8.1 (Continued)

Azalea Middle School Plan for Improvement, 2004-05 (Continued)

GOAL 2: *Improve student learning and achievement through the use of technology.*

OBJECTIVES:
- ▼ Expand and integrate the use of technology as measured by teacher self-assessments, student work, and questionnaires.
- ▼ Increase teachers' technology proficiency as measured by the district technology self-assessment.
- ▼ Use information literacy skills with appropriate technology as measured by student work.

Strategy/Action	Person Responsible	Measurement	Resources Needed	Due Date	Aug	Sept	Oct	Nov	Dec	Jan	Feb	Mar	Apr	May	Jun	Jul
I. Students will expand and integrate knowledge through technology																
Support increased knowledge and alignment of content standards and the state content standards through classroom instruction to:																
◆ Exhibit legal and ethical behaviors when using information and technology.	Principal, Instructional Coach, Media Specialist	Staff development paperwork, sign-in sheets	Computer lab, standards, Internet	May 2005		X	X	X	X	X	X	X	X	X		
◆ Use content-specific tools, software and simulations (environmental probes, graphing calculators, and web tools) to support learning and research.	Instructional Coach, Media Specialist, Webmaster	Assessment results, needs identified, changes made in plan	*One Computer, software*	Ongoing		X	X	X	X	X	X	X	X	X		
◆ Apply productivity/multimedia tools and peripherals to support individual learning and group collaboration through the state content standards.	Instructional Coach, Media Specialist, Webmaster	Assessment results, needs identified, changes made in plan	*Hyperstudio,* etc.	Ongoing		X	X	X	X	X	X	X	X	X		
◆ Design, develop, publish, and present products (WebPages, videotapes, CDs), using technology resources that demonstrate and communicate curriculum concepts to audiences, both within the school and outside the school.	Instructional Coach, Media Specialist, Webmaster	Staff development sign-in sheets / Lesson plans show increased use of these applications	*Hyperstudio,* etc.	Ongoing		X	X	X	X	X	X	X	X	X		
◆ Collaborate with peers, experts, and others using e-mail to investigate real world problems, issues, information to develop solutions or products (limited during 2004-05).	Instructional Coach, Media Specialist, Webmaster	Plan developed	E-mail, Internet	Ongoing												
◆ Develop an *Academic Showcase* on Azalea's intranet to showcase student work by grade and subject.	Instructional Coach	Showcase developed	Disks, CDs, web/photo software	May 2005	X	X	X	X	X	X	X	X	X	X		
II. Teachers and staff will increase their technology proficiency																
Support the increased knowledge of teacher and administrator technology standards and the state content standards.																
◆ Provide professional development opportunities during school and after-school on appropriate technology use with the state content standards, as determined by their technology self-assessment.	Principal, Instructional Coach, Media Specialist, Webmaster	Staff development paperwork, sign-in sheets / Assessment results	Computer lab, standards, Internet, lab data analyzed	May 2005	X	X	X	X	X	X	X	X	X	X		

HOW CAN WE GET TO WHERE WE WANT TO BE?

Figure 8.1 (Continued)

Azalea Middle School Plan for Improvement, 2004-05 *(Continued)*

Strategy/Action	Person Responsible	Measurement	Resources Needed	Due Date	Timeline											
					Aug	Sept	Oct	Nov	Dec	Jan	Feb	Mar	Apr	May	Jun	Jul
II. Teachers and staff will increase their technology proficiency *(Continued)*																
Increase knowledge and use of *MS Office* applications: *Word; Excel; PowerPoint; Inspiration;* presentation devices and software.	Instructional Coach, Media Specialist, Webmaster	Sign-in sheets, lesson plans, advanced courses taken	*One Computer,* software, scanners, cameras, web/photo software	May 2005		X	X	X	X	X	X	X	X	X		
Provide continued support and training for e-mail and teacher WebPages.	Instructional Coach, Media Specialist, Webmaster	Attendance at trainings	Networked location for teachers to work on WebPages, e-mail	May 2005		X	X	X	X	X		X	X	X		
Provide opportunities for support staff to attend technology training required for their job responsibilities.	Principal	Attendance at training	Time away from duties	May 2005		X	X	X	X	X		X	X	X		
Plan, purchase and prepare for increased use of technology:																
Develop a plan for the effective use of an instructional computer lab and other future technologies for teachers in 2005-06.	Technology Committee	Plan developed	Local and state instructional technology resources	February 2005		X	X	X	X	X	X					
Update school technology plan.	Technology Coordinator	Updated technology plan	Time	March 2005						X	X					
III. Use information literacy skills with appropriate technology																
Support increased knowledge of information literacy and the state content standards.																
Use information literacy skills and understand the appropriate technology associated with it: • Task definition • Information seeking strategies • Location and access • Use of information • Synthesis • Evaluation	Media Specialist	Lesson plans/units completed with classes Student work	Information literacy materials, handouts for teachers and students, time to plan	May 2005	X	X	X	X	X	X		X	X	X		
Provide training for teachers about information literacy and the use of appropriate technology associated with it.	Media Specialist	Sign-in sheets	Paper, time	January 2005		X	X			X						

Figure 8.1 (Continued)

Azalea Middle School Plan for Improvement, 2004-05 (Continued)

GOAL 3: *Provide a school environment supportive of learning.*

OBJECTIVES:
- Develop a professional learning community as measured by involvement in focused study groups and perception questionnaires.
- Develop quality arts-focused and teaching strategies as measured by teacher self-assessments, lessons, and student work.
- Increase parent/partnership involvement at Azalea each year as measured by questionnaires completed by parents and business partners.
- Develop a safe and nurturing school environment as measured by perception questionnaires.

Strategy/Action	Person Responsible	Measurement	Resources Needed	Due Date	Aug	Sept	Oct	Nov	Dec	Jan	Feb	Mar	Apr	May	Jun	Jul
I. Develop a professional learning community																
Utilize a professional development plan focused on staff needs as determined by Student Achievement section of the school portfolio and professional development.																
◆ Survey teachers by team to determine their specific needs for professional development, which is from the list in the *Student Achievement* section (small group teaming, technology, *Learning focus*, arts integration, standards, assessment, etc.).	Professional Development Team	Professional development plan	To be determined after the questionnaires are completed and goals are set	October 2005			X									
◆ Teams set professional development goals for their team plan time, based on schoolwide focus and/or specific team needs.	Team Leaders	Goals set by teams, turned into Principal Records kept of professional development hours and focus			X											
Support teachers as learners in small collegial groups.																
◆ Establish study groups focused on specific curriculum/learning needs, from *Student Achievement* section of the portfolio, such as curriculum mapping, closing the gap, assessment, writing, portfolios, literacy, technology, and arts integration, etc. These will meet throughout the year.	Team Leaders, Arts Teachers, Arts Coordinator	Study groups agendas, sign-in sheets Improved student achievement	Materials purchased or checked-out from professional library, based on needs	October 2004			X									
◆ Increase the number of teachers in *Critical Friend's Groups.*	Instructional Coach	Increase members of *Critical Friend's Groups*	Books, professional periodicals	November 2004				X								
◆ Increase collaborative curriculum development in teams.	Team Leaders, Principal	Team minutes focused on curriculum/assessment		May 2005		X	X	X	X	X	X	X	X	X		
II. Develop quality arts-focused lessons and strategies																
Teacher development of arts-integration strategies and lessons/units.																
◆ Conduct individual and small groups to plan and develop arts-integration strategies for lessons/units.	Arts Coordinator	Documentation of planning, evaluation of lessons	Professional library resources Internet sites Purchase materials	May 2005	X	X	X	X	X	X	X	X	X	X		

Figure 8.1 (Continued)

Azalea Middle School Plan for Improvement, 2004-05 (Continued)

Strategy/Action	Person Responsible	Measurement	Resources Needed	Due Date	Timeline											
					Aug	Sept	Oct	Nov	Dec	Jan	Feb	Mar	Apr	May	Jun	Jul
III. Increase parent/partnership involvement																
Increase communication between home, school, and the community.																
◆ Teachers will maintain and increase the information on school/teacher websites.	Principal, Webmaster	Self-evaluation of teacher websites	Webpage training, photo software and training, networked computers, materials	May 2005	X	X	X	X	X	X	X	X	X	X		
◆ Increase the subscription of the e-newsletter to parents/partners.	Media Specialist	Increased e-newsletter subscriptions		April 2005	X	X	X	X	X	X	X	X	X			
◆ Increase attendance at all PTA and School Improvement Committee (SIC) meetings.	PTA President/SIC Chair	Attendance at joint PTA/SIC meetings		May 2005	X	X	X	X	X	X	X	X	X	X		
Improve parent/business partnerships.																
◆ Increase the number of parents and business community members in the development of the school portfolio.	PTA President, Principal	Meeting attendance	Partnership evaluation team	May 2005	X	X	X	X	X	X	X	X	X	X		
◆ Increase the number of parents and business community involvement in the classroom supporting student achievement.	Partnership Team	Parent/partnership questionnaire	Partnership log	May 2005	X	X	X	X	X	X	X	X	X	X		
◆ Create a win-win partnership plan.	Leadership, Partnership Team	Creation of plan	Time	May 2005	X	X	X	X	X	X	X	X	X	X		
IV. Provide a safe and nurturing environment																
◆ Update and maintain our school safety plan during the school construction/remodeling phase.	Principal, Assistant Principal	Updated safety plan	School Resource Officer	September 2004	X	X	X									
◆ Develop a sense of community within teams, grades, and as a professional learning community. • Teachers, School Improvement Committee, and PTA brainstorm and select ways to keep a sense of community during construction.	School Improvement Committee/PTA/Team Leaders, parents	Meeting agenda, attendance Documentation of brainstorming, results, and implementation	Money for signs on portables, room numbers, team/grade signs, etc.	October 2004	X	X	X									
◆ Study the causes of suspensions and discipline.	Assistant Principal	Results of study	Time, team	September 2004	X	X										
◆ Study why students feel they are not being respected by other students and by the adults.	Assistant Principal	Results of study	Time	October 2004			X									
◆ Implement *Character Education* plan.	Every teacher	Implementation and questionnaires	Time	May 2005	X	X	X	X	X	X	X	X	X	X		

Implementing the Plan: The Leadership Structure

It is hard to create a comprehensive plan—no doubt. Making sure everyone on staff implements the plan in the manner intended is even harder. A leadership structure can ensure that a plan is truly implemented. Leadership structures must look like the vision. Azalea's vision is new. Their new leadership structure looks like their plan and will help them implement that shared vision.

The Azalea Middle School Leadership Plan emerged from the plan. (LeadPlan.pdf) The Leadership Structure and a narrative follow.

Azalea Leadership Plan, 2003-04

Azalea Middle School's principal has been the primary decision maker for the past three years. Under her successful leadership, Azalea began to implement the goals and objectives mandated under the school district's *"Raising the Bar for Student Achievement in Middle Schools."* The primary focus of the plan is to raise the level of academic challenge, expectation, and achievement for every student in the district; all efforts towards reaching each objective are directed to that end. The framework for the plan includes four primary objectives and action steps with which to accomplish each objective. Because Azalea previously operated as a site-based school, many teachers prefer having a more active role in the decision-making process, while others feel decisions should be made by the administration.

After completing the leadership section of the *Continuous Improvement Continuums,* with scores of two in *Approach, Implementation,* and *Outcome,* it was evident that staff did not feel included in the decision-making process that could lead to substantial school improvement. The faculty felt that a shared decision-making structure would help implement our vision.

In order to improve this area, team leaders were established, regular meetings were held to discuss the future direction of the teams, and potential stumbling blocks were identified. Administrators meet with team leaders (academic, special education, and related arts team leaders) each month to help guide decisions. Teachers communicate with the administration through the collection of weekly team minutes, e-mails, individual conferences, and regular, open, informal discussions initiated by staff members or the administrator.

A school's leadership structure, professional development strategies, and partnership development plan are important components of the answer to the question, "How can we get to where we want to be?"

The administration communicates with the staff through various resources including the publication of team leader handbooks, staff handbooks, meeting agendas, regular use of e-mail, published weekly bulletins, and monthly calendars. These efforts keep the staff informed of changes and decisions that will affect them.

Decision-making Structure: The Leadership Team

The current administration at Azalea Middle School includes the principal, assistant principal, and administrative assistant. Azalea's principal is directly responsible to the area superintendent, associate superintendent of student performance, and to the superintendent of the school district. Principals meet as a group with the area superintendents monthly. Our principal meets weekly (on Tuesdays) after school with her leadership team which includes the assistant principal, administrative assistant, arts coordinator, two guidance counselors, media specialist, school secretary, and instructional coach. The leadership team is a new concept developed to improve communication. These meetings provide the time to conduct a "calendar check" to coordinate events on school and district calendars and to discuss school processes, district initiatives, the vision, and opportunities for faculty and staff. School district management memos as well as other publications are shared and discussed. Effective faculty meetings are also planned using this information.

These delegated duties and responsibilities of the leadership team include, but are not limited to:

▼ staff evaluations related to the school vision and goals

▼ walk-throughs related to the school vision and goals

▼ IEP or other parent conferences

▼ duty rosters

▼ bell schedule changes

▼ substitutes/class coverage

▼ programs during and after school

- ▼ discipline
- ▼ safety and transportation issues
- ▼ district-funded after-school programs
- ▼ athletics events and schedules
- ▼ staff facilitators
- ▼ textbook coordinators
- ▼ members of School Improvement Council, Leadership Team, and Portfolio Leadership Team

Leadership team members also take on the role of facilitators for the faculty and staff. Textbooks, safety plans and evacuation procedures, duty rosters, transportation, special education meetings, and athletic decisions and scheduling are responsibilities of the assistant principal. After-school academic programs, school pictures, dress code violations, special education meetings, and other teacher support, including morale issues, are handled by the administrative assistant.

Staff development is spearheaded by the arts program coordinator and instructional coach. Our arts program coordinator facilitates many of our communication arts initiatives that have won many awards. She is also in charge of public relations for our school. The instructional coach is held responsible by the district and the principal for instructional improvement, data support, school planning, and accountability.

Azalea counselors also have many responsibilities in the management and leadership of the school: Developing scheduling for students; testing security and facilitation; permanent records; communication to other schools; and the never-ending counseling of students.

The secretary and bookkeeper assists all staff members with securing and ordering materials and supplies, receipts all money, and oversees all fund-raising projects. She follows all auditing procedures in the handling of money and supervises the expenditures of all monies with the approval of the principal.

Leadership through Portfolio Leadership Team

The Portfolio Leadership Team (PLT) was formed in the spring of 2003, to begin the formal school-based leadership training needed to implement the school portfolio. Most of Azalea's PLT members are department heads or leaders in the school. Members attended a three-day portfolio leadership training provided by the school district in July 2003. The PLT has met regularly (every fourth and fifth Wednesday) to develop the school portfolio. PLT members are responsible for informing their committee of meeting discussions and bringing concerns back to the PLT. Almost all teachers serve on one of the seven committees.

The Portfolio Leadership Team meet regularly to:

▼ coordinate the work of the different portfolio committees

▼ keep everyone informed about the work of all portfolio committees

▼ investigate the findings and recommendations of committees

▼ schedule time during faculty meetings for discussion or recommendations as they are being developed, therefore, allowing input into the recommendation early in the process

Leadership through Small Group Teaming

Small academic teams were implemented in 2003-04 as a result of the District's Education Plan, goals, and objectives. The 2002-03 school year was spent preparing for this change to small group teaming. Teachers went to observe three schools that were successful in teaming. The principal, arts coordinator, and instructional coach also visited two award-winning schools in a neighboring district that have successfully implemented small group teaming. "Turning Points 2000" was read and discussed by staff during planning times, and after-school meetings were held by teacher representatives to share concerns and views on how to implement teaming at Azalea. A teaming handbook was developed and published for team leaders to assist them in leading their teams.

Grades six through eight are composed of two equally balanced academic teams, as much as the course schedule allows. Teams are comprised of Language Arts, Math, Science, and Social Studies from which leaders are chosen. The related arts team is composed of the fine arts, physical education, and communication arts teachers. Special education teachers are also represented by a team leader. Small group teaming provides opportunities for teachers to lead and make decisions regarding the students they teach. Team leadership has enabled teams to develop consistent discipline plans, celebrations or rewards for students, and more effective ways of communicating with parents and planning instruction. The assistant principal and administrative assistant provide support and guidance with the development of the team discipline plans which each team enforces.

The small group team met on Wednesdays during 2002-03 to establish how Azalea was going to do this. In 2003-04, this team will meet to communicate how the implementation is coming along in all parts of the school.

Leadership through the School Improvement Councils

School Improvement Councils (SIC), required by state law, work collaboratively with the school to develop and implement the school improvement plan (school portfolio), monitor and evaluate success in reaching the plan's goals and objectives, and write an annual report to parents and the community about the progress of the plan. Councils also assist the principal in writing the narrative for the school report card. In addition, Councils advise on the use of school incentive awards and provide assistance as required by the principal. School Improvement Councils do not have any of the powers and duties reserved by the local school board.

The SIC meets monthly and is composed of elected teachers, parents and appointed community/business representatives. Ex-officio members of the SIC currently include administration and our arts coordinator. Setting goals focused on an area of school improvement is an example of SIC leadership. A School Improvement Council goal set for 2002-03 and 2003-04 was to improve communication between our parents and between home and school. Three informal parent workshops were presented by the principal during 2002-03. During 2003-04, the SIC and PTA worked together to assist in providing three parent workshops on *"Living with a Middler," "Understanding PACT,"* and *"Middle School Teaming."* The parent workshops held in 2003-04 were different and included participation of the administrative team, a team of teachers from each grade level, guidance counselors, instructional coach, and the arts coordinator. This was the first joint effort of the PTA and SIC focused on school improvement. During 2004-05, the SIC and PTA will focus on Goal 3: *To provide a school environment supportive of learning.*

Leadership through the Parent-Teacher Association

The Parent-Teacher Association (PTA) promotes the welfare of children, works with the school and community to provide quality education for all children and youth, and participates in the decision-making process establishing school policy. Our PTA is a part of the larger state and National Parents and Teachers (National PTA) which is the largest and oldest volunteer association working exclusively on behalf of children and youth. The PTA seeks to promote collaboration between parents, the school, and the community at large. The efforts of the PTA are promoted through an advocacy and education program directed toward parents, teachers, and the general public which were developed through conferences, committees, projects, and programs. Our pool of volunteers supports the educational efforts of the faculty,and assists the staff in various roles, including planning and other leadership needs. The net earnings of the PTA are used entirely to benefit the school, its students, staff, and programs.

Azalea's PTA administrative board officers meet monthly to discuss issues relating to PTA and its support of the school. During 2003-04, PTA provided 1,177 volunteers, 8,264 hours of volunteer service, and raised over $32,000 for the school. The PTA board meets to prioritize fund raising and to stay informed of district and school issues.

Leadership through Departments

Departments (Language Arts, Math, Social Studies, Science, Related Arts, and Special Education) meet the second Wednesday each month to focus on issues relating to their specific curriculum area. Each department submits minutes to the principal. In addition to the vertical articulation in our departments at Azalea, our administrators and teachers expand this discussion when they meet annually with our main feeder elementary and high school administrators and teachers to discuss state standards and how to improve the transition from elementary to middle, and from middle to high school.

Meeting Times

All staff members have committed to meet every Wednesday and every other Thursday after school, with the leadership team meeting every Tuesday after school. Dates and times for leadership meetings follow:

Day	Time	Teams
Every Tuesday	3:30 to 5:00 PM	Leadership Team
1st/3rd Wednesdays	3:30 to 5:00 PM	Faculty
2nd Wednesday	3:30 to 5:00 PM	Department
4th Wednesday	3:30 to 5:00 PM	Grade Level/School Portfolio
5th Wednesday	3:30 to 5:00 PM	School Portfolio
1st Tuesday	7:00 to 8:30 PM	Parent-Teacher Association
3rd Friday	Noon to 1:00 PM	School Improvement Committee
2nd/4th Thursdays	3:30 to 5:00 PM	Critical Friends Group

Implementing the Plan:
The Professional Development Plan/Schedule

The Professional Development Schedule that reinforces the Leadership Structure and overall plan can help staff know if the plan is possible and what adjustments are necessary. It also serves as a document of commitment. It is one thing to see the activities in a plan; it is another thing to see the activities listed in chronological order, with the time commitments and expectations clearly laid out. Below is Azalea's Professional Development Plan for 2003-04, and their Calendar for Fall 2004, extracted from the overall plan (Figure 8.1). (PrDevPlan.pdf and PrDevCal.pdf)

Also on the CD is a table of *Powerful Professional Development Designs* and a folder of activities related to these designs. (Designs.pdf and Powerful Professional Development Designs Folder) Most school improvement plans that get implemented include at least thirty *Powerful Professional Development Designs* to assist with implementation.

> *Most school improvement plans that get implemented include at least thirty "Powerful Professional Development Designs" to assist with implementation.*

Azalea Professional Development Plan, 2003-04

At the beginning of the 2003-04 year, the Azalea Middle School staff rated the school a 3 in *Approach*, a 3 in *Implementation*, and a 3 in *Outcome* with respect to *Professional Development* on the *School Portfolio Continuous Improvement Continuums*. According to this rating, the staff viewed Azalea, at that time, as a school where student needs are used to target professional development for employees, and where there is year-round professional development on relevant instructional and leadership strategies, many of which begin to lead in the direction of shared decision making, team building, and data analysis. However, it was apparent from the rating that the staff did not view professional development at Azalea as the driver of learning at all levels or as a tool aligned to the achievement of student learning standards. The consensus seemed to be that, though Azalea's multiple professional development opportunities may be seen as a strength, this plethora of opportunities may also be seen as a weakness, as it accentuates a lack of focus and connection; the volume of professional development opportunities does not allow for adequate feedback, continuity, and time to implement the strategies learned.

Next steps were determined. They included asking staff for input on professional development and looking for a schoolwide unified focus. In creating a shared vision, two areas of focus were agreed upon: improving student achievement and improving school climate.

Professional development continued throughout the year, and the staff was surveyed to evaluate the effectiveness of this professional development.

The results of a staff survey on professional development, shown with the other questionnaires in Chapter 5, indicate a few trends. According to the survey, 67% of the staff view the professional development opportunities at Azalea as somewhat helpful. Fourteen percent view the professional development as very helpful, and 17% view it as not helpful. According to the comments that were recorded on the surveys, some of the same weaknesses noted at the beginning of the year are still weaknesses: opportunities are too broad and unfocused, time constraints make implementation very difficult, and there is little follow-through or feedback on the professional development opportunities that could give the continuity necessary for the effective implementation thereof.

The staff indicated that small group settings for professional development, such as grade level or department meetings, are preferred over the entire faculty sessions. Other indications were that teachers' comfort levels and frequency of use of standards-based instruction as well as arts-focused instruction were high. On the other hand, the comfort level and frequency of use of learner-focused strategies, differentiated instructional strategies, and technology were lower. The indication was that the staff would benefit greatly from focused professional development on a few areas in small group settings.

Therefore, much of Azalea's professional development in 2004-05 will be held in meetings of:

▼ Grade levels

▼ Subject areas (vertical/horizontal)

▼ Articulation with elementary and high schools

▼ Study groups

Meetings will focus on standards and technology implementation, effective instruction for all students, curriculum calibration, and using data. Staff will use demonstration lessons and peer coaching to implement the concepts. The vision implementation assessment tool will help grade levels/content areas know where all teachers are every month, with respect to implementing standards (including Technology and The Arts).

All other professional development that teachers will attend will be related to these same topics.

2004-05

After the school plan was created, the Professional Development Committee captured the professional development activities in a calendar. The Fall 2004 calendar is shown in Figure 8.2. This calendar caused staff to adapt the plan to make it more doable. It was a good "check and balance." The calendar also helped staff see how all the parts of the vision and leadership structure come together and support each other.

Figure 8.2

Azalea Middle School Professional Development Calendar

Fall 2004		
Date	**Type of Meeting**	**Topics**
August 25 8:00 to 4:00 PM	Professional Development	Review vision, standards, curriculum articulation, *Character Education*, and *Learning Focus implementation*
August 26 8:00 to 4:00 PM	Professional Development	Review vision, standards, curriculum articulation, *Character Education*, and *Learning Focus implementation*
August 27 8:00 to 4:00 PM	Professional Development	Review vision, standards, curriculum articulation, *Character Education*, and *Learning Focus implementation*
September 1 3:30 to 5:00 PM	Faculty Meeting	Peer observation and demonstration lesson scheduling
September 2 3:30 to 5:00 PM	Professional Development	Aligning our standards-based curriculum
September 2 7:00 to 8:30 PM	PTA	Partnership plan
September 7 3:30 to 5:00 PM	Leadership Team	Shared decision making; standards alignment; partnerships
September 8 3:30 to 5:00 PM	Department Meetings	Check alignment to standards; shared decision making
September 9 3:30 to 5:00 PM	Critical Friends Group Small Group Teams	*Learning Focus* strategies and demonstration lessons
September 10 12:00 to 1:00 PM	School Improvement Committee (SIC)	School Plan: Developing a sense of community within teams and grade levels
September 13 3:30 to 5:00 PM	Professional Development	Technology: e-newsletters and placing information on the school website
September 14 3:30 to 5:00 PM	Leadership Team	Standards alignment and implementation
September 15 3:30 to 5:00 PM	Faculty Meeting	*Learning Focus*— suspensions/discipline/*Character Education*
September 16 3:30 to 5:00 PM	Professional Development	Differentiating standards-based instruction
September 21 3:30 to 5:00 PM	Leadership Team	Standards-based instruction and teaching students who live in poverty

Figure 8.2 (Continued)

Azalea Middle School Professional Development Calendar

Fall 2004		
Date	**Type of Meeting**	**Topics**
September 22 3:30 to 5:00 PM	Grade Level/ Portfolio Meetings	Standards-based instruction and teaching students who live in poverty
September 23 3:30 to 5:00 PM	Critical Friends Group Small Group Teams	Standards-based instruction and teaching students who live in poverty
September 28 3:30 to 5:00 PM	Leadership Team	Standards alignment and technology implementation
September 29 3:30 to 5:00 PM	Portfolio Meetings	School Portfolio
October 5 3:30 to 5:00 PM	Leadership Team	*Learning Focus* and strategies that work to close gaps
October 6 3:30 to 5:00 PM	Faculty Meeting	*Learning Focus* and strategies that work to close gaps
October 7 7:00 to 8:30 PM	PTA	Partnership plan
October 8 12:00 to 1:00 PM	School Improvement Committee	School plan
October 12 3:30 to 5:00 PM	Leadership Team	*Learning Focus* and strategies that work to close gaps implementation
October 13 3:30 to 5:00 PM	Department Meetings	*Learning Focus* and strategies that work to close gaps implementation
October 14 3:30 to 5:00 PM	Critical Friends	Integrating the arts across the curriculum
October 19 3:30 to 5:00 PM	Leadership Team	Arts and standards-based integration
October 20 3:30 to 5:00 PM	Faculty Meeting	Arts and standards-based integration
October 21 3:30 to 5:00 PM	Critical Friends Group	Integrating the arts across the curriculum
October 25 8:00 to 4:00 PM	Professional Development	*A Framework for Understanding Poverty*
October 26 3:30 to 5:00 PM	Leadership Team	Implementation of poverty concepts
October 27 3:30 to 5:00 PM	Grade Level/ Portfolio Meetings	Learning focus, portfolio
October 28 3:30 to 5:00 PM	Critical Friends	Integrating the arts across the curriculum
October 30 3:30 to 5:00 PM	Professional Development	Technology—classroom technology software and tools
November 2 3:30 to 5:00 PM	Leadership Team	Update on where teachers are with ongoing assessments and closing the gap
November 3 3:30 to 5:00 PM	Faculty Meeting	Update on where teachers are with ongoing assessments and closing the gap and next steps
November 4 7:00 to 8:30 PM	PTA	Partnership plan
November 9 3:30 to 5:00 PM	Leadership Team	Reviewing student data and student work
November 10 3:30 to 5:00 PM	Department Meetings	Reviewing student data and student work
November 11 3:30 to 5:00 PM	Critical Friends Group	Reviewing student data and student work
November 12 12:00 to 1:00 PM	School Improvement Committee	School plan
November 16 3:30 to 5:00 PM	Leadership Team	Vision implementation tool results update

Figure 8.2 (Continued)

Azalea Middle School Professional Development Calendar

Fall 2004		
Date	**Type of Meeting**	**Topics**
November 17 3:30 to 5:00 PM	Faculty Team	Learning focus
November 18 3:30 to 5:00 PM	Professional Development	Technology
November 22 8:00 to 4:00 PM	Professional Development	Differentiating instruction with technology
November 23 3:30 to 5:00 PM	Leadership Team	Implementing differentiated instruction with technology
November 24 3:30 to 5:00 PM	Grade Level / Portfolio Meetings	Implementing differentiated instruction with technology
November 25 3:30 to 5:00 PM	Critical Friends Group	*Learning Focus*
November 30 3:30 to 5:00 PM	Leadership Team	Status of vision and standards implementation
December 1 3:30 to 5:00 PM	Faculty Meeting	Implementing differentiated instruction/standards with technology: demonstration lesson
December 2 7:00 to 8:30 PM	PTA	Report on partnerships
December 7 3:30 to 5:00 PM	Leadership Team	Status of vision implementation
December 8 3:30 to 5:00 PM	Department Meeting	Standards and vision implementation
December 9 3:30 to 5:00 PM	Critical Friends Group	Closing the gap with all students/effective strategies/results
December 10 12:00 to 1:00 PM	School Improvement Committee	School plan
December 14 3:30 to 5:00 PM	Leadership Team	Where are we with the vision and standards implementation?
December 15 3:30 to 5:00 PM	Faculty Meeting	Where are we with the vision and standards implementation?
December 16 3:30 to 5:00 PM	Professional Development	Technology
December 21 3:30 to 5:00 PM	Leadership Team	Where are we with the vision and standards implementation and closing the gap? Reviewing the data and celebrating success.
December 22 3:30 to 5:00 PM	Grade Level/ Portfolio Meetings	School portfolio

In addition to the leadership structure and professional development calendar, a vision assessment tool was created for self-assessing where each teacher is in implementing the vision. Staff knows the tool will evolve over time. The first draft of this tool follows as Figure 8.3.

Figure 8.3

Teacher Assessment Tool Related to the Azalea Middle School Vision

To what degree are you implementing these processes and strategies in your classroom? Circle the number that represents the degree of implementation right now (1 = not at all; 2 = not all the time; 3 = about half of the time; 4 = almost all the time; 5 = all the time). Add comments about what would help you implement the different strategies, or notes about what you did that you would like to share with others

Implementation *Teachers will—*	Classroom	Comments
• Create lesson plans and syllabi that address the standards.	1 2 3 4 5	
• Use district pacing guides for grade-level students and adjust pacing and activities as appropriate to accommodate low-performing students, new students, students with IEPs, and above-standards-level students.	1 2 3 4 5	
• Maximize instructional time to help every student meet content standards and the school to accomplish its shared vision.	1 2 3 4 5	
• Provide students with opportunities to use higher-order thinking and problem-solving skills.	1 2 3 4 5	
• Provide students opportunities to demonstrate knowledge of content in a variety of ways.	1 2 3 4 5	
• Assess student knowledge on an ongoing basis, using multiple strategies.	1 2 3 4 5	
• Use standards-based instruction congruent with what the assessment data say.	1 2 3 4 5	
• Utilize technology for content-area learning and research.	1 2 3 4 5	
• Provide students with opportunities to use technology to support learning.	1 2 3 4 5	
• Provide students with opportunities for sufficient practice of technology skills.	1 2 3 4 5	
• Apply productivity/multimedia tools and peripherals to support individual learning and group collaboration through the state content standards.	1 2 3 4 5	
• Design, develop, publish, and present products (Webpages, videotapes, CDs) using technology resources that demonstrate and communicate curriculum concepts to audiences, both within the school and outside the school.	1 2 3 4 5	
• Collaborate with peers, experts, and others using e-mail to investigate real world problems, issues, and information to develop solutions or products.	1 2 3 4 5	
• Showcase student work on the Intranet by grade and subject.	1 2 3 4 5	
• Create flexible instructional groupings.	1 2 3 4 5	
• Implement *Character Education* concepts in the classroom.	1 2 3 4 5	
• Implement arts-focused strategies that raise student achievement.	1 2 3 4 5	

How many times in the past month have you—
    Observed a colleague teach? _____
    Been observed by a colleague? _____
When will you be willing to provide a demonstration lesson
    at a faculty meeting? _____
    Topic? _____

Overall comments and needs:

Implementing the Plan: The Partnership Plan

Similar to the leadership structure and professional development plan, a partnership plan can be extracted from the overall plan. 🔘 (PartPlan.pdf)

When extracting the partnership plan from the overall plan, Azalea realized they did not have enough meaningful partnerships. They reviewed their goals and objectives and brainstormed how they could work with parents, business, and the community to achieve their main goal to have all students proficient in the standards. They came up with these ideas:

Azalea Partnership Plan, 2003-04

Azalea Middle School envisions our families, staff, and community working together to strengthen instruction and learning as a shared responsibility. We are committed to exploring and developing new strategies for our school, which will help us to help our students meet the challenges of a fast-paced, ever changing world.

Recognizing that parental involvement is one of the greatest contributors to student success in school, our staff decided to convene a team to develop strategies for increased parental and community involvement. Ultimately, we would like to have a clearly articulated partnership structure for the school, so that our partners' efforts directly impact our goals and standards for our students' success in school and in life.

Our developing partnership plan, as a part of our comprehensive schoolwide improvement plan, works to ensure that our partners have the opportunity to contribute to and benefit from these endeavors. It is our belief that our students have much to give to, as well as learn from, their community. We are actively seeking reciprocal partnerships.

Our current partnerships are described below:

A reciprocal relationship currently exists between parents and the school. New and perspective parents are invited to tour the school and to see students and staff in action. Each fall all parents and students are invited to Back-to-School Night, where they meet teachers and receive syllabi aligned with state standards. They also receive information regarding our PTA, e-newsletter, e-mail addresses for staff websites, and ways to become involved in the school community. Four times a school year the PTA newsletter is mailed home. The newsletter contains information regarding all aspects of the current school program and activities, including a calendar of upcoming school events.

In February of each year, the SIC publishes an annual report to the parents. This report provides a summary of standardized test scores, the School Report Card, academic goals for school improvement, and awards for students and teachers. Azalea Middle School parents attend meetings, tutor students, chaperone field trips and school dances, raise funds for special projects, run copies, and landscape. PTA and SIC collaborate to sponsor a welcoming open house for sixth-grade parents and grade-level meetings that address specific grade level concerns.

Community/business involvement includes members of the community who participate in our writing programs, representatives from Ford, General Electric, and the local credit union teach Junior Achievement to social studies classes once a week for eight weeks; our supermarket loans plants for assemblies and donates food and beverages; the "Magnolia City News" features weekly school activities and student profiles, and offers free and discount subscriptions of class sets of newspapers. Three professors and a director from State University, the vice-president of The Bank of Magnolia City, career mothers, and educators serve on our SIC. Azalea has its own police resource officer who counsels all students and teaches the seventh graders "Code Blue," which is a drug abuse program. The Urban League provides us with a Teen Connection Coordinator who counsels "at risk" students. Our Teen Connection students participate in college visits, step team competitions, and host an open house to present an original play for parents.

Summary of Progress

This has been an exciting year! We have identified some of the *"who"* currently partnering at Azalea. We feel that we have just begun a list that will be much longer. We hope to expand this base of information in 2004-05. In reviewing the list developed this year, we became aware that we do not have an established business partnership. Instead, we have *"events"* that call for community involvement. We have been fortunate to have excellent volunteers from both our parents and our community. At this time we are ready to initiate and build partnerships that are sustained and focused for increased student learning with The Bank of Magnolia City and State University. We are working to start two meaningful relationships for our students with those currently investing in our school's culture. We realize this team's work has the potential to change the school in very dramatic and positive ways. Our team has grown to include not only faculty, but also parents and community representatives. This inclusive team is determined to focus on the school's vision, goals, and students' learning as we build partnerships. The future success depends a great deal on the alignment of all of our efforts with the standards and the quality of our communication with everyone. We are committed to building two new partnerships in 2004-05 that will be sustained and assessed while building our information base.

Next Steps

▼ We need to define, initiate, and assess partnerships built around student learning standards and the school vision.

▼ We need to be clear on what we mean by and want for partnership involvement in order to increase participation in student learning.

▼ We need to make sure that all of our partners feel appreciated and see the results of their work with our students.

▼ We need to enlarge our base of information regarding current interaction with volunteers and community members in order to develop true partnerships.

Evaluating the Plan

Also in the Azalea Middle School Action Plan is a column indicating how strategies and activities will be evaluated. By condensing the measurement column into a comprehensive evaluation plan (Figure 8.4), the persons responsible for the measurement of the plan can see the overall evaluation and plan accordingly. (EvalPlan.pdf) If one looks only at the measurement of individual strategies and activities in isolation of each other, she/he could miss ways to efficiently measure the entire plan.

Figure 8.4

Azalea Middle School Evaluation Plan

The evaluation of the Azalea Middle School action plan is designed around achieving adequate yearly progress toward 100% proficiency of all students in all subject areas, and the measurement of the strategies and activities to achieve the school's three main goals, which are to:

- Raise the academic challenge and performance of each student.
- Improve student learning through the use of technology.
- Provide a school environment supportive of learning.

In addition to the measurement of events as spelled out in the action plan, the following will be used to measure student learning progress.

Evaluation of the Plan

Goal 1: *Raise the academic challenge and performance of each student.*

Measurable Objectives:

Objective 1: *By 2013-14, all Azalea Middle School students will show proficiency in every tested standards-based subject, as measured by SCAT scores (No Child Left Behind Act).*

Objective 2: *By the end of 2005-06, we will decrease by 20% the number of students (2003-04) scoring "Below Basic" in Mathematics and English Language Arts, as measured by SCAT.*

Objective 3: *Azalea will maintain or improve SCAT English Language Arts and Mathematics scores for cohort groups.*

The following are key performance measures for Goal 1, Objectives 1–3:

- The implementation of content and performance standards, aligned with the State Curriculum Standards for all courses and grade levels, as measured by the Standards Assessment Instrument.
- The establishment and implementation of a set of program standards for measuring and improving the quality of schoolwork offered to students, as measured by:
  - ★ Modification of course content and curriculum offerings to meet program quality standards, appropriate revisions of existing courses, deletions of courses that do not meet standards, and additions of new courses and requirements that provide both challenging and diverse learning opportunities for students.
  - ★ Increasing numbers of students who enroll and succeed in a rigorous, comprehensive schedule of coursework (including foreign language).
- Districtwide programs for improving Mathematics instruction effectively implemented, as measured by:
  - ★ Algebra I established as the standard Math curriculum in eighth grade.
  - ★ Increasing numbers of certified Math teachers at the middle school level.
  - ★ Increasing levels of student achievement on the Algebraic strands of SCAT in grade six through eight.
  - ★ Increasing percentages of students passing the end-of-course test for Algebra I.
- A system of districtwide performance assessments, accompanied by increased use of effective educational practices and appropriate support for diverse students' learning needs, established and effectively implemented, as measured by:
  - ★ Increasing scores on SCAT for all subjects and grade levels tested.
  - ★ Increasing percentages of students who excel in mastering challenging subject matter and "real-world" competencies as demonstrated through instructional assessment tasks in classrooms and indicated by school records of academic achievement
  - ★ Decreasing gaps in achievement between identified groups of students on SCAT and other local and national assessments.
  - ★ Increasing percentages of students scoring at or above the 50th percentile on national standardized tests.
- Documenting professional development provided for teaching effectively in heterogeneous classrooms, and documenting related actions by the district and specific schools to demonstrate and research the efficacy of heterogeneous grouping.

Figure 8.4 (Continued)

Azalea Middle School Evaluation Plan *(Continued)*

Goal 2: *Improve student learning through the use of technology.*

Measurable Objectives:

Objective 1: *Expand and integrate the use of technology, as measured by teacher self-assessments, student work, and questionnaires.*

Objective 2: *Teachers will increase their technology proficiency, as measured by the district technology self-assessment.*

Objective 3: *Use information literacy skills with appropriate technology, as measured by student work.*

The following are key performance measures for Goal 2, Objectives 1–3:

- ♦ School technology plan designed, related training conducted, technical support needs addressed, and classroom technologies installed and available for teaching and learning, with effectiveness measured by:
  - ★ Documented use of technology as a tool for improving student learning, as specified by the objectives and performance measures of Goal 1
  - ★ Documented use of technology as a tool for accomplishing the quality personnel objectives specified for Goal 2
  - ★ Documented use of technology as a tool for accomplishing communications objectives
  - ★ Decreasing numbers of behavior referrals and suspensions

Goal 3: *Provide a school environment supportive of learning.*

Measurable Objectives:

Objective 1: *Develop a professional learning community, as measured by involvement in focused study groups.*

Objective 2: *Develop quality arts-focused lessons and teaching strategies, as measured by teacher self-assessments, lessons, and student work.*

Objective 3: *Increase meaningful parent/partnership involvement at Azalea each year, as measured by questionnaires completed by parents and business partners.*

Objective 4: *Develop a safe and nurturing school environment, as measured by perception questionnaires.*

The following are key performance measures for Goal 3, Objectives 1–4:

- ♦ School safety and crisis management plans established and related training effectively implemented as evidenced by routine documentation and an excellent safety record.
- ♦ School maintenance standards and procedures established and effectively implemented as evidenced by routine inspections and an excellent record of clean and well-maintained buildings and grounds.
- ♦ District character education plan developed and effectively implemented, as measured by:
  - ★ Reduced disruptive behavior
  - ★ Increased community involvement
  - ★ Increased number of service learning projects
  - ★ Reduced vandalism
  - ★ Student questionnaire results

> *A continuous school improvement plan includes objectives for reaching the school goals, strategies, and actions to achieve the objectives, person responsible, how each strategy and action will be measured, resources needed, due date, and timeline.*

Summary

With the strengths, challenges, gap analyses, and root cause analyses complete, one can integrate findings to create a continuous school improvement plan that is informed by the data and a school vision, and that will lead to student achievement increases. A continuous school improvement plan that is based on quality data can eliminate root causes. Identifying and then eliminating the root causes of the gaps in student achievement by using the data will almost surely guarantee student learning increases.

A continuous school improvement plan includes objectives for reaching the school goals, strategies, and actions to achieve the objectives, person responsible, how each strategy and action will be measured, resources needed, due date, and timeline.

From the overall continuous school improvement plan, one can pull out a leadership structure, evaluation plan, professional development schedule/plan, and even a partnership plan that will reinforce roles, responsibilities, meeting times, and the overall approach to continuous improvement and evaluation.

On the CD Related to this Chapter

▼ *Azalea Shared Vision* (AZVision.pdf)
This read-only file is Azalea's Guiding Principles and Shared Vision, and also shown on pages 201-204 in Chapter 8.

▼ *Facilitator's Agenda for Creating a Shared Vision* (AgendaFa.pdf)
This read-only file provides an annotated agenda for taking staff through a visioning process in one day. Typical time requirements for the different activities are provided.

▼ *Agenda for Creating a Shared Vision* (Agenda.doc)
This is an example agenda for creating a vision in one day. It accompanies the facilitator's agenda for creating a vision. Add your school's name.

▼ *Shared Vision Template* (VTemplte.doc)
This is a template for staff to use when creating their shared vision. It allows staff to document their personal ideas before they are merged into core principles for the whole school.

▼ *Vision Notetaking Form* (VNotes.doc)
This notetaking form is for staff to use when creating a shared vision. It allows staff to write down their anecdotal stories, questions, comments, or concerns to share later as opposed to during the process.

▼ *Vision Quote Posters* (VPosters.pdf)

These read-only files contain motivating quotes to have enlarged for visioning day. The quotes show how to get to the vision, ground rules, and words of wisdom by Peter Senge and Joel Barker.

▼ *Azalea School Plan for Improvement* (SchlPlan.pdf)

This read-only file is the first draft of the Azalea Middle School Plan and is shown as Figure 8.1 in Chapter 8.

▼ *Planning Template* (APForm.doc)

A quality action plan to implement the vision consists of goals, objectives, strategies, actions, persons responsible, resources required, due dates, and timelines. A template with these components is provided in *Microsoft Word,* ready to be completed.

▼ *Azalea Leadership Plan* (LeadPlan.pdf)

This read-only file is the Azalea Leadership Plan and Structure, created from the overall action plan, and is shown on pages 213-218 in Chapter 8.

▼ *Azalea Professional Development Plan* (PrDevPlan.pdf)

This read-only file is the 2003-04 Azalea Professional Development Plan shown on pages 219-221 in Chapter 8.

▼ *Azalea Professional Development Calendar* (PrDevCal.pdf)

This read-only file Azalea's 2004-05 Fall/Winter Calendar, also shown as Figure 8.2 in Chapter 8.

▼ *Professional Development Calendar Template* (PrDevCal.doc)

This *Microsoft Word* document is a template for creating your school Professional Development Calendar.

▼ *Azalea Partnership Plan* (PartPlan.pdf)

This read-only file is the Azalea Partnership Plan, created from the overall action plan, and is shown on pages 225-227 in Chapter 8.

▼ *Establishing a Partnership Plan* (EstPPlan.pdf)

This read-only file describes the steps in creating a partnership plan that will become a part of the continuous school improvement plan.

▼ *Azalea Evaluation Plan* (EvalPlan.pdf)

This read-only file, the Azalea Evaluation Plan, condenses the measurement column of the action plan into a comprehensive evaluation plan, and is shown as Figure 8.4 in Chapter 8.

▼ *Evaluating a Program Activity* (ACTEval.pdf)

The purpose of this activity is to get many people involved in creating a comprehensive evaluation design to determine the impact of a program and to know how to improve the program.

▼ *Powerful Professional Development Designs* (Designs.pdf)

This read-only file describes numerous ways to embed professional development into the learning community.

▼ *Powerful Professional Development Designs Folder*

Powerful Professional Development Designs are those that are embedded into the daily operations of a staff. They are ongoing and lead to improvement of instruction and increases in student learning.

◆ *Action Research Activity* (ACTRsrch.pdf)

Teachers and/or administrators raise questions about the best way to improve teaching and learning, systematically study the literature to answer the questions, implement the best approach, and analyze the results.

◆ *Cadres or Action Teams Activity* (ACTCdres.pdf)

Organizing cadres or teams allows for the delegation of responsibilities so teams of educators can study new approaches, plan for the implementation of new strategies or programs, and get work done without every staff member's involvement.

◆ *Case Studies Activity* (ACTCases.pdf)

Staff members review case studies of student work, and/or of another teacher's example lessons, which can lead to quality discussions and improved practices.

◆ *Coaching Activity* (ACTCoach.pdf)

Teachers form teams of two or three to observe each other, plan together, and to talk and encourage each other in meaningful ways, while reflecting on continuously improving instructional practices.

◆ *Examining Student Data: Teacher Analysis of Test Scores Table One* (Table1.doc)

Examining student data consists of conversations around individual student data results and the processes that created the results. This approach can be a significant form of professional development when skilled team members facilitate the dialogue.

◆ *Examining Student Work Activity* (ACTSWork.pdf)

Examining student work as professional development ensures that what students learn is aligned to the learning standards. It also shows teachers the impact of their processes.

- *Example Lessons: Birds of a Feather Unit Example* (UnitEx.pdf)

  Some teachers need to see what a lesson that implements all aspects of the school vision would look like. Providing examples for all teachers to see can reward the teacher who is doing a good job of implementing the vision and provide a template for other teachers. It is very effective to store summary examples in a binder or on a website for everyone to peruse at any time.

- *Example Lessons: Unit Template* (UnitTmpl.doc)

  This *Microsoft Word* template provides the outline for creating instructional units that implement the vision.

- *Immersion Activity* (ACTImrsn.pdf)

  Immersion is a method for getting teachers engaged in different content through hands-on experiences as a learner.

- *Journaling Activity* (ACTJourn.pdf)

  Journal writing helps teachers construct meaning for, and reflect on, what they are teaching and learning.

- *Listening to Students Activity* (ACTListn.pdf)

  Students' perceptions of the learning environment are very important for continuous improvement. Focus groups, interviews, and questionnaires can be used to discover what students are perceiving.

- *Needs Assessment: Professional Development Needs Related to Technology Example* (TechnEx.pdf)

  Needs assessments help staff understand the professional development needs of staff. At the same time, if done well, a tool can lead to quality staff conversations and sharing of knowledge.

- *Needs Assessment: Professional Development Plan Related to Technology Template* (TechTmpl.doc)

  This template provides the outline for doing your own professional development needs assessment.

- *Networks Activity* (ACTNtwrk.pdf)

  Purposeful grouping of individuals/schools to further a cause or commitment.

- *Partnerships: Creating Partnerships Activity* (ACTParts.pdf)

  Teachers partnering with businesses in the community, scientists, and/or university professors can result in real-world applications for student learning and deeper understandings of content for the teacher.

- *Process Mapping: Charting School Processes Activity* (ACTProcs.pdf)
  School processes are instruction, curriculum, and assessment strategies used to ensure the learning of all students. Mapping or flowcharting school processes can help staff objectively look at how students are being taught.

- *Reflection Log Activity* (ACTLog.pdf)
  Reflective logs are recordings of key events in the educators' work days to reflect on improvement and/or to share learnings with colleagues.

- *Scheduling Activity* (ACTSchdl.pdf)
  A real test for whether or not a vision is realistic is to have teachers develop a day's schedule. This would tell them immediately if it is doable, or what needs to change in the vision and plan to make it doable.

- *School Meetings: Running Efficient Meetings* (Meetings.pdf)
  Staff, department, grade level, and cross-grade level meetings can promote learning through study or sharing best practice, while focusing on the implementation of the vision.

- *Self-Assessment: Teacher Assessment Tool Related to the Azalea Middle School Vision* (AssessEx.pdf)
  This read-only file is shown as Figure 8.3 in Chapter 8. Staff self-assessments on tools to measure progress toward the vision, such as the *Continuous Improvement Continuums,* will help them see where their school is as a system and what needs to improve for better results.

- *Self-Assessment: Teacher Assessment Tool Related to Our School Vision Template* (AssessEx.doc)
  This template file for staff self-assessments on tools to measure progress toward the vision, such as the *Continuous Improvement Continuums,* will help them see where their school is as a system and what needs to improve for better results.

- *Self-Assessment: Our School Shared Vision Implementation Rubric Example* (StRubric.pdf)
  Staff self-assessments on tools to measure progress toward the vision, such as the *Continuous Improvement Continuums,* will help them see where their school is as a system and what needs to improve for better results.

◆ *Self-Assessment: Our School Shared Vision Implementation Rubric Template* (StRubric.doc)

This template file for staff self-assessments on tools to measure progress toward the vision, such as the *Continuous Improvement Continuums,* will help them see where their school is as a system and what needs to improve for better results.

◆ *Self-Assessment: Staff-Developed Rubric Activity* (ACTRubric.pdf)

This activity for staff self-assessments on tools to measure progress toward the vision, such as the *Continuous Improvement Continuums,* will help them see where their school is as a system and what needs to improve for better results.

◆ *Shadowing Students Activity* (ACTShadw.pdf)

Purposefully following students and systematically recording the students' instructional experiences is a wonderful job-embedded approach to understanding what students are experiencing in school.

◆ *Storyboarding Activity* (ACTStory.pdf)

Storyboarding is an activity that will allow participants to share previous knowledge, while reflecting on the topic. It is a structure for facilitating conversations.

◆ *Study Groups Activity* (ACTStudy.pdf)

Groups of educators meet to learn new strategies and programs, to review new publications, or to review student work together.

◆ *Teacher Portfolio Activity* (ACTTcher.pdf)

Teacher portfolios can be built to tell the story of implementing the vision in the classroom, and its impact on student learning. Portfolios are excellent for reflection, understanding, and showing progress. Portfolios can be used for many things including self-assessment, employment, supervision to replace traditional teacher evaluation, and peer collaboration.

◆ *Train the Trainers Activity* (ACTTrain.pdf)

Train the Trainers is an approach to saving time and money. Individuals are trained and return to the school or school district to train others.

◆ *Tuning Protocols Activity* (ACTTune.pdf)

A tuning protocol is a formal process for reviewing, honoring, and fine tuning colleagues' work through presentation and reflection.

> *Your best defense against others drawing incorrect or incomplete assumptions about your school is to provide complete analyses.*

The main purpose of *Using Data to Improve Student Learning in Middle Schools* is to show analyses of a real middle school's data, using a continuous school improvement planning model to understand, explain, and continuously improve learning for all students.

In this book, an analysis of data has been presented. Many of you might consider the analysis to be massive. However, this example was created using only the state criterion-referenced assessments, some perceptions, some demographics, and some process data. The data shown here and on the CD, therefore, are not exhaustive. More comprehensive data analyses would use other measures of student learning in addition to state assessments, such as grades, authentic assessments, and additional process measures such as degree of program or process implementation. Additionally, comprehensive data analyses would have multiple years of data—ideally, we want to follow students throughout their K-12 education experiences. This is not very realistic for all schools and districts at this point in time. Three years of consistent measures are good—five years are better. Most schools have plenty of data. Most do not need to gather more data—where effort is needed is in organizing, graphing, analyzing, and using what they already have.

What the Example Shows

From the example, I hope you can see how much a person can learn about a school through data—even when only little data are available. I hope you can also see that one person alone cannot analyze all the data. Everybody sees something different in the results, so many perspectives are necessary and valuable.

The demographic analyses of this school show us that we could get a very good understanding of the context of education for students at Azalea. The way the school organizes itself to provide for its students is shown in the demographic data, and it tells a story. My hope is that school personnel reviewing these data will take the time to comprehensively analyze their own system's demographic data. There are times when others must read about your school. Remember how easy it would be, when reviewing this school's data, to start "making up" parts of the story when it was not complete. Your best defense against others drawing incorrect or incomplete assumptions about your school is to provide complete analyses.

With regard to perceptions data, we viewed four different types of perceptual data—a *Continuous Improvement Continuum* assessment, student, staff, and parent climate questionnaire data, standards assessment data, and an assessment of Azalea's professional development. These data helped the school see itself from different perspectives. A major caution in looking at the questionnaire results is to make sure one does not over-interpret differences in subgroups—even though a gap in averages appears, there might not be a *real* difference if both averages indicate agreement. It just might be the degree of the agreement that is different. Real differences would show agreement-disagreement. We are not concerned with looking for "significant differences." We want to know about "educational or perceptual differences," because these differences are significant in the learning of students.

The *Continuous Improvement Continuums* are a powerful self-analysis tool. These assessments help whole staffs talk the same talk and walk the same walk. Over time, they show staffs that they are making improvement, which keeps them moving ahead.

In analyzing student learning results, Azalea used its state criterion-referenced assessment test (SCAT). Because we are only looking at middle school data, we do not know about the educational experiences of students before these grade levels that contributed to the grade level results. We also do not know how well the students did after middle school. One can see through this example, however, that analyzing data over time for each grade level can give powerful information about which students are not being reached.

As far as gap analyses are concerned, Azalea Middle School was able to indicate gaps. It was not able to find *one* root cause, which is very common.

If working directly with a school staff, one would be able to analyze processes more comprehensively. All programs or processes used to deliver instruction could be described and eventually coded in the data warehouse so impact can be determined, since the way in which instruction is delivered is the one element over which schools have complete control. Demographic, perceptual, and student learning data show some process impact and data.

Data Warehouses

Done well, data analysis is a massive activity requiring the technical support of knowledgeable people and a data warehouse. Districts are coming on board with acquiring data warehouses that will enable the storage of a large number of data elements, and the analysis of data quickly, easily, accurately, and meaningfully. (See *Designing and Using Databases for School Improvement* [Bernhardt, 2000].) On the CD is an article entitled *Databases Can Help Teachers with Standards Implementation* (Bernhardt, 1999), summarizing how databases can help with standards implementation. (Dbases.pdf)

> *Done well, data analysis is a massive activity requiring the technical support of knowledgeable people and a data warehouse.*

School districts or schools that do not have such a tool right now must begin looking and preparing to buy a data warehouse, because they need one. It simply is no longer an option not to have one. When looking for a database or data warehouse, districts need to keep at least six considerations in mind:

1. *Accessibility at different levels.* We would like the data stored at the district, possibly even regional or state levels, and have it accessible from the school and classroom levels. Small districts can form consortia.

2. *Build graphs automatically.* We want to be able to look over the data tables to check for accuracy; however, we want the data analysis tool to build graphs as well. Because we want staffs to review the data, it is wise to put the data in picture form so everyone can see the resulting information in the same way. Trends are often easier to detect in graphs than in tables. However, sometimes we need tables to display the data. (The CD has graphing templates for use with an analysis tool or paper data.)

3. *Disaggregation on the fly.* When performing analyses that are starting to show interesting data, we want to be able to analyze quickly and easily at the next deeper levels. The easier and quicker this is to do, the deeper one can get into the data, and the more likely we are to get to root causes.

4. *Point and click or drag and drop technology that is intuitive.* We want anyone to be able to use the database without requiring a manual every time it is used.

5. *The ability to create standard reports with a click of a button.* Some reports have to be created every year, such as a School Accountability Report Card or a Title 1 report. If the same information is required each year, the programming should allow one to push a button the next year to create the report without spending a lot of time on it.

6. *The ability to follow cohorts.* Following the same groups of students as they progress through their educational careers will provide a great deal of information about one's school processes.

For the analyses in this book, I used a data warehouse tool called *EASE-E Data Analyzer* by *TetraData (www.tetradata.com)*. With this tool, I am able to analyze an entire district's data and all of its schools at the same time, as quickly and easily as analyzing one school. I do the analyses for all the schools at the same time, and then use graphing templates, such as the ones provided on the accompanying CD, to build the graphs quickly and easily. (*Point of clarification:*

EASE-E builds graphs. I use graphing templates for the fastest production. Teachers and administrators can also access specific school and classroom data from this warehouse.)

Because of their commitment to help make data analysis easier, especially for schools, *TetraData* has included the analyses made in this work as standard queries and the school profiles as standard reports. In other words, if you own *EASE-E Data Analyzer*, you will be able to create a school report similar to Azalea's, with a few clicks of buttons. You will have to verify that what you named as elements are similar to those in this study.

Who Does the Data Analysis Work?

For the types of data analyses shown here in the example, or described above as comprehensive data analyses, it would be ideal if someone at the district level did the major analyses. With a good strong data analysis tool, the district person can analyze the data for all the schools, at all grade levels, for all the subtests, disaggregated by demographics, in one query. A clerk can then copy and paste the individual results into charting templates, perhaps even into the templates provided on the CD with this book.

With a strong data analysis tool, standard queries and standard reports, such as a school report card, can be created for each of the schools by one person. Our passion with data analysis is getting the results into the hands of teachers and giving them professional development in understanding the results and the time to study the *results* of the analyses, instead of having them use their time performing the analyses. In our ideal world, at minimum, teachers would start the school year with historical data on each student in their class(es). They would have the demographic data and would know what the students know and what they need to know. Also in our ideal world, teachers would be using ongoing measurements in their classrooms to make sure all students are progressing and mastering the standards/outcomes.

Let's say your district does not have a data warehouse and provides only the state assessment results on paper; you can still use these data in meaningful ways. At minimum, schools can use the templates on the CD to graph the content and proficiency levels over time. If there have been positive improvements in the school, you should see increases in scores. If the school is making a positive impact on students, student cohort scores should increase over time.

> *Our passion with data analysis is getting the results into the hands of teachers and giving them professional development in understanding the results and the time to study the results of the analyses, instead of having them use their time performing the analyses.*

> *A school's performance cannot improve without the building administrator(s) being totally dedicated to and engaged in this process.*

The Role of the Administrator

Research shows that there are three preconditions to school/district performance improvement: instructional coherence, a shared vision for school improvement, and data-driven decision making (Armstrong, 2002). Data are necessary, but not sufficient. All three—instructional coherence, a shared vision, and data-driven decision making—must work together. We believe the link for these three preconditions is the administrator. The administrator must lead the way, challenging processes through the study of school results, inspiring the shared vision, enabling others to act through planning, modeling the way through consistent actions, and encouraging the heart by reminding teachers of the purpose of the school, why they got into teaching in the first place, and celebrating successes (Kouzes & Posner, 2002). A school's performance cannot improve without the building administrator(s) being totally dedicated to and engaged in this process.

Evaluation

Just a word about evaluation. *Continuous Improvement and Evaluation* is required to assess the alignment of all parts of the system to the vision and to check the results the learning organization is getting compared to what is being implemented. If schools or districts conduct the analyses described in this book, they will have a fairly comprehensive evaluation. An evaluation does not have to be different from data analysis. You might organize an evaluation around school goals, objectives, or even purpose and vision, by asking the basic question, *What do we have as evidence that we are doing these things?* This might take reorganizing the data already analyzed, or simply answering questions, using the data already analyzed.

Summary: Review of Steps in Using Data to Improve Student Learning in Middle Schools

Continuous school improvement planning for increasing student learning can be organized through answering a series of logical questions.

One of the first questions we want to answer is *Who are we?* Demographic data can answer this question. The answers set the context for the school, have huge implications for the direction the continuous school improvement plan will take, and can help explain how the school gets the results it is getting. In fact, there is no way any school can understand another number without the context.

The second question, *How do we do business?,* tells us about perceptions of the learning environment from student, staff, and parent perspectives. Understanding these perceptions can help a school know what is possible and what is appropriate, needed, and doable in the continuous school improvement plan.

Answering the question, *How are we doing?* takes the data analysis work into the student learning realm. Analyzing required norm-referenced and/or criterion-referenced tests is an excellent way to begin answering this question. Looking across all measures can be useful and informative—another way to think about what students know and are able to do, giving us a glimpse of *how* students learn.

Gap analyses are critical for answering the question, *What are the gaps?* Gap analyses help schools see the differences between where they are (current results) and where they want to be (vision and goals). To be effective, gap analyses must dig layers deep into the data to truly understand the results and to begin to uncover root causes.

A root cause, as used in this continuous school improvement planning model, refers to the deep underlying reason for the occurrence of a specific situation, the gap. While a symptom may become evident from a needs assessment or gap analysis—the symptom (low student scores) is not the cause. To find a root cause, one often has to ask *why* at least five levels down to uncover the root reason for the symptom. Root causes are not easy to uncover, but the information that is uncovered in the process of uncovering root causes is well worth the effort.

With the strengths, challenges, gap analyses, and root cause analyses complete, one can integrate findings to create a continuous school improvement plan that is informed by the data, and that will lead to student achievement increases. Additionally, a continuous school improvement plan based on data will eliminate root causes.

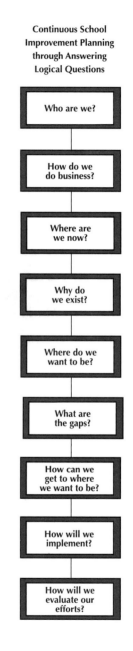

Continuous School Improvement Planning through Answering Logical Questions

Who are we?

How do we do business?

Where are we now?

Why do we exist?

Where do we want to be?

What are the gaps?

How can we get to where we want to be?

How will we implement?

How will we evaluate our efforts?

A continuous school improvement plan to eliminate root causes can answer the question, *How will we get there?* A continuous school improvement plan focused on data lays out the strategies and activities to implement. Required professional development, a leadership structure, a design for partnerships with parents, communities, and businesses, and the evaluation of the plan are vital components of the plan.

Gather your schoolwide data, graph it in a manner similar to the examples in this book; this will give you a good look at where your school is right now. To understand what to improve in your system, you have to know as much about your systems as you possibly can; study your demographic data, and your perceptual and student learning results, along with your current processes.

Time and time again, the differences in results by classroom or by school come down to the fact that some teachers are teaching to the standards and some are not. I can almost guarantee that if all teachers in your school know what the students know when they start a grade level and subject area, focus their effective instructional strategies on teaching what they want students to know and be able to do to meet the standards, measure in an ongoing fashion to know if the students are improving, student learning results for all students will increase in a very short period of time.

Final Notes

In the past, the usual way typical school personnel dealt with school data was to analyze the dickens out of their annual state assessment results, develop a plan to increase the lowest scores, and then wait for the next year's results to come out to know if their plan made a difference. Many found they could improve their assessment results in that area, only to discover that other subject-area scores declined. With *No Child Left Behind,* this approach is no longer plausible. To move all students to proficiency, school personnel must have a complete understanding of the whole system the students experience and work on improving the system that creates the results.

In the example, we started with demographic and perceptual data, which gave us a view of the system that student learning data alone cannot give. There were definite student learning issues that would be missed had we only looked at student learning results. My recommendations for getting student learning increases at the schoolwide level include:

▼ Gather and analyze your demographic data to understand clearly the students you are serving and who is teaching them, by grade level and by content area. Make sure your processes are set up for success.

▼ Listen to the *voices* of students, parents, and staff through questionnaires.

▼ Analyze your student achievement results by student groups, by grade level, and by following cohorts.

▼ Align and monitor your curriculum and instructional strategies to meet content standards.

▼ Incorporate into all teaching ongoing assessments related to standards acquisition (e.g., diagnostics, benchmarking, grade level indicators).

▼ Pull these data together to learn what needs to change to get different results.

▼ Create a vision that is shared and a plan to implement the vision and close the gaps.

The data are not the hardest part of creating this scenario. Getting staffs to work together to share and implement a shared vision and plan takes strong and consistent leadership from the school administrator(s) and leadership teams, as well as the district leadership teams.

Best wishes to you as you continuously improve your systems for the students. You are creating the future in which the next generation will live.

On the CD Related to this Chapter

▼ *Databases Can Help Teachers with Standards Implementation* (Dbases.pdf) This read-only article, by Victoria L. Bernhardt, describes how databases can help with standards implementation.

> *It's easy to get the players. Getting 'em to play together, that's the hard part.*
> **Casey Stengel**

Appendix A
Overview of the CD Contents

The Appendix provides a list of the files as they appear on the accompanying CD. These files are listed by section, along with a description of the file's content and file type. (This list appears as the Index file [Index.pdf] on the CD.)

▼ **WHAT DATA ARE IMPORTANT?**

The files in this section support Chapter 2 in the book and provide an overview of what data are important in understanding if a school is effectively carrying out its purpose and assessing if *all* students are learning.

Multiple Measures of Data Graphic | MMgraphc.pdf | Acrobat Reader

This is Figure 2.1 in a PDF (portable document file) for printing.

Summary of Data Intersections | IntrscTbl.pdf | Acrobat Reader

This is Figure 2.2 in a PDF for your use with staff.

Data Discovery Activity | ACTDiscv.pdf | Acrobat Reader

The purpose of this activity is to look closely at examples of data and to discover specific information and patterns of information, both individually and as a group.

Intersections Activity | ACTIntrs.pdf | Acrobat Reader

The purpose of this activity is to motivate school improvement teams to think about the questions they can answer when they cross different data variables. It is also designed to help teams focus their data-gathering efforts so they are not collecting everything and anything.

Creating Intersections Activity | ACTCreat.pdf | Acrobat Reader

This activity is similar to the *Intersections Activity*. The purpose is to have participants "grow" their intersections.

Data Analysis Presentation | DASlides.ppt | Microsoft PowerPoint

This *Microsoft PowerPoint* presentation is an overview to use with your staffs in getting started with data analysis. The script of the presentation can be found under "view notes" and by setting the print option to "notes pages." Handouts can be created by setting the print option to "handouts" (three slides to a page).

Articles

These read-only articles, by Victoria L. Bernhardt, will be useful in workshops or in getting started on data with staff.

Multiple Measures | MMeasure.pdf | Acrobat Reader

This article by Victoria L. Bernhardt, in read-only format, summarizes why, and what, data are important to continuous school improvement.

Intersections: New Routes Open when One Type of Data Crosses Another | Intersct.pdf | Acrobat Reader

This article by Victoria L. Bernhardt, in read-only format, published in the *Journal of Staff Development* (Winter 2000), discusses how much richer your data analyses can be when you intersect multiple data variables.

No Schools Left Behind | NoSchls.pdf | Acrobat Reader

This article by Victoria L. Bernhardt, in read-only format, published in *Educational Leadership* (February 2003), summarizes how to improve learning for *all* students.

Study Questions Related to *What Data are Important?* | Ch2Qs.pdf | Acrobat Reader

These study questions will help you better understand the information provided in Chapter 2. This file can be printed for use with staffs as they think through the data questions they want to answer and the data they will need to gather to answer the questions.

The files in this section support Chapter 3 in the book and provide an overview of how a school can get started with comprehensive data analysis work.

Continuous School Improvement Planning via the School Portfolio Graphic	CSIPlang.pdf	Acrobat Reader

This read-only graphic displays the questions that can be answered to create a continuous school improvement plan. The data that can answer the questions, and where the answers would appear in the school portfolio, also appear on the graphic. In the book, it is Figure 3.1.

Continuous School Improvement Planning via the School Portfolio Description	CSIdscr.pdf	Acrobat Reader

This read-only file shows Figure 3.1, along with its description.

The School Portfolio Presentation	SPSlides.ppt	Microsoft PowerPoint

This *Microsoft PowerPoint* presentation is an overview to use with your staffs in getting started on the school portfolio. The script of the presentation can be found under "view notes" and by setting the print option to "notes pages." Handouts can be created by setting the print option to "handouts" (three slides to a page).

Study Questions Related to *Getting Started*	Ch3Qs.pdf	Acrobat Reader

These study questions will help you better understand the information provided in Chapter 3. This file can be printed for use with staffs as you begin continuous school improvement planning. Answering the questions will help staff determine the data needed to answer the questions discussed in this chapter.

▼ ANALYZING THE DATA: *WHO ARE WE?*

The files in this section support Chapter 4 in the book and are tools to create a demographic profile of your school in order to answer the question, *Who are we?*

Study Questions Related to *Who Are We?*	Ch4Qs.pdf	Acrobat Reader

These study questions will help you better understand the information provided in Chapter 4. This file can be printed for use as you study the case study or to use with staff as you study your own demographic data.

Demographic Graphing Templates	MiddDemog.xls	Microsoft Excel

All of the *Microsoft Excel* files that were used to create the demographic graphs in the Azalea example in Chapter 4 appear on the CD in this section. Use these templates by putting your data in the data source table and changing the title/labels to reflect your data. Your graphs will build automatically. This file also explains how to use the templates.

Demographic Data Table Templates for Azalea Middle School	MiddDemog.doc	Microsoft Word

All of the *Microsoft Word* files that were used to create the demographic data tables in the Azalea example in Chapter 4 appear on the CD in this section. Use these templates by putting your data in the data table and changing the title/labels to reflect your data.

School Data Profile Template	MiddProfil.doc	Microsoft Word

This *Microsoft Word* file provides a template for creating your own school data profile like the one in the example, using the graphing and table templates provided. Create your graphs in the graphing and table templates, then copy and paste them into the *School Profile Template*.

School Profile	ProfilSc.doc	Microsoft Word

The *School Profile* is a template for gathering and organizing data about your school, prior to graphing. Please adjust the profile to add data elements you feel are important for describing the context of your school. This information is then graphed and written into a narrative form. If creating a school portfolio, the data graphs and narrative would appear in *Information and Analysis*. (If you already have your data organized and just need to graph it, you might want to skip this step and use the graphing templates described above.)

Community Profile   ProfilCo.doc   Microsoft Word

The *Community Profile* is a template for gathering and organizing data about your community, prior to graphing. Please adjust the profile to add data elements you feel are important for describing the context of your community. It is important to describe how the community has changed over time, and how it is expected to change in the near future. This information is then graphed and written into a narrative form. If creating a school portfolio, the data graphs and narrative would appear in *Information and Analysis*. (If you already have your data organized and just need to graph it, you might want to skip this step and use the graphing templates described on the previous page.)

Administrator Profile   ProfilAd.doc   Microsoft Word

The *Administrator Profile* is a template for gathering and organizing data about your school administrators, prior to graphing. Please adjust the profile to fully describe your administrators. This information is then graphed and written into a narrative form. If creating a school portfolio, the data graphs and narrative will appear in *Information and Analysis* and *Leadership* sections. (If you already have your data organized and just need to graph it, you might want to skip this step and use the graphing templates described on the previous page.)

Teacher Profile   ProfilTe.doc   Microsoft Word

The *Teacher Profile* is a template for gathering and organizing data about your school's teachers, prior to graphing. Please adjust the profile to fully describe your teachers. The synthesis of this information is then graphed and written into a narrative form. If creating a school portfolio, the data graphs and narrative would appear in *Information and Analysis*. (If you already have your data organized and just need to graph it, you might want to skip this step and use the graphing templates described on the previous page.)

Staff (Other than Teacher) Profile   ProfilSt.doc   Microsoft Word

The *Staff (Other than Teacher) Profile* is a template for gathering and organizing data about school staff who are not teachers, prior to graphing. Please adjust the profile to fully describe your non-teaching staff. The synthesis of this information is then graphed and written into a narrative form. If creating a school portfolio, the data graphs and narrative would appear in *Information and Analysis*. (If you already have your data organized and just need to graph it, you might want to skip this step and use the graphing templates described on the previous page.)

History Gram Activity   ACTHstry.pdf   Acrobat Reader

A team-building activity that will "write" the history of the school, which could help everyone see what staff has experienced since coming to the school and how many school improvement initiatives have been started over the years. It is helpful for understanding what it will take to keep this current school improvement effort going.

Questions to Guide the Analysis of Demographic Data   QsDemogr.doc   Microsoft Word

This *Microsoft Word* file provides a guide for interpreting your demographic data. Adjust the questions to better reflect the discussion you would like to have with your staff about the gathered demographic data.

What I Saw in the Example   Ch4Saw.pdf   Acrobat Reader

What I Saw in the Example is a file, organized by the demographic study questions, that summarizes what the author saw in the demographic data provided by Azalea Middle School.

Demographic Data to Gather to Create the Context of the School   DemoData.pdf   Acrobat Reader

This file defines the types of demographic data that are important to gather to create the context of the school and describe *Who are we?*

▼ **ANALYZING THE DATA:** *HOW DO WE DO BUSINESS?*

The files in this section support Chapter 5 in the book and include tools to help staff understand the organization and climate of the school from the perspective of students, staff, and parents. The resulting analyses can help answer the question, *How do we do business?*

Continuous Improvement Continuums for Schools	CICs.pdf	Acrobat Reader

This read-only file contains the seven *School Portfolio Continuous Improvement Continuums* for schools. These can be printed as is and enlarged for posting individual staff opinions during staff assessments.

Continuous Improvement Continuums for Districts	CICsDstrct.pdf	Acrobat Reader

This read-only file contains the seven *School Portfolio Continuous Improvement Continuums* for assessing the district level. These can be printed as is and enlarged for posting individual staff opinions during staff assessments.

Azalea School Baseline CIC Results	AZBase.pdf	Acrobat Reader

This read-only file is the summary of Azalea's baseline assessment on the *School Portfolio Continuous Improvement Continuums*.

Continuous Improvement Continuum Tools

These files are tools for assessing on the CICs and for writing the CIC report.

Continuous Improvement Continuums Self-Assessment Activity	ACTCIC.pdf	Acrobat Reader

Assessing on the *Continuous Improvement Continuums* will help staffs see where their systems are right now with respect to continuous improvement and ultimately will show they are making progress over time. The discussion has major implications for the *Continuous School Improvement (CSI) Plan*.

Coming to Consensus	Consenss.pdf	Acrobat Reader

This read-only file provides strategies for coming to consensus, useful when assessing on the *Continuous Improvement Continuums*.

Continuous Improvement Continuums Report Example	ExReprt1.pdf	Acrobat Reader

This read-only file shows a real school's assessment on the *School Portfolio Continuous Improvement Continuums,* as an example.

Continuous Improvement Continuums Report Example for Follow-Up Years	ExReprt2.pdf	Acrobat Reader

This read only file shows a real school's assessment on the *School Portfolio Continuous Improvement Continuums* over time, as an example.

Continuous Improvement Continuums Baseline Report Template	ReptTemp.doc	Microsoft Word

This *Microsoft Word* file provides a template for writing your school's report of its assessment on the *School Portfolio Continuous Improvement Continuums*.

Continuous Improvement Continuums Graphing Templates	CICGraph.xls	Microsoft Excel

This *Microsoft Excel* file is a template for graphing your assessments on the seven *School Portfolio Continuous Improvement Continuums*.

Study Questions Related to *How Do We Do Business?*	Ch5Qs.pdf	Acrobat Reader

These study questions will help you better understand the information provided in Chapter 5. This file can be printed for use with staffs as you answer the question, *How do we do business?,* through analyzing Azalea's perceptual data.

What I Saw in the Example	Ch5Saw.pdf	Acrobat Reader

What I Saw in the Example is a file, organized by the perceptual study questions, that summarizes what the author saw in the perceptual data provided by Azalea Middle School.

Analysis of Questionnaire Data Table	QTable.doc	Microsoft Word

This *Microsoft Word* file is a tabular guide for interpreting your student, staff, and parent questionnaires, independently and interdependently. It will help you see the summary of your results and write the narrative.

Full Narratives of Questionnaire Results Used in the Example

Azalea Student Questionnaire Results	StuNarr.doc	Microsoft Word

This template file is the full narrative of student questionnaire results used in the school example.

Azalea Staff Questionnaire Results	StfNarr.doc	Microsoft Word

This template file is the full narrative of staff questionnaire results used in the school example.

Azalea Parent Questionnaire Results	ParNarr.doc	Microsoft Word

This template file is the full narrative of parent questionnaire results used in the school example.

Education for the Future Perception Questionnaires Used in the Example

Student Questionnaire	AZStudntQ.pdf	Acrobat Reader

This read-only file is the *Education for the Future* student perception questionnaire used in the example.

Staff Questionnaire	AZStaffQ.pdf	Acrobat Reader

This read-only file is the *Education for the Future* staff perception questionnaire used in the example.

Staff Standards Assessment Questionnaire	AZStndrdsQ.pdf	Acrobat Reader

This read-only file is the *Education for the Future* staff standards assessment questionnaire used in the example.

Parent Questionnaire	AZParentQ.pdf	Acrobat Reader

This read-only file is the *Education for the Future* parent perception questionnaire used in the example.

School IQ Graphing Templates	School IQ Folder

School Improvement Questionnaire Solutions (School IQ) is a powerful tool for analyzing *Education for the Future* questionnaires. *School IQ* reduces an otherwise technical and complicated process to one that can be navigated with pushbutton ease. There are different versions of *IQ* for each of the eleven standard *Education for the Future* questionnaires. *School IQ* includes online questionnaire templates, all 11 questionnaires in PDF format, the analysis tool, the *School IQ,* and graphing templates.

Other Popular Education for the Future Questionnaires

Student (Kindergarten to Grade 3) Questionnaire	StQKto3.pdf	Acrobat Reader

This read-only file is the *Education for the Future* perception questionnaire for students in kindergarten through grade three.

Student (Grades 1 to 6) Questionnaire	StQ1to6.pdf	Acrobat Reader

This read-only file is the *Education for the Future* perception questionnaire for students in grades one through six.

Student (Grades 6 to 12) Questionnaire	StQ6to12.pdf	Acrobat Reader

This read-only file is the *Education for the Future* perception questionnaire for students in grades six through twelve.

Student (High School) Questionnaire	StQHS.pdf	Acrobat Reader

This read-only file is the *Education for the Future* perception questionnaire for high school students.

Staff Questionnaire	StaffQ.pdf	Acrobat Reader

This read-only file is the *Education for the Future* perception questionnaire for staff.

Administrator Questionnaire	Admin.pdf	Acrobat Reader

This read-only file is the *Education for the Future* perception questionnaire for administrators.

Teacher Predictions of Student Responses (Grades 1 to 6) Questionnaire	TchPr1.pdf	Acrobat Reader

This read-only file is the *Education for the Future* perception questionnaire for teachers of students in grades one through six.

Teacher Predictions of Student Responses
(Grades 6 to 8) Questionnaire TchPr2.pdf Acrobat Reader

This read-only file is the *Education for the Future* perception questionnaire for teachers of students in grades six through eight.

Parent Questionnaire ParntK12.pdf Acrobat Reader

This read-only file is the *Education for the Future* perception questionnaire for parents of kindergarten through grade twelve students.

High School Parent Questionnaire ParntHS.pdf Acrobat Reader

This read-only file is the *Education for the Future* perception questionnaire for parents of high school students.

Alumni Questionnaire Alumni.pdf Acrobat Reader

This read-only file is the *Education for the Future* perception questionnaire for high school graduates.

How to Analyze Open-ended Responses OEanalz.pdf Acrobat Reader

This read-only file discusses how to analyze responses to the open-ended questions on questionnaires.

Questions to Guide the Analysis of Perceptions Data PerceptQ.doc Microsoft Word

This *Microsoft Word* file is a tabular guide for interpreting your perceptions data. You can change the questions if you like or use the file to write in the responses. It will help you write the narrative for your results.

▼ ANALYZING THE DATA: *WHERE ARE WE NOW?*

The tools in this section support Chapter 6 in the book, help staffs determine the results of their current processes, particularly student achievement results, and can help staffs answer the question, *Where are we now?*

Study Questions Related to *Where Are We Now?* Ch6Qs.pdf Acrobat Reader

These study questions will help you better understand the information provided in Chapter 6. This file can be printed for use with staffs as you begin to explore your own student learning results.

Arguments For and Against Standardized Testing TestArgu.pdf Acrobat Reader

This table summarizes the most common arguments for and against the use of standardized testing.

Standardized Test Score Terms TestTerm.pdf Acrobat Reader

This table shows the different standardized testing terms, their most effective uses, and cautions for their uses.

Arguments For and Against Performance Assessments PerfArgu.pdf Acrobat Reader

This table shows the most common arguments for and against the use of performance assessments.

Arguments For and Against Teacher Grading GradeArg.pdf Acrobat Reader

This table shows the most common arguments for and against the use of teacher grading.

Terms Related to Analyzing Student Achievement
Results, Descriptively SAterms1.pdf Acrobat Reader

This table shows the different terms related to analyzing student achievement results, descriptively, their most effective uses, and cautions for their uses.

Terms Related to Analyzing Student Achievement
Results, Inferentially SAterms2.pdf Acrobat Reader

This table shows the different terms related to analyzing student achievement results, inferentially, their most effective uses, and cautions for their uses.

What I Saw in the Example Ch6Saw.pdf Acrobat Reader

What I Saw in the Example is a file, organized by the student learning study questions, that summarizes what the author saw in the student learning data provided by Azalea Middle School.

Student Achievement Graphing Templates   MiddSA.xls   Microsoft Excel

> All of the *Microsoft Excel* files that were used to create the student achievement graphs in the Azalea example (Chapter 6) appear on the CD. Use these templates by putting your data in the data table and changing the title/labels to reflect your data. The graphs will build automatically. This file also explains how to use the templates.

Student Achievement Data Table Templates   MiddSA.doc   Microsoft Word

> All of the *Microsoft Word* files that were used to create the student achievement data tables in the Azalea example (Chapter 6) appear on the CD in this section. Use these templates by putting your data in the data table and changing the title/labels to reflect your data.

Questions to Guide the Analysis of Student Achievement Data   QsStachv.doc   Microsoft Word

> This *Microsoft Word* file consists of questions to guide the interpretation of your student learning data. You can write your responses into this file.

▼ ANALYZING THE DATA: *WHAT ARE THE GAPS?* AND *WHAT ARE THE ROOT CAUSES OF THE GAPS?*

The tools in this section support Chapter 7 in the book and help staffs analyze their data to determine the gaps and the root causes of the gaps. These files and tools can help answer the questions, *What are the gaps?* and *What are the root causes of the gaps?*

Goal Setting Activity   ACTGoals.pdf   Acrobat Reader

> By setting goals, a school can clarify its end targets for the school's vision. This activity will help a school set goals for the future.

Gap Analysis and Objectives Activity   ACTGap.pdf   Acrobat Reader

> The purpose of this activity is to look closely at differences between current results and where the school wants to be in the future. It is this gap that gets translated into objectives that guide the development of the action plan.

Root Cause Analysis Activity   ACTRoot.pdf   Acrobat Reader

> Root causes are the real causes of our educational problems. We need to find out what they are so we can eliminate the true cause and not just address the symptom. This activity asks staff teams to review and analyze data, and ask probing questions to uncover the root cause(s).

Cause and Effect Analysis Activity   ACTCause.pdf   Acrobat Reader

> This activity will help teams determine the relationships and complexities between an effect or problem and all the possible causes.

Problem-Solving Cycle Activity   ACTCycle.pdf   Acrobat Reader

> The purpose of the *Problem-Solving Cycle Activity* is to get all staff involved in thinking through a problem before jumping to solutions. This activity can also result in a comprehensive data analysis design.

Study Questions Related to the Gaps and the Root Causes of the Gaps   Ch7Qs.pdf   Acrobat Reader

> These study questions will help you better understand the information provided in Chapter 7. This file can be printed for use with staffs as you analyze their data to determine the gaps and the root causes of the gaps.

What I Saw in the Example   Ch7Saw.pdf   Acrobat Reader

> *What I Saw in the Example* is a file, organized by the demographic study questions, that summarizes what the author saw in the demographic data provided by Azalea Middle School.

Gap Analyses Data Table Templates   Gaps.doc   Microsoft Word

> All of the *Microsoft Word* files that were used to create the gap analyses data tables in the Azalea example (Chapter 7) appear on the CD. Use these templates by putting your data in the data table and changing the title/labels to reflect your data.

No Child Left Behind (NCLB) Templates

Table templates for analyzing student learning data for NCLB are provided on the CD .

NCLB Language Scores Template	LangTbl.doc	Microsoft Word

This *Microsoft Word* file is a table template to use in capturing your *No Child Left Behind* (NCLB) Language scores analysis.

NCLB Reading Scores Template	ReadTbl.doc	Microsoft Word

This *Microsoft Word* file is a table template to use in capturing your *No Child Left Behind* (NCLB) Reading scores analysis.

NCLB Math Scores Template	MathTbl.doc	Microsoft Word

This *Microsoft Word* file is a table template to use in capturing your *No Child Left Behind* (NCLB) Math scores analysis.

NCLB Student Achievement Reading Results Template	ProfLaEl.doc	Microsoft Word

This *Microsoft Word* file is a table template to use in summarizing your *No Child Left Behind* (NCLB) disaggregated student achievement Reading proficiency results.

NCLB Student Achievement Math Results Template	ProfMaEl.doc	Microsoft Word

This *Microsoft Word* file is a table template to use in summarizing your *No Child Left Behind* (NCLB) disaggregated student achievement Math proficiency results.

Group Process Tools and Activities

The files include read-only documents, examples, templates, tools, activities, and strategy recommendations. Many of the group process tools and activities can be used throughout the analysis of data.

Affinity Diagram Activity		Acrobat Reader

The affinity diagram encourages honest reflection on the real underlying root causes of a problem and its solutions, and encourages people to agree on the factors. This activity assists teams in discussing and resolving problems, using a nonjudgmental process.

Fishbowl Activity	ACTFish.pdf	Acrobat Reader

The *Fishbowl Activity* can be used for dynamic group involvement. The most common configuration is an inner ring, which is the discussion group, surrounded by an outer ring, which is the observation group. Just as people observe the fish in the fishbowl, the outer ring observes the inner ring.

Forcefield Analysis Activity	ACTForce.pdf	Acrobat Reader

The *Forcefield Analysis Activity* helps staffs think about the ideal state for the school and the driving and restraining forces regarding that ideal state.

Placemat Activity	ACTPlace.pdf	Acrobat Reader

The *Placemat Activity* was developed to invite participants to share their knowledge about the school portfolio, data, a standard, an instructional strategy, a concept, etc.

T-Chart Activity	ACTTChrt.pdf	Acrobat Reader

A *T-Chart* is a simple tool to organize material into two columns. Use a T-Chart to compare and contrast information or to show relationships. Use it to help people see the opposite dimension of an issue.

"X" Marks the Spot Activity	ACTXSpot.pdf	Acrobat Reader

This activity helps staff understand levels of expertise or degrees of passion about a topic.

Quadrant Diagram Activity	ACTQuadr.pdf	Acrobat Reader

A quadrant diagram is a method to determine which solution best meets two goals at once, such as low cost and high benefit.

▼ ANALYZING THE DATA: *HOW CAN WE GET TO WHERE WE WANT TO BE?*

The files in this section support Chapter 8 in the book, helping staffs answer the question, *How can we get to where we want to be?* through comprehensive planning to implement the vision and eliminate the gaps, using powerful professional development, leadership, partnership development, and continuous improvement and evaluation.

Azalea Shared Vision	AZVision.pdf	Acrobat Reader

This read-only file is Azalea's Guiding Principles and Shared Vision, also shown on pages 201-204 in Chapter 8.

Facilitator's Agenda for Creating a Shared Vision	AgendaFa.pdf	Acrobat Reader

This read-only file provides an annotated agenda for taking staff through a visioning process in one day. Typical time requirements for the different activities are provided.

Agenda for Creating a Shared Vision	Agenda.pdf	Acrobat Reader

This is an example agenda for creating a vision in one day. It accompanies the facilitator's agenda for creating a vision. Add your school's name.

Shared Vision Template	VTemplte.doc	Microsoft Word

This is a template for staff to use when creating their shared vision. It allows staff to document their personal ideas before they are merged into core principles for the whole school.

Vision Notetaking Form	VNotes.doc	Microsoft Word

This notetakin form is for staff to use when creating a shared vision. It allows staff to write down their anecdotal storiesk, questions, comments, or concerns to share later as opposed to during the process.

Vision Quote Posters	VPosters.pdf	Acrobat Reader

These read-only files contain motivating quotes to have enlarged for visioning day. The quote show how to get to the vision, ground rules, and words of wisdom by Peter Senge and Joel Barker.

Azalea School Plan for Improvement	SchlPlan.pdf	Acrobat Reader

This read-only file is the first draft of the Azalea Middle School Plan and is shown as Figure 8.1 in Chapter 8.

Planning Template	APForm.doc	Microsoft Word

A quality action plan to implement the vision consists of goals, objectives, strategies/actions, persons responsible, resources needed, due dates, and timelines. A template with these components is provided in *Microsoft Word,* ready to be completed.

Azalea Leadership Plan	LeadPlan.pdf	Acrobat Reader

This read-only file is the Azalea Leadership Plan, created from the overall action plan, and is shown on pages 213-218 in Chapter 8.

Azalea Professional Development Plan	PrDevPlan.pdf	Acrobat Reader

This read-only file is the 2003-04 Azalea Professional Development Plan shown on pages 219-221 in Chapter 8.

Azalea Professional Development Calendar	PrDevCal.pdf	Acrobat Reader

This read-only file is Azalea's 2004-05 Fall/Winter Professional Development Calendar, also shown as Figure 8.2 in Chapter 8.

Professional Development Calendar Template	PrDevCal.doc	Microsoft Word

This *Microsoft Word* document is a template for creating your school Professional Development Calendar.

Azalea Partnership Plan	PartPlan.pdf	Acrobat Reader

This read-only file is the Azalea Partnership Plan, created from the overall action plan, and is shown on pages 225-227 in Chapter 8.

| Establishing a Partnership Plan | EstPPlan.pdf | Acrobat Reader |

This read-only file describes the steps in creating a partnership plan that will become a part of the continuous school improvement plan.

| Azalea Evaluation Plan | EvalPlan.pdf | Acrobat Reader |

This read-only file, the Azalea Evaluation Plan, condenses the measurement column of the action plan into a comprehensive evaluation plan, and is shown as Figure 8.4 in Chapter 8.

| Evaluating a Program Activity | ACTEval.pdf | Acrobat Reader |

The purpose of this activity is to get many people involved in creating a comprehensive evaluation design to determine the impact of a program and to know how to improve the program.

| Powerful Professional Development Designs | Designs.pdf | Acrobat Reader |

This read-only file describes numerous ways to embed professional development into the learning community.

Powerful Professional Development Designs Folder

Powerful Professional Development Designs are those that are embedded into the daily operations of a staff. They are ongoing and lead to improvement of instruction and increases in student learning.

| Action Research Activity | ACTRsrch.pdf | Acrobat Reader |

Teachers and/or administrators raise questions about the best way to improve teaching and learning, systematically study the literature to answer the questions, implement the best approach, and analyze the results.

| Cadres or Action Teams Activity | ACTCdres.pdf | Acrobat Reader |

Organizing cadres or teams allows for the delegation of responsibilities so teams of educators can study new approaches, plan for the implementation of new strategies or programs, and get work done without every staff member's involvement.

| Case Studies Activity | ACTCases.pdf | Acrobat Reader |

Staff members review case studies of student work, and/or of another teacher's example lessons, which can lead to quality discussions and improved practices.

| Coaching Activity | ACTCoach.pdf | Acrobat Reader |

Teachers form teams of two or three to observe each other, plan together, and to talk and encourage each other in meaningful ways, while reflecting on continuously improving instructional practices.

| Examining Student Data: *Teacher Analysis of Test Scores Table One* | Table1.doc | Microsoft Word |

Examining student data consists of conversations around individual student data results and the processes that created the results. This approach can be a significant form of professional development when skilled team members facilitate the dialogue.

| Examining Student Work Activity | ACTSWork.pdf | Acrobat Reader |

Examining student work as professional development ensures that what students learn is aligned to the learning standards. It also shows teachers the impact of their processes.

| Example Lessons: *Birds of a Feather Unit Example* | UnitEx.pdf | Acrobat Reader |

Some teachers need to see what a lesson that implements all aspects of the school vision would look like. Providing examples for all teachers to see can reward the teacher who is doing a good job of implementing the vision and provide a template for other teachers. It is very effective to store summary examples in a binder or on a website for everyone to peruse at any time.

| Example Lessons: *Unit Template* | UnitTmpl.doc | Microsoft Word |

This template provides the outline for creating instructional units that implement the vision.

| Immersion Activity | ACTImrsn.pdf | Acrobat Reader |

Immersion is a method for getting teachers engaged in different content through hands-on experiences as a learner.

| Journaling Activity | ACTJourn.pdf | Acrobat Reader |

Journal writing helps teachers construct meaning for, and reflect on, what they are teaching and learning.

| Listening to Students Activity | ACTListn.pdf | Acrobat Reader |

Students' perceptions of the learning environment are very important for continuous improvement. Focus groups, interviews, and questionnaires can be used to discover what students are perceiving.

Needs Assessment: *Professional Development Needs*
Related to Technology Example   TechnEx.pdf   Acrobat Reader

Needs assessments help staff understand the professional development needs of staff. At the same time, if done well, a tool can lead to quality staff conversations and sharing of knowledge.

Needs Assessment: *Professional Development Needs*
Related to Technology Template   TechTmpl.doc   Microsoft Word

This template provides the outline for doing your own professional development needs assessment.

| Networks Activity | ACTNtwrk.pdf | Acrobat Reader |

Purposeful grouping of individuals/schools to further a cause or commitment.

| Partnerships: *Creating Partnerships Activity* | ACTParts.pdf | Acrobat Reader |

Teachers partnering with businesses in the community, scientists, and/or university professors can result in real world applications for student learning and deeper understandings of content for the teacher.

| Process Mapping: *Charting School Processes Activity* | ACTProcs.pdf | Acrobat Reader |

School processes are instruction, curriculum, and assessment strategies used to ensure the learning of all students. Mapping or flowcharting school processes can help staff objectively look at how students are being taught.

| Reflection Log Activity | ACTLog.pdf | Acrobat Reader |

Reflective logs are recordings of key events in the educators' work days to reflect on improvement and/or to share learnings with colleagues.

| Scheduling Activity | ACTSchdl.pdf | Acrobat Reader |

A real test for whether or not a vision is realistic is to have teachers develop a day's schedule. This would tell them immediately if it is doable, or what needs to change in the vision and plan to make it doable.

| School Meetings: *Running Efficient Meetings* | Meetings.pdf | Acrobat Reader |

Staff, department, grade level, and cross-grade level meetings can promote learning through study or sharing best practice, while focusing on the implementation of the vision.

Self-Assessment: *Teacher Assessment Tool Related*
to the Azalea Middle School Vision   AssessEx.pdf   Acrobat Reader

This read-only file is shown as Figure 8.3 in Chapter 8. Staff self-assessments on tools to measure progress toward the vision, such as the *Continuous Improvement Continuums,* will help them see where their school is as a system and what needs to improve for better results.

Self-Assessment: *Teacher Assessment Tool Related*
to Our School Vision   AssessEx.doc   Microsoft Word

This template file for staff self-assessments on tools to measure progress toward the vision, such as the *Continuous Improvement Continuums,* will help them see where their school is as a system and what needs to improve for better results.

Self-Assessment: *Our School Shared Vision*
Implementation Rubric Example   StRubric.pdf   Acrobat Reader

Staff self-assessments on tools to measure progress toward the vision, such as the *Continuous Improvement Continuums,* will help them see where their school is as a system and what needs to improve for better results.

Self-Assessment: *Our School Shared Vision*
        Implementation Rubric Template   StRubric.doc   Microsoft Word

This template file for staff self-assessments on tools to measure progress toward the vision, such as the *Continuous Improvement Continuums,* will help them see where their school is as a system and what needs to improve for better results.

Self-Assessment: *Staff-Developed Rubric Activity*   ACTRubric.pdf   Acrobat Reader

This activity for staff self-assessments on tools to measure progress toward the vision, such as the *Continuous Improvement Continuums,* will help them see where their school is as a system and what needs to improve for better results.

Shadowing Students Activity   ACTShadw.pdf   Acrobat Reader

Purposefully following students and systematically recording the students' instructional experiences is a wonderful job-embedded approach to understanding what students are experiencing in school.

Storyboarding Activity   ACTStory.pdf   Acrobat Reader

Storyboarding is an activity that will allow participants to share previous knowledge, while reflecting on the topic. It is a structure for facilitating conversations.

Study Groups Activity   ACTStudy.pdf   Acrobat Reader

Groups of educators meet to learn new strategies and programs, to review new publications, or to review student work together.

Teacher Portfolio Activity   ACTTcher.pdf   Acrobat Reader

Teacher portfolios can be built to tell the story of implementing the vision in the classroom, and its impact on student learning. Portfolios are excellent for reflection, understanding, and showing progress. Portfolios can be used for many things including self-assessment, employment, supervision to replace traditional teacher evaluation, and peer collaboration.

Train the Trainers Activity   ACTTrain.pdf   Acrobat Reader

Train the trainers is an approach to saving time and money. Individuals are trained and return to the school or school district to train others.

Tuning Protocols Activity   ACTTune.pdf   Acrobat Reader

A tuning protocol is a formal process for reviewing, honoring, and fine-tuning colleagues' work through presentation and reflection.

▼ **ANALYZING THE DATA:** *CONCLUSIONS AND RECOMMENDATIONS*
The files in this section support Chapter 9 in the book and help staffs evaluate their programs and processes.

Databases Can Help Teachers with Standards Implementation   Dbases.pdf   Acrobat Reader

This read-only article, by Victoria L. Bernhardt, describes how databases can help with standards implementation.

These *Education for the Future Continuous Improvement Continuums,* adapted from the *Malcolm Baldrige Award Program for Quality Business Management,* provide an authentic means for measuring schoolwide improvement and growth. Schools use these Continuums as a vehicle for ongoing self-assessment. They use the results of the assessment to acknowledge their accomplishments, to set goals for improvement, and to keep school districts and partners apprised of the progress they have made in their school improvement efforts.

Understanding the Continuums

These Continuums, extending from *one* to *five* horizontally, represent a continuum of expectations related to school improvement with respect to an *Approach* to the Continuum, *Implementation* of the approach, and the *Outcome* that results from the implementation. A *one* rating, located at the left of each Continuum, represents a school that has not yet begun to improve. *Five,* located at the right of each Continuum, represents a school that is one step removed from "world class quality." The elements between *one* and *five* describe how that Continuum is hypothesized to evolve in a continuously improving school. Each Continuum moves from a reactive mode to a proactive mode—from fire fighting to prevention. The *five* in *outcome* in each Continuum is the target.

Vertically, the *Approach, Implementation,* and *Outcome* statements, for any number one through five, are hypotheses. In other words, the implementation statement describes how the approach might look when implemented, and the outcome is the "pay-off" for implementing the approach. If the hypotheses are accurate, the outcome will not be realized until the approach is actually implemented.

Using the Continuums

Use the *Continuous Improvement Continuums* (CICs) to understand where your school is with respect to continuous improvement. The results will hopefully provide that sense of urgency needed to spark enthusiasm for your school improvement efforts.

The most beneficial approach to assessing on the Continuums is to gather the entire staff together for the assessment. When assessing on the Continuums for the first time, plan for three hours to complete all seven categories.

Start the assessment by stating or creating the ground rules, setting the tone for a safe and confidential assessment, and explaining why you are doing this. Provide a brief overview of the seven sections, taking each section one at a time, and having each staff member read the related Continuum and make independent assessments of where she/he believes the school is with respect to *Approach, Implementation,* and *Outcome.* We recommend using individual 8 1/2 x 11 copies of the Continuums for individual assessments. (CICs.pdf) Then, have each staff member note where she/he believes the school is with a colorful sticker or marker on a large poster of each Continuum. The markers allow all staff to see how much they are in agreement with one another. If only one color is used for the first assessment, another color can be used for the next assessment, and so forth, to help gauge growth over time, or you can plan to use two different charts for gauging progress over time such as in the photos below.

When all dots or marks have been placed on the enlarged Continuum, look at the agreement or disagreement of the ratings. Starting with *Approach,* have staff discuss why they believe the school is where they rated it. Keep discussing until the larger group comes to consensus on one number that reflects where the school is right now. You might need to make a quick check on where staff is with respect to coming to consensus, using a thumbs up, thumbs down "vote." Keep discussing the facts until consensus is reached. (Consenss.pdf) Do not average the results—it does not produce a sense of urgency for improvement. We cannot emphasize this enough! Keep discussing until agreement is reached by everyone on a number that represents where "we" are right now. When that consensus is reached, record the number and move to *Implementation* and then *Outcome.* Determine *Next Steps.* Proceed in the same way through the next six categories.

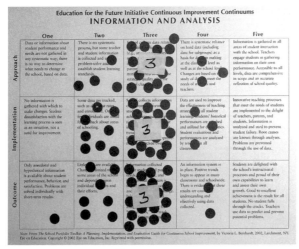

Fall Assessment

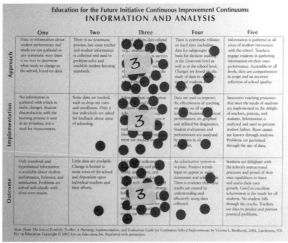

Spring Assessment

During the assessments, make sure someone records the discussions of the Continuum assessments. Schools might want to exchange facilitators with a neighboring school or district to have someone external to the school facilitate the assessments. This will enable everyone in the school to participate and provide an unbiased and competent person to lead the consensus-building piece. Assessing over time will help staff see that they are making progress. The decision of how often to assess on the *Continuous Improvement Continuums* is certainly up to the school. We recommend twice a year—about mid-fall and mid-spring—when there is time (or has been time) to implement next steps.

Using these Continuums will enable you and your school to stay motivated, to shape and maintain your shared vision, and will assist with the continuous improvement of all elements of your school. Take pictures of the resulting charts. Even if your consensus number does not increase, the dots will most probably come together over time showing shifts in whole staff thinking.

Remember that where your school is at any time is just where it is. The important thing is what you do with this information. Continuous improvement is a never-ending process which, when used effectively, will ultimately lead your school toward providing a quality program for all children.

School Continuous Improvement Continuums
INFORMATION AND ANALYSIS

	One	Two	Three	Four	Five
Approach	Data or information about student performance and needs are not gathered in any systematic way; there is no way to determine what needs to change at the school, based on data.	There is no systematic process, but some teacher and student information is collected and used to problem solve and establish student learning standards.	School collects data related to student performance (e.g., attendance, achievement) and conducts surveys on student, teacher, and parent needs. The information is used to drive the strategic quality plan for school change.	There is systematic reliance on hard data (including data for subgroups) as a basis for decision making at the classroom level as well as at the school level. Changes are based on the study of data to meet the needs of students and teachers.	Information is gathered in all areas of student interaction with the school. Teachers engage students in gathering information on their own performance. Accessible to all levels, data are comprehensive in scope and an accurate reflection of school quality.
Implementation	No information is gathered with which to make changes. Student dissatisfaction with the learning process is seen as an irritation, not a need for improvement.	Some data are tracked, such as drop-out rates and enrollment. Only a few individuals are asked for feedback about areas of schooling.	School collects information on current and former students (e.g., student achievement and perceptions), analyzes and uses it in conjunction with future trends for planning. Identified areas for improvement are tracked over time.	Data are used to improve the effectiveness of teaching strategies on all student learning. Students' historical performances are graphed and utilized for diagnostics. Student evaluations and performances are analyzed by teachers in all classrooms.	Innovative teaching processes that meet the needs of students are implemented to the delight of teachers, parents, and students. Information is analyzed and used to prevent student failure. Root causes are known through analyses. Problems are prevented through the use of data.
Outcome	Only anecdotal and hypothetical information is available about student performance, behavior, and satisfaction. Problems are solved individually with short-term results.	Little data are available. Change is limited to some areas of the school and dependent upon individual teachers and their efforts.	Information collected about student and parent needs, assessment, and instructional practices is shared with the school staff and used to plan for change. Information helps staff understand pressing issues, analyze information for "root causes," and track results for improvement.	An information system is in place. Positive trends begin to appear in many classrooms and schoolwide. There is evidence that these results are caused by understanding and effectively using data collected.	Students are delighted with the school's instructional processes and proud of their own capabilities to learn and assess their own growth. Good to excellent achievement is the result for all students. No student falls through the cracks. Teachers use data to predict and prevent potential problems.

Copyright © 1991–2004 Education for the Future Initiative, Chico, CA.

School Continuous Improvement Continuums
STUDENT ACHIEVEMENT

	One	Two	Three	Four	Five
Approach	Instructional and organizational processes critical to student success are not identified. Little distinction of student learning differences is made. Some teachers believe that not all students can achieve.	Some data are collected on student background and performance trends. Learning gaps are noted to direct improvement of instruction. It is known that student learning standards must be identified.	Student learning standards are identified, and a continuum of learning is created throughout the school. Student performance data are collected and compared to the standards in order to analyze how to improve learning for all students.	Data on student achievement are used throughout the school to pursue the improvement of student learning. Teachers collaborate to implement appropriate instruction and assessment strategies for meeting student learning standards articulated across grade levels. All teachers believe that all students can learn.	School makes an effort to exceed student achievement expectations. Innovative instructional changes are made to anticipate learning needs and improve student achievement. Teachers are able to predict characteristics impacting student achievement and to know how to perform from a small set of internal quality measures.
Implementation	All students are taught the same way. There is no communication with students about their academic needs or learning styles. There are no analyses of how to improve instruction.	Some effort is made to track and analyze student achievement trends on a school-wide basis. Teachers begin to understand the needs and learning gaps of students.	Teachers study effective instruction and assessment strategies to implement standards and to increase their students' learning. Student feedback and analysis of achievement data are used in conjunction with implementation support strategies.	There is a systematic focus on implementing student learning standards and on the improvement of student learning schoolwide. Effective instruction and assessment strategies are implemented in each classroom. Teachers support one another with peer coaching and/or action research focused on implementing strategies that lead to increased achievement and the attainment of the shared vision.	All teachers correlate critical instructional and assessment strategies with objective indicators of quality student achievement. A comparative analysis of actual individual student performance to student learning standards is utilized to adjust teaching strategies to ensure a progression of learning for all students.
Outcome	There is wide variation in student attitudes and achievement with undesirable results. There is high dissatisfaction among students with learning. Student background is used as an excuse for low student achievement.	There is some evidence that student achievement trends are available to teachers and are being used. There is much effort, but minimal observable results in improving student achievement.	There is an increase in communication between students and teachers regarding student learning. Teachers learn about effective instructional strategies that will implement the shared vision, including student learning standards, and meet the needs of their students. They make some gains.	Increased student achievement is evident schoolwide. Student morale, attendance, and behavior are good. Teachers converse often with each other about preventing student failure. Areas for further attention are clear.	Students and teachers conduct self-assessments to continuously improve performance. Improvements in student achievement are evident and clearly caused by teachers' and students' understandings of individual student learning standards, linked to appropriate and effective instructional and assessment strategies. A continuum of learning results. No students fall through the cracks.

Copyright © 1991–2004 Education for the Future Initiative, Chico, CA.

School Continuous Improvement Continuums
QUALITY PLANNING

	One	Two	Three	Four	Five
Approach	No quality plan or process exists. Data are neither used nor considered important in planning.	The staff realize the importance of a mission, vision, and one comprehensive action plan. Teams develop goals and timelines, and dollars are allocated to begin the process.	A comprehensive school plan to achieve the vision is developed. Plan includes evaluation and continuous improvement.	One focused and integrated schoolwide plan for implementing a continuous improvement process is put into action. All school efforts are focused on the implementation of this plan that represents the achievement of the vision.	A plan for the continuous improvement of the school, with a focus on students, is put into place. There is excellent articulation and integration of all elements in the school due to quality planning. Leadership team ensures all elements are implemented by all appropriate parties.
Implementation	There is no knowledge of or direction for quality planning. Budget is allocated on an as-needed basis. Many plans exist.	School community begins continuous improvement planning efforts by laying out major steps to a shared vision, by identifying values and beliefs, the purpose of the school, a mission, vision, and student learning standards.	Implementation goals, responsibilities, due dates, and timelines are spelled out. Support structures for implementing the plan are set in place.	The quality management plan is implemented through effective procedures in all areas of the school. Everyone commits to implementing the plan aligned to the vision, mission, and values and beliefs. All share responsibility for accomplishing school goals.	Schoolwide goals, mission, vision, and student learning standards are shared and articulated throughout the school and with feeder schools. The attainment of identified student learning standards is linked to planning and implementation of effective instruction that meets students' needs. Leaders at all levels are developing expertise because planning is the norm.
Outcome	There is no evidence of comprehensive planning. Staff work is carried out in isolation. A continuum of learning for students is absent.	The school community understands the benefits of working together to implement a comprehensive continuous improvement plan.	There is evidence that the school plan is being implemented in some areas of the school. Improvements are neither systematic nor integrated schoolwide.	A schoolwide plan is known to all. Results from working toward the quality improvement goals are evident throughout the school. Planning is ongoing and inclusive of all stakeholders.	Evidence of effective teaching and learning results in significant improvement of student achievement attributed to quality planning at all levels of the school organization. Teachers and administrators understand and share the school mission and vision. Quality planning is seamless and all demonstrate evidence of accountability.

Copyright © 1991–2004 Education for the Future Initiative, Chico, CA.

School Continuous Improvement Continuums
PROFESSIONAL DEVELOPMENT

	One	Two	Three	Four	Five
Approach	There is no professional development. Teachers, principals, and staff are seen as interchangeable parts that can be replaced. Professional development is external and usually equated to attending a conference alone. Hierarchy determines "haves" and "have-nots."	The "cafeteria" approach to professional development is used, whereby individual teachers choose what they want to take, without regard to an overall school plan.	The shared vision, school plan, and student needs are used to target focused professional development for all employees. Staff is inserviced on relevant instructional and leadership strategies.	Professional development and data-gathering methods are used by all teachers and are directed toward the goals of the shared vision and the continuous improvement of the school. Teachers have ongoing conversations about student achievement data. Other staff members receive training in their content areas. Systems thinking is considered in all decisions.	Leadership and staff continuously improve all aspects of the learning organization through an innovative, data-driven, and comprehensive continuous improvement process that prevents student failures. Effective job-embedded professional development is ongoing for implementing the vision for student success. Traditional teacher evaluations are replaced by collegial coaching and action research focused on student learning standards. Policies set professional development as a priority budget line-item. Professional development is planned, aligned, and lead to the achievement of student learning standards.
Implementation	Teacher, principal, and staff performance is controlled and inspected. Performance evaluations are used to detect mistakes.	Teacher professional development is sporadic and unfocused, lacking an approach for implementing new procedures and processes. Some leadership training begins to take place.	Teachers are involved in year-round quality professional development. The school community is trained in shared decision making, team building concepts, effective communication strategies, and data analysis at the classroom level.	Teachers, in teams, continuously set and implement student achievement goals. Leadership considers these goals and provides necessary support structures for collaboration. Teachers utilize effective support approaches as they implement new instruction and assessment strategies. Coaching and feedback structures are in place. Use of new knowledge and skills is evident.	Teams passionately support each other in the pursuit of quality improvement at all levels. Teachers make bold changes in instruction and assessment strategies focused on student learning standards and student learning styles. A teacher as action researcher model is implemented. Staffwide conversations focus on systemic reflection and improvement. Teachers are strong leaders.
Outcome	No professional growth and no staff or student performance improvement. There exists a high turnover rate of employees, especially administrators. Attitudes and approaches filter down to students.	The effectiveness of professional development is not known or analyzed. Teachers feel helpless about making schoolwide changes.	Teachers, working in teams, feel supported and begin to feel they can make changes. Evidence shows that shared decision making works.	A collegial school is evident. Effective classroom strategies are practiced, articulated schoolwide, are reflective of professional development aimed at ensuring student achievement, and the implementation of the shared vision, that includes student learning standards.	True systemic change and improved student achievement result because teachers are knowledgeable of and implement effective, differentiated teaching strategies for individual student learning gains. Teachers' repertoire of skills are enhanced, and students are achieving. Professional development is driving learning at all levels.

Copyright © 1991–2004 Education for the Future Initiative, Chico, CA.

School Continuous Improvement Continuums
LEADERSHIP

	One	Two	Three	Four	Five
Approach	Principal as decision maker. Decisions are reactive to state, district, and federal mandates. There is no knowledge of continuous improvement.	A shared decision-making structure is put into place and discussions begin on how to achieve a school vision. Most decisions are focused on solving problems and are reactive.	Leadership team is committed to continuous improvement. Leadership seeks inclusion of all school sectors and supports study teams by making time provisions for their work.	Leadership team represents a true shared decision-making structure. Study teams are reconstructed for the implementation of a comprehensive continuous improvement plan.	A strong continuous improvement structure is set into place that allows for input from all sectors of the school, district, and community, ensuring strong communication, flexibility, and refinement of approach and beliefs. The school vision is student focused, based on data, and appropriate for school/community values, and meeting student needs.
Implementation	Principal makes all decisions, with little or no input from teachers, the community, or students. Leadership inspects for mistakes.	School values and beliefs are identified; the purpose of school is defined; a school mission and student learning standards are developed with representative input. A structure for studying approaches to achieving student learning standards is established.	Leadership team is active on study teams and integrates recommendations from the teams' research and analyses to form a comprehensive plan for continuous improvement within the context of the school mission. Everyone is kept informed.	Decisions about budget and implementation of the vision are made within teams, by the principal, by the leadership team, and by the full staff as appropriate. All decisions are communicated to the leadership team and to the full staff.	The vision is implemented and articulated across all grade levels and into feeder schools. Quality standards are reinforced throughout the school. All members of the school community understand and apply the quality standards. Leadership team has systematic interactions and involvement with district administrators, teachers, parents, community, and students about the school's direction. Necessary resources are available to implement and measure staff learning related to student learning standards.
Outcome	Decisions lack focus and consistency. There is no evidence of staff commitment to a shared vision. Students and parents do not feel they are being heard. Decision-making process is clear and known.	The mission provides a focus for all school improvement and guides the action to the vision. The school community is committed to continuous improvement. Quality leadership techniques are used sporadically.	Leadership team is seen as committed to planning and quality improvement. Critical areas for improvement are identified. Faculty feel included in shared decision making.	There is evidence that the leadership team listens to all levels of the organization. Implementation of the continuous improvement plan is linked to student learning standards and the guiding principles of the school. Leadership capacities for implementing the vision among teachers are evident.	Site-based management and shared decision making truly exists. Teachers understand and display an intimate knowledge of how the school operates. Teachers support and communicate with each other in the implementation of quality strategies. Teachers implement the vision in their classrooms and can determine how their new approach meets student needs and leads to the attainment of student learning standards. Leaders are standards-driven at all levels.

Copyright © 1991–2004 Education for the Future Initiative, Chico, CA.

School Continuous Improvement Continuums
PARTNERSHIP DEVELOPMENT

	One	Two	Three	Four	Five
Approach	There is no system for input from parents, business, or community. Status quo is desired for managing the school.	Partnerships are sought, but mostly for money and things.	School has knowledge of why partnerships are important and seeks to include businesses and parents in a strategic fashion related to student learning standards for increased student achievement.	School seeks effective win-win business and community partnerships and parent involvement to implement the vision. Desired outcomes are clearly identified. A solid plan for partnership development exists.	Community, parent, and business partnerships become integrated across all student groupings. The benefits of outside involvement are known by all. Parent and business involvement in student learning is refined. Student learning *regularly* takes place beyond the school walls.
Implementation	Barriers are erected to close out involvement of outsiders. Outsiders are managed for least impact on status quo.	A team is assigned to get partners and to receive input from parents, the community, and business in the school.	Involvement of business, community, and parents begins to take place in some classrooms and after school hours related to the vision. Partners begin to realize how they can support each other in achieving school goals. School staff understand what partners need from the partnership.	There is a systematic utilization of parents, community, and businesses schoolwide. Areas in which the active use of these partnerships benefit student learning are clear.	Partnership development is articulated across all student groupings. Parents, community, business, and educators work together in an innovative fashion to increase student learning and to prepare students for the 21st Century. Partnerships are evaluated for continuous improvement.
Outcome	There is little or no involvement of parents, business, or community at-large. School is a closed, isolated system.	Much effort is given to establishing partnerships. Some spotty trends emerge, such as receiving donated equipment.	Some substantial gains are achieved in implementing partnerships. Some student achievement increases can be attributed to this involvement.	Gains in student satisfaction with learning and school are clearly related to partnerships. All partners benefit.	Previously non-achieving students enjoy learning with excellent achievement. Community, business, and home become common places for student learning, while school becomes a place where parents come for further education. Partnerships enhance what the school does for students.

Copyright © 1991–2004 Education for the Future Initiative, Chico, CA.

School Continuous Improvement Continuums

CONTINUOUS IMPROVEMENT AND EVALUATION

	One	Two	Three	Four	Five
Approach	Neither goals nor strategies exist for the evaluation and continuous improvement of the school organization or for elements of the school organization.	The approach to continuous improvement and evaluation is problem solving. If there are no problems, or if solutions can be made quickly, there is no need for improvement or analyses. Changes in parts of the system are not coordinated with all other parts.	Some elements of the school organization are evaluated for effectiveness. Some elements are improved on the basis of the evaluation findings.	All elements of the school's operations are evaluated for improvement and to ensure congruence of the elements with respect to the continuum of learning students experience.	All aspects of the school organization are rigorously evaluated and improved on a continuous basis. Students, and the maintenance of a comprehensive learning continuum for students, become the focus of all aspects of the school improvement process.
Implementation	With no overall plan for evaluation and continuous improvement, strategies are changed by individual teachers and administrators only when something sparks the need to improve. Reactive decisions and activities are a daily mode of operation.	Isolated changes are made in some areas of the school organization in response to problem incidents. Changes are not preceded by comprehensive analyses, such as an understanding of the root causes of problems. The effectiveness of the elements of the school organization, or changes made to the elements, is not known.	Elements of the school organization are improved on the basis of comprehensive analyses of root causes of problems, client perceptions, and operational effectiveness of processes.	Continuous improvement analyses of student achievement and instructional strategies are rigorously reinforced within each classroom and across learning levels to develop a comprehensive learning continuum for students and to prevent student failure.	Comprehensive continuous improvement becomes the way of doing business at the school. Teachers continuously improve the appropriateness and effectiveness of instructional strategies based on student feedback and performance. All aspects of the school organization are improved to support teachers' efforts.
Outcome	Individuals struggle with system failure. Finger pointing and blaming others for failure occurs. The effectiveness of strategies is not known. Mistakes are repeated.	Problems are solved only temporarily and few positive changes result. Additionally, unintended and undesirable consequences often appear in other parts of the system. Many aspects of the school are incongruent, keeping the school from reaching its vision.	Evidence of effective improvement strategies is observable. Positive changes are made and maintained due to comprehensive analyses and evaluation.	Teachers become astute at assessing and in predicting the impact of their instructional strategies on individual student achievement. Sustainable improvements in student achievement are evident at all grade levels, due to continuous improvement.	The school becomes a congruent and effective learning organization. Only instruction and assessment strategies that produce quality student achievement are used. A true continuum of learning results for all students and staff. The impact of improvements is increasingly measurable.

Copyright © 1991–2004 Education for the Future Initiative, Chico, CA.

Glossary of Terms

The Glossary provides brief definitions of data analysis and testing terms used throughout *Using Data to Improve Student Learning in Middle Schools*.

▼ **Achievement**

The demonstration of student performance measured against learning goals, learning objectives, or standards.

▼ **Achievement Gap**

The difference between how well low-income and minority children perform on standardized tests, as compared with their peers. For many years, low-income and minority children have been falling behind their white peers in terms of academic achievement.

▼ **Accountability**

The act of being responsible to somebody else or to others. It also means capable of being explained.

▼ **Action**

Specific steps, tasks, or activity used to implement a strategy.

▼ **Action Plan**

The part of continuous school improvement planning that describes the tasks that must be performed, when they will be performed, who is responsible, and how much they will cost to implement.

▼ **Action Research**

Teachers and/or administrators raise questions about the best way to improve teaching and learning, systematically study the literature to answer the questions, implement the best approach(es), and analyze the results.

▼ **Adequate Yearly Progress (AYP)**

An individual state's measure of yearly progress toward achieving state academic standards. *Adequate Yearly Progress* is the minimum level of improvement that states, school districts, and schools must achieve each year to fulfill the requirement of the *No Child Left Behind Act*.

▼ **Affinity Diagram**

A visual picture or chart of reflective thinking. The result is that more participants are likely to deal with problems that emerge.

▼ **Aggregate**

Combining the results of all groups that make up the sample or population.

▼ **Alignment**

An arrangement of groups or forces in relation to one another. In continuous school improvement planning, we align all parts of the system to the vision. With curriculum, we align instruction and materials to student learning standards.

▼ **Analysis**

The examination of facts and data to provide a basis for effective decisions.

▼ **Analysis of Variance (ANOVA)**

ANOVA is an inferential procedure to determine if there is a significant difference among sample means.

▼ **Anticipated Achievement Scores**

An estimate of the average score for students of similar ages, grade levels, and academic aptitude. It is an estimate of what we would expect an individual student to score on an achievement test.

▼ **Articulation**

The varied process of integrating the district/school aligned curriculum across disciplines and between grade levels and connecting it to real-life situations; also presenting it to all stakeholders and implementing it district/school wide.

▼ **Assessment**

Gathering and interpretation of student performance, primarily for the purpose of enhancing learning. Also used for the improvement of a program and/or strategies.

▼ **Authentic Assessment**

Refers to a variety of ways to assess a student's demonstration of knowledge and skills. Authentic assessments may include performances, projects, exhibitions, and portfolios.

▼ **Bar Graph**

A pictorial representation that uses bars to display data, usually frequencies, percentages, and averages.

▼ **Baseline Data**

Information collected to comprise a reference set for comparison of a second set of data collected at a later time; used to interpret changes over time, usually after some condition has been changed for research purposes that sets the standard for any research that follows in the same project.

▼ **Benchmark**

A standard against which something can be measured or assessed.

▼ **Brainstorming**

The act of listing ideas without judgment. Brainstorming generates creative ideas spontaneously.

▼ **Cadres or Action Teams**

Groups or teams of educators who agree to accept responsibility to study new approaches, plan for the implementation of new strategies or programs, and get work done without every staff member's involvement.

▼ **Case Studies**

Reviewing student's work, and/or another teacher's example lessons, which can lead to quality discussions and improved practices.

▼ **Cause and Effect**

The relationship and complexities between a problem or effect and the possible causes.

▼ **Coaching**

Teachers form teams of two or three to observe each other, plan together, and talk and encourage each other in meaningful ways while reflecting on continuously improving instructional practices.

▼ **Cognitive Abilities or Skills Index**

An age-dependent, normalized standard score based on a student's performance on a cognitive skills test with a mean of 100 and standard deviation of 16. The score indicates a student's overall cognitive ability or academic aptitude relative to students of similar age, without regard to grade level.

▼ **Cohort**

A group of individuals sharing a particular statistical or demographic characteristic, such as the year they were in a specific school grade level. Following cohorts over time helps teachers understand the effects particular circumstances may have on results. Matched cohort studies follow the same individuals over time, and unmatched cohort studies follow the same group over time.

▼ **Cohort Analysis**

The reorganization of grade level data to look at the groups of students progressing through the grades together over time.

▼ **Collaboration**

Evidence of two of more concerned groups (i.e., teachers, aides, itinerant and resource teachers, parents, community representatives, etc.), working together to improve the school program.

▼ **Collaborative**

Working jointly with others, especially in an intellectual endeavor.

▼ **Comprehensive Action Plan**

Defining the specific actions needed to implement the vision, setting forth when the actions will take place, designating who is responsible for accomplishing the action, how much it will cost, and where to get the funds.

▼ **Confidence Interval**

Used in inferential statistics, a range of values that a researcher can estimate, with a certain level of confidence, where the population parameter is located.

▼ **Congruent**

Corresponding to, or consistent with, each other or something else.

▼ **Consensus**

Decision making where a group finds a proposal acceptable enough that all members can support it; no member actively opposes it.

▼ **Content Standard**

Description of the knowledge or skills that educators want students to learn.

▼ **Continuous**

In the context of continuous school improvement, continuous means the ongoing review of the data, the implementation of the plan, and the progress being made.

▼ **Continuous Improvement**

Keeping the process of planning, implementing, evaluating, and improving alive over time.

▼ **Continuous Improvement and Evaluation**

The section of the school portfolio that assists schools to further understand where they are and what they need to do to move forward in the big picture of continuous school improvement.

▼ Continuous Improvement Continuums (CICs)

As developed by *Education for the Future Initiative,* CICs are seven rubrics that represent the theoretical flow of systemic school improvement. The *Continuous Improvement Continuums* take the theory and spirit of continuous school improvement, interweave educational research, and offer practical meaning to the components that must change simultaneously and systematically.

▼ Continuous School Improvement

By *continuous school improvement,* we mean measuring and evaluating processes on an ongoing basis to identify and implement improvement.

▼ Continuous School Improvement Plan

A plan for improvement, based on data, that will help create and manage change. The process of answering the following questions: *Who are we? How do we do business? What are our strengths and areas for improvement? Why do we exist? Where do we want to be? What are the gaps? What are the root causes of the gaps? How can we get to where we want to be? How will we implement? How will we evaluate our efforts?*

▼ Control Groups

Control groups serve as a baseline in making comparisons with treatment groups and are necessary when general effectiveness of the treatment is unknown. During an experiment, the control group is studied the same as the experimental groups, except that it does not receive the treatment of interest.

▼ Convenience Sampling

Convenience sampling is done when one wants to survey people who are ready and available, and not hassle with trying to get everyone in the population ready and willing to complete the questionnaire.

▼ Correlation

A statistical analysis that helps one see the relationship of scores in one distribution to scores in another distribution. Correlation coefficients have a range of −1.0 to +1.0. A correlation of around zero indicates no relationship. Correlations of .8 and higher indicate strong relationships.

▼ Criteria

Characteristics or dimensions of student performance.

▼ Criterion-referenced Tests

Tests that judge how well a test taker does on an explicit objective, learning goal, or criteria relative to a pre-determined performance level. There is no comparison to any other test takers.

▼ Culture

Attitudes, values, beliefs, goals, norms of behavior, and practices that characterize a group.

▼ Curriculum Alignment

A curriculum in which what is taught, how it is taught, and how it is assessed is intentionally based on, but not limited to, the state *Core Curriculum Content Standards and Assessment*—the sequence of learning in an aligned curriculum is articulated and constantly discussed, monitored, and revised.

▼ **Curriculum Development and Implementation**

The way content is designed and delivered. Teachers must think deeply about the content, student-learning standards, and how it must be managed and delivered, or put into practice.

▼ **Curriculum Implementation**

Putting the curriculum into practice.

▼ **Curriculum Mapping and Webbing**

Approaches that require teachers to align the curriculum and student learning standards by grade levels, and then across grade levels, to ensure a continuum of learning that makes sense for all students.

▼ **Data Cleansing**

The process of ensuring that all values in a database are consistent and correctly recorded.

▼ **Data-driven Decision Making**

Making decisions based on demographic, student learning, perceptions, and school process data. True data-driven decision making has the guiding principles of the learning organization at the center of every decision.

▼ **Data Mining**

Techniques for finding patterns and trends in large data sets. The process of automatically extracting valid, useful, previously unknown, and ultimately comprehensible information from large databases. Just doing common data analysis is not data mining.

▼ **Data Table**

The source of data for tables and graphs. In building graphs with a software program, one would need to create a data table from which to create the graphs or tables.

▼ **Data Warehouse**

A single, large database that has collected relevant information from several other sources into a single, accessible format designed to be used for decision making. The data warehouse is created to house data imported from many other data sources that are not designed to work together or to share information.

▼ **Database**

A storage mechanism for data that eliminates redundancy and conflict among multiple data files. Data is entered once and is then available to all programs that need it.

▼ **Deciles**

The values of a variable that divide the frequency distribution into ten equal frequency groups. The ninth decile shows the number (or percentage) of the norming group that scored between 80 and 89 NCE, for example.

▼ **Demographics**

Statistical characteristics of a population, such as average age, number of students in a school, percentages of ethnicities, etc. Disaggregation with demographic data allows us to isolate variations among different subgroups.

▼ **Derived Score**

A score that is attained by performing some kind of mathematical operation on a raw score for comparison within a particular grade (e.g., T-scores, NCE, etc.).

▼ Descriptive Statistics

Direct measurement (i.e. mean, median, percent correct) of each member of a group or population. Descriptive statistics can include graphing.

▼ Diagnostic

Assessment/evaluation carried out prior to instruction that is designed to determine a student's attitude, skill, or knowledge in order to identify specific student needs.

▼ Diagnostic Tests

Usually standardized and normed, diagnostic tests are given before instruction begins to help the instructor(s) understand student learning needs. Many different score types are used with diagnostic tests.

▼ Different Ways of Knowing (DWOK)

A standards-based, interdisciplinary, arts-infused curriculum that promotes collaborative learning and higher–order thinking.

▼ Disaggregate

Separating the results of different groups that make up the sample or population.

▼ Disaggregated Data

To *disaggregate* means separating the results of different groups or separating a whole into its parts. In education, this term means that test results are sorted into groups of students by gender, those who are economically disadvantaged, by racial and ethnic minority groups, disabilities, or by English fluency. This practice allows administrators and teachers to see more than just the average score for the school. Instead, administrators and teachers can see how each student group is performing.

▼ Diverse/Diversity

The inclusion of differences based on gender, race, disability, age, national origin, color, economic status, religion, geographic regions, and other characteristics. Achieving diversity requires respect of differences; valuing differences; supporting, encouraging, and promoting differences; and affirmation initiatives, such as recruitment, placement, and retention.

▼ Educationally Significant

Gains in student achievement, school, or program results can be considered educationally significant, even though they are not statistically significant.

▼ Evaluation

Making judgments about the quality of overall student performance for the purpose of communicating student achievement. Evaluation also is the study of the impact of a program or process.

▼ Examining Student Data

Conversations around individual student data results and the processes that created the results. This approach can be a significant form of professional development when skilled team members facilitate the discussions.

▼ Examining Student Work

Ensures that what students learn is aligned to the learning standards. It also shows teachers the impact of their actions.

▼ **Exemplars**

Models or examples of excellent work that meet stated criteria or levels of performance.

▼ **Experimental Design**

The detailed planning of an experiment, made beforehand, to insure the data collected is appropriate and obtained in a way that will lead to an objective analysis, with valid inferences. Preferably, the design will maximize the amount of information that can be gained, given the amount of effort expended.

▼ **Fluency**

The capacity to read text accurately and quickly.

▼ **Flow Chart**

A flowchart illustrates the steps in a process. By visualizing the process, a flow chart can quickly help identify bottlenecks or inefficiencies where a process can be streamlined or improved.

▼ **Focus Group**

A group convened to gather information about processes or practices that need to be examined.

▼ **Formative**

Assessments at regular intervals of a student's progress, with accompanying feedback in order to help the student's performance and to provide direction for improvement of a program for individual students or for a whole class.

▼ **Frequency**

The number of times a given score occurs in a distribution.

▼ **Frequency Distribution**

Describes how often observations fall within designated categories. It can be expressed as numbers, percents, and deciles, to name just a few possibilities.

▼ **Gain Score**

The difference between two administrations of the same test. Gain scores are calculated by subtracting the previous score from the most recent score. One can have negative gains, which are actually losses.

▼ **Gaps**

The difference between where the school is now and where the school wants to be in the future. It is this gap that gets translated into goals, objectives, strategies, and actions in the action plan.

▼ **Goals**

Achievements or end results. Goal statements describe the intended outcome of the vision and are stated in terms that are broad, general, abstract, and non-measurable. Schools should have only two or three goals.

▼ **Grade-level Analysis**

Looking at the same grade level over time.

▼ **Grade-level Equivalent**

The grade and month of the school year for which a given score is the actual or estimated average. Based on a 10-month school year, scores would be noted as 6.1 for grade six, first month, 8.10 for grade eight, tenth month, etc.

▼ **Grades**
   Subjective scores given by teachers to students for performance.

▼ **Guiding Principles**
   The vision of the school, or district, that is based on the purpose and mission of the organization, created from the values and beliefs of the individuals to make up the organization. Everything that is done in the organization ought to be aligned to its guiding principles.

▼ **Holistic**
   Emphasizing the organic or functional relation between parts and the whole.

▼ **Horizontal Articulation or Coordination**
   Indicates that the curriculum is carefully planned within grade levels. In effect, this would mean that every primary grade throughout the school/district will teach the same curriculum—also every grade six social studies class; every grade ten health class; every grade twelve physics class, and so on.

▼ **Inferential Statistics**
   Statistical analysis concerned with the measurement of only a sample from a population and then making estimates, or inferences, about the population from which the sample was taken; inferential statistics help generalize the results of data analyses.

▼ **Information and Analysis**
   Establishes systematic and rigorous reliance on data for decision making in all parts of the organization. This section of the school portfolio sets the context of the learning organization.

▼ **Intersections**
   Analyzing the intersections or overlapping of measures (demographics, perceptions, school processes, student learning) enables schools to predict what they must do to meet the needs of all the students they have, or will have in the future.

▼ **Interval Scale**
   Intervals are meaningful with a relative zero point. Can calculate mode, median, mean, range, standard deviation, etc.

▼ **Item Analysis**
   Reviewing each item on a test or assessment to determine how many students missed the particular item. A general term for procedures designed to access the usefulness of a test item.

▼ **Latent Trait Scale**
   A scaled score obtained through one of several mathematical approaches collectively known as Latent-trait procedures or Item Response Theory. The particular numerical values used in the scale are arbitrary, but higher scores indicate more knowledgeable test takers or more difficult items.

▼ **Leadership**
   Providing needed assistance to schools to think through and plan for their vision, shared decision making, and other structures that will work with their specific population.

▼ **Learner-Centered**
   An environment created by educators focusing on the needs and learning styles of all students.

Learning
   A process of acquiring knowledge, skills, understanding, and/or new behaviors.

▼ **Learning Environment**

Any setting or location, inside or outside the school, used to enhance the instruction of students.

▼ **Learning Goal**

A target for learning: a desired skill, knowledge, or behavior.

▼ **Line Graph**

Line graphs give a lot of flexibility and are exceptionally good for showing a series of numbers over time. Line graphs can display complex data more effectively than bar graphs.

▼ **Matched Cohorts**

Looking at the same students (individual, not groups) progressing through the grades over time.

▼ **Maximum**

The highest actual score or the highest possible score on a test.

▼ **Mean**

Average score in a set of scores; calculated by summing all the scores and dividing by the total number of scores.

▼ **Means**

Methods, strategies, actions, and processes by which a school plans to improve student achievement.

▼ **Measures**

A way of evaluating something; how we know we have achieved the objective.

▼ **Median**

The score that splits a distribution in half: 50 percent of the scores lie above and 50 percent of the scores lie below the median. If the number of scores is odd, the median is the middle score. If the number of scores is even, one must add the two middle scores and divide by two to calculate the median.

▼ **Minimum**

The lowest score or the lowest possible score on a test.

▼ **Mission**

A brief, clear, and compelling statement that serves to unify an organization's efforts. A mission has a finish line for its achievement and is proactive. A mission should walk the boundary between the possible and impossible.

▼ **Mobility**

The reference to the movement of students in and out of a school or district.

▼ **Mode**

The score that occurs most frequently in a scoring distribution.

▼ **Multiple Measures**

Using more than one method of assessment, gathered from varying points of view, in order to understand the multifaceted world of school from the perspective of everyone involved.

▼ **N**

The number of students in the group being described, such as the number taking a test or completing a questionnaire.

▼ Needs Assessment

Questions that help staff understand their professional development needs. At the same time, if done well, this assessment can lead to quality staff conversations and sharing of knowledge.

▼ No Child Left Behind (NCLB)

The No Child Left Behind Act of 2001 reauthorized the 1965 Elementary and Secondary Education Act. NCLB calls for increased accountability for states, school districts, and schools; choices for parents and students; greater flexibility for states, school districts, and schools regarding Federal education funds; establishing a Reading First initiative to ensure every child can read by end of grade three; and improving the quality of teachers.

▼ Nominal Scale

Qualitative, categorical information. Numbers represent categories, e.g., 1=male, 2=female.

▼ Normal Curve

The bell-shaped curve of the normal distribution.

▼ Normal Curve Equivalent (NCE)

Equivalent scores are standard scores with a mean of 50, a standard deviation of 21.06, and a range of 1 to 99.

▼ Normal Distribution

A distribution of scores or other measures that in graphic form has a distinctive bell-shaped appearance. In a normal distribution, the measures are distributed symmetrically about the mean. Cases are concentrated near the mean and decrease in frequency, according to a precise mathematical equation, the farther one departs from the mean. Also known as a normal curve.

▼ Normalized Standard Score

A transformation procedure used to make scores from different tests more directly comparable. Not only are the mean and the standard deviation of the raw score distribution changed, as with a linear standard score transformation, but the shape of the distribution is converted to a normal curve. The transformation to a normalized z-score involves two steps: 1) compute the exact percentile rank of the raw score; and 2) determine the corresponding z-score for that exact percentile rank from a table of areas under the normal curve.

▼ Norming Group

A representative group of students whose results on a norm-referenced test help create the scoring scales with which others compare their performance. The norming group's results are professed to look like the normal curve.

▼ Norm-referenced Test

Any test in which the score acquires additional meaning by comparing it to the scores of people in an identified norming group. A test can be both norm- and criterion-referenced. Most standardized achievement tests are referred to as norm-referenced.

▼ Norms

The distribution of test scores and their corresponding percentile ranks, standard scores, or other derived scores of some specified group called the norming group. For example, this may be a national sample of all fourth graders, a national sample of all fourth-grade males, or perhaps all fourth graders in some local district.

▼ **Norms versus Standards**

Norms are not standards. Norms are indicators of what students of similar characteristics did when confronted with the same test items as those taken by students in the norming group. Standards, on the other hand, are arbitrary judgments of what students should be able to do, given a set of test items.

▼ **Objectives**

Goals that are redrafted in terms that are clearly tangible. Objective statements are narrow, specific, concrete, and measurable. When writing objectives, it is important to describe the intended results, rather than the process or means to accomplish them, and state the time frame.

▼ **Observation**

Teacher and observer agree on what is being observed, the type of information to be recorded, when the observation will take place, and how the information will be analyzed. The observee is someone implementing strategies and actions that others want to know. Observer might be a colleague, a supervisor, or a visitor from another location.

▼ **Open-ended Response Items**

Questions that require students to combine content knowledge and application of process skills in order to communicate an answer.

▼ **Ordinal**

Ordinal provides information about size or direction; numbers ordered along underlying dimension, but no information about distance between points.

▼ **Outcome**

Successful demonstration of learning that occurs at the culmination point of a set learning experiences.

▼ **Over Time**

No less than three years.

▼ **Parameter**

A parameter is a population measurement that characterizes one of its features. An example of a parameter is the mode. The mode is the value in the population that occurs most frequently. Other examples of parameters are a population's mean (or average) and its variance.

▼ **Partnerships**

Teachers developing relationships with parents, businesses in the community, scientists, and/or university personnel to help students achieve student learning standards, and to bring about real world applications for student learning and deeper understandings of content.

▼ **Pearson Correlation Coefficient**

The most widely-used correlation coefficient determines the extent to which two variables are proportional to each other; measures the strength and direction of a linear relationship between the x and y variables.

▼ **Percent Correct**

A calculated score implying the percentage of students meeting and exceeding some number, usually a cut score, or a standard. Percent passing equals the number passing the test divided by the number taking the test.

▼ **Percent Proficient**

Percent Proficient, Percent Mastery, or Percent Passing are terms that represent the percentage of students who pass a particular test at a level above a cut score, as defined by the test creators or the test interpreters.

▼ **Percentile**

A point on the normal distribution below which a certain percentage of the scores fall. For example, if 70 percent of the scores fall below a raw score of 56, then the score of 56 is at the 70th percentile. The term *local percentile* indicates that the norm group is obtained locally. The term *national percentile* indicates that the norm group represents a national group.

▼ **Percentile Rank (PR)**

Percentage of students in a norm group (e.g., national or local) whose scores fall below a given score. Range is from 1 to 99. A 50th percentile ranking would mean that 50 percent of the scores in the norming group fall below a specific score.

▼ **Perceptions Data**

Information that reflects opinions and views of questionnaire respondents.

▼ **Performance Assessment**

Refers to assessments that measure skills, knowledge, and ability directly—such as through performance. In other words, if you want students to learn to write, you assess their ability on a writing activity.

▼ **Performance Standard**

Identification of the desired level of proficiency at which educators want a content standard to be mastered.

▼ **Pie Chart or Pie Graph**

A graph in a circular format, used to display percentages of something, such as the percentage of a school or district population, by ethnicity.

▼ **Population**

Statisticians define a population as the entire collection of items that is the focus of concern. Descriptive Statistics describe the characteristics of a given population by measuring each of its items and then summarizing the set of measures in various ways. Inferential Statistics make educated inferences about the characteristics of a population by drawing a random sample and appropriately analyzing the information it provides.

▼ **Press Release**

Article written by school public information official or an education reporter for a local newspaper.

▼ **Process Mapping**

School processes are instruction, curriculum, and assessment strategies used to ensure the learning of all students. Mapping or flow charting school processes can help staff objectively look at how students are being taught.

▼ **Processes**

Measures that describe what is being done to get results, such as programs, strategies, and practices.

▼ **Professional Development**

Planned activities that help staff members, teachers, and administrators change the manner in which they work, i.e., how they make decisions; gather, analyze, and use data; plan, teach, and monitor achievement; evaluate personnel; and assess the impact of new approaches to instruction and assessment on students.

▼ **Program Evaluation**

The examination of a program to understand its quality and impact.

▼ **Purpose**

The aim of the organization; the reason for existence.

▼ **Quality Planning**

Developing the elements of a strategic plan including a vision, mission, goals, action plan, outcome measures, and strategies for continuous improvement and evaluation. Quality planning is a section of the school portfolio.

▼ **Quality**

A standard for excellence.

▼ **Quartiles**

Three quartiles—Q1, Q2, Q3—divide a distribution into four equal groups (Q1=25th percentile; Q2=50th percentile; Q3=75th percentile).

▼ **Query**

A request one makes to a database that is returned to the desktop. Understanding and knowing how to set up queries or to ask questions of the database is very important to the information discovery process.

▼ **Quota Sampling**

Divides the population being studied into subgroups such as male and female, or young, middle, and old, to ensure that you set a quota of responses.

▼ **Range**

A measure of the spread between the lowest and the highest scores in a distribution, calculated by subtracting the lowest score from the highest score.

▼ **Ratio**

A proportional relationship between two different numbers or quantities.

▼ **Raw Scores**

A person's observed score on a test or subtest. The number of questions answered correctly on a test or subtest. A raw score is simply calculated by adding the number of questions answered correctly.

▼ **Regression**

An analysis that results in an equation that describes the nature of the relationship among variables. Simple regressions predict an object's value on a criterion variable when given its value on one predictor variable. Multiple regressions predict an object's value on a criterion variable when given its value on each of several predictor variables.

▼ **Relational Database**

A type of database that allows the connection of several databases to each other. The data and relations between them are stored in table form. Relational databases are powerful because they require few assumptions about how data are related and how they will be extracted from the database.

▼ **Relationships**

Looking at two or more sets of analyses to understand how they are associated or what they mean to each other.

▼ **Reliability**

The consistency with which an assessment measures what it intends to measure.

▼ **Research**

The act of methodically collecting information about a particular subject to discover facts or to develop a plan of action based on the facts discovered.

▼ **RIT Scale Scores**

Named for George Rasch, who developed the theory of this type of measurement, RIT scores are scaled scores that come from a series of tests created by the Northwest Evaluation Association (NWEA). The tests that draw from an item bank are created to align with local curriculum and state standards.

▼ **Root Cause**

As used in the continuous school improvement plan, root cause refers to the deep underlying reason for a specific situation. While a symptom may be made evident from a needs assessment or gap analysis—the symptom (low student scores) is not the cause. To find a root cause or causes one often has to ask Why? at least five levels down to uncover the root reasons for the symptom.

▼ **Rubric**

A scoring tool that rates performance according to clearly stated levels of criteria. The scales can be numeric or descriptive.

▼ **Sample**

In statistical terms, a random sample is a set of items that have been drawn from a population in such a way that each time an item is selected, every item in the population has an equal opportunity to appear in the sample. In practical terms, it is not so easy to draw a random sample.

▼ **Scaled Scores**

A mathematical transformation of a raw score. It takes the differences in the difficulty of test forms into consideration and is useful for teaching changes over time.

▼ **School Improvement Planning**

Planning to implement the vision requires studying the research, determining strategies that will work with the students, and determining what the vision would look like, sound like, and feel like when the vision is implemented, and how to get all staff members implementing the vision.

▼ **School Portfolio**

A professional development tool that gathers evidence about the way work is done in the school and a self-assessment tool to ensure the alignment of all parts of the learning organization to the vision. A school portfolio can also serve as a principal portfolio.

▼ School Processes

Instruction, curriculum, and assessment strategies used to ensure the learning of all students.

▼ School Profile

A two to four page summary that presents a picture of a school. Usually includes demographic and achievement information, as well as analysis of other available data.

▼ Scientifically-based Research

The revised *Elementary and Secondary Education Act,* recently approved by Congress and also known as the *No Child Left Behind Act of 2001,* mandates that educators base school programs and teaching practices on Scientifically Based Research. This includes everything from teaching approaches to drug abuse prevention. Scientifically Based Research means research that involves the application of rigorous, systematic, and objective procedures to obtain reliable and valid knowledge relevant to education activities and programs.

▼ Self-assessment

Assessment by the individual performing the activity.

▼ Shared Decision Making

A process whereby all stakeholders within a school are engaged and meaningfully involved in the planning and decision-making process of that school.

▼ Simple Sample

A smaller version of the larger population that can be considered representative of the population. One classroom of students can be a simple sample, or one school in the district. This is typically used when administering a very large questionnaire.

▼ Skewed Distribution

Most of the scores are found near one end of the distribution. When most of the scores are grouped at the lower end, it is positively skewed. When most of the scores are grouped at the upper end, it is negatively skewed.

▼ Snowball Sampling

Relies on members of one group completing the questionnaire to identify other members of the population to complete the questionnaire.

▼ Socioeconomic Status (SES)

An indication of the level of poverty in which a student lives. Most school districts use whether or not a student qualifies for free/reduced lunch as an indicator. Other school districts use more complex equations that include mother's level of education and the like.

▼ Standard

A guideline or description that is used as a basis for judgment—exemplary performance; an objective ideal; a worthy and tangible goal.

▼ Standard Deviation

Measure of variability in a set of scores. The standard deviation is the square root of the variance. Unlike the variance, the standard deviation is stated in the original units of the variable. Approximately 68 percent of the scores in a normal distribution lie between plus one and minus one standard deviation. The more scores cluster around the mean, the smaller the variance.

▼ Standard Scores

A group of scores having a desired mean and standard deviation. A z-score is a basic standard score. Other standard scores are computed by first converting a raw score to a z-score (sometimes normalized), multiplying the transformation by the desired standard deviation, and then adding the desired mean to the product. The raw scores are transformed this way for reasons of convenience, comparability, and ease of interpretation.

▼ Standardized Tests

Tests that are uniform in content, administration, and scoring. Standardized tests can be used for comparing results across classrooms, schools, school districts, and states.

▼ Standards

Consistent expectations of all learners.

▼ Standards-based Assessments

A collection of items that indicate how much students know and/or are able to do with respect to specific standards.

▼ Stanines

A nine-point normalized standard score scale. It divides the normal curve distribution of scores into nine equal points: 1 to 9. The mean of a stanine distribution is 5, and the standard deviation is approximately 2.

▼ Statistically Significant

Statistical significance of a result is the probability that the observed relationship in a sample occurred by pure chance; indicates that there is at least a 95% probability of the result that did not happen by chance.

▼ Strategies

Procedures, methods, or techniques to accomplish an objective.

▼ Stratified Random Sample

One which divides the population into subgroups, and then a random sample is selected from each of the groups. This approach would be used when you want to make sure that you hear from all the groups of people you want to study.

▼ Student Achievement Data

Information that reflects a level of knowledge, skill, or accomplishment, usually in something that has been explicitly taught.

▼ Study Groups

Teams or groups of educators meet to learn new strategies or programs, to review new publications, or to review student work together.

▼ Summative

Assessment or evaluation designed to provide information; used in making judgments about a student's achievement at the end of a period of instruction.

▼ Symptom

A symptom is the outward (most visible) indicator of a deeper root cause.

▼ System

A system is the sum of the interactions between and among its component parts. School districts are systems.

▼ **Systemic**

Affecting or relating to a system as a whole.

▼ **Systematic**

Refers to approaches that are repeatable and that use data and information so that improvement and learning are possible.

▼ **Systems Perspective**

Viewing the school or school district as a whole or perceiving the combination of related structures/components of the school and community (i.e., indicators and standards for school improvement), organized into a complex whole.

▼ **Systems Thinking**

Systems thinking would have continuous improvement teams focusing on improving how the parts of the system interact and support one another towards achievement of common goals.

▼ **T-Chart**

Used to compare and contrast information or to show relationships. It is used to help people see the opposite dimension of an issue.

▼ **T-Scores**

A calculated standard score with a mean of 50 and a standard deviation of 10. T-scores are obtained by the following formula: $T=10z+50$. T-scores are sometimes normalized.

▼ **Table**

A data structure comprised of rows and columns, like a spreadsheet.

▼ **Teacher Portfolios**

The process and product of documenting a teacher as learner; includes reflections, observations, and evidence. Portfolios can be used for many things, such as, self-assessment, employment, supervision to replace traditional teacher evaluation, and for peer collaboration.

▼ **Tests of Significance**

Procedures that use samples to test claims about population parameters. Significance tests can estimate a population parameter, with a certain amount of confidence, from a sample.

▼ **Trends**

Direction that is given from a learning organization's data. Usually need three years of data to see a trend.

▼ **Triangulation**

The term used for combining three or more student achievement measures to get a more complete picture of student achievement.

▼ **Validity**

The degree to which an assessment strategy measures what it is intended to measure.

▼ **Values and Beliefs**

The core of who we are, what we do, and how we think and feel. Values and beliefs reflect what is important to us; they describe what we think about work and how we think it should operate. Core values and beliefs are the first step in reaching a shared vision.

▼ **Variance**

A measure of the dispersion, or variability, of scores about their mean. The population variance is calculated by taking the average of the squared deviations from the mean—a deviation being defined as an individual score minus the mean.

▼ **Variation**

All systems and processes vary. It is essential to understand what type of variation is present before trying to correct or improve the system. Two types of variation are *common cause* and *special cause*. Special cause variation must be eliminated before a system can be improved.

▼ **Vertical Articulation or Alignment**

Indicates that the curriculum is carefully planned and sequenced from beginning learning and skills to more advanced learning and skills. Vertical articulation speaks to what is taught from pre-school through upper grades and is sometimes noted simply as "K-12 Curriculum."

▼ **Vision**

A specific description of what the learning organization will be like when the mission is achieved. A vision is a mental image. It must be written in practical, concrete terms that everyone can understand and see in the same way.

▼ **z-Scores**

A standard score with a mean of zero and a standard deviation of one. A z-score is obtained by the following formula: z = raw score (x) minus the mean, divided by the standard deviation (sd). A z-score is sometimes normalized.

References and Resources

The references used in this book, along with other resources that will assist busy school administrators and teachers in conducting quality data analyses, appear below.

Airasian, P. W. (1994). *Classroom assessment.* New York, NY: McGraw-Hill, Inc.

Ammerman, M. (1998). *The root cause analysis handbook: A simplified approach to identifying, correcting, and reporting workplace errors.* New York, NY: Quality Resources.

Ardovino, J., Hollingsworth, J., & Ybarra, S. (2000). *Multiple measures: Accurate ways to assess student achievement.* Thousand Oaks, CA: Corwin Press, Inc.

Armstrong, J. (2002). *What is an accountability model?* Denver, CO: Education Commission of the States. Available: http://www.ecs.org.

Armstrong, J., & Anthes, K. (2001). How data can help: Putting information to work to raise student achievement. In *American School Board Journal,* 38-41.

Arter, J. (1999). *Teaching about performance assessment.* Portland, OR: Northwest Regional Educational Laboratory.

Arter, J., & The Classroom Assessment Team, Laboratory Network Program. (1998). *Improving classroom assessment: A toolkit for professional developers: Alternative Assessment.* Aurora, CO: MCREL.

Arter, J., & Busick, K. (2001). *Practice with student-involved classroom assessment.* Portland, OR: Assessment Training Institute, Inc.

Arter, J., & McTighe, J. (2001). *Scoring rubrics in the classroom: Using performance criteria for assessing and improving student performance.* In Guskey, T.R., & Marzano, R.J. (Series Eds.). *Experts in Assessment.* Thousand Oaks, CA: Corwin Press, Inc.

Aschbacher, P. R., & Herman, J. L. (1991). *Guidelines for effective score reporting.* (CSE Technical Report No. 326). Los Angeles, CA: University of California, Center for Research on Evaluation, Standards and Student Testing (CRESST).

Baldrige National Quality Program. (2004). *Education criteria for performance excellence.* Gaithersburg, MD: National Institute of Standards and Technology. Available: www.quality.nist.gov

Barth, P., Haycock, K., Jackson, H., Mora, K., Ruiz, P., Robinson, S., & Wilkins, A. (Eds.). (1999). *Dispelling the myth: High poverty schools exceeding expectations.* Washington, DC: Education Trust in Cooperation with the Council of Chief State School Officers and partially funded by the U.S. Department of Education.

Bernhardt, V. L. (2004). *Data analysis for continuous school improvement* (2nd ed.). Larchmont, NY: Eye on Education, Inc.

Bernhardt, V. L. (1999). *The school portfolio: A comprehensive framework for school improvement* (2nd ed.). Larchmont, NY: Eye on Education, Inc.

Bernhardt, V.L. (1999, June). *Databases can help teachers with standards implementation.* Monograph No. 5. California Association for Supervision and Curriculum Development (CASCD).

Bernhardt, V. L. (2000). *Designing and using databases for school improvement.* Larchmont, NY: Eye on Education, Inc.

Bernhardt, V. L. (2000). Intersections: New routes open when one type of data crosses another. *Journal of Staff Development,* 21(1), 33-36.

Bernhardt, V. L. (2002). *The school portfolio toolkit: A planning, implementation, and evaluation guide for continuous school improvement.* Larchmont, NY: Eye on Education, Inc.

Bernhardt, V. L. (2003). *Using Data to Improve Student Learning in Elementary Schools.* Larchmont, NY: Eye on Education, Inc.

Bernhardt, V. L. (2003). No Schools Left Behind. *Educational Leadership,* 60(5), 26-30.

Bernhardt, V. L., von Blanckensee, L., Lauck, M., Rebello, F., Bonilla, G., & Tribbey, M. (2000). *The example school portfolio, A companion to the school portfolio: A comprehensive framework for school improvement.* Larchmont, NY: Eye on Education, Inc.

Blythe, T., & Associates. (1998). *The teaching for understanding guide.* San Francisco, CA: Jossey-Bass, Inc.

Bobko, P. (2001). *Correlation and regression: Applications for industrial/organizational psychology and management.* (2nd ed.). Thousand Oaks, CA: Sage Publications, Inc.

Carr, N. (2001). Making data count: Transforming schooling through data-driven decision making. *American School Board Journal,* 34-37.

Cawelti, G. (Ed.). (1999). *Handbook of research on improving student achievement* (2nd ed.). Arlington, VA: Educational Testing Service.

Chenoweth, T., & Everhart, R.B. (1993). *The restructured school: How do you know if something is happening* (Report No. ISSN-0032-0684). East Lansing, MI: National Center for Research on Teacher Learning. (ERIC Document Reproduction Service No. EJ462413)

Clarke, D. (1997). *Constructive assessment in mathematics: Practical steps for classroom teachers.* Berkeley, CA: Key Curriculum Press.

Clune, B., & Webb, N. (2001-02). WCER Highlights. Madison, WS: University of Wisconsin-Madison, Wisconsin Center for Education Research.

Commission on Instructionally Supportive Assessment. (2001). *Building tests to support instruction and accountability.* Available: http://www.aasa.org.

Conzemius, A., & O'Neill, J. (2001). *Building shared responsibility for student learning.* Alexandria, VA: Association for Supervision and Curriculum Development.

Creighton, T. B. (2001). *Schools and data: The educator's guide for using data to improve decision-making.* Thousand Oaks, CA: Corwin Press, Inc.

Creswell, J. W. (2003). *Research design: Qualitative, quantitative, and mixed methods approaches.* Thousand Oaks, CA: SAGE publications.

Dann, R. (2002). *Promoting assessment as learning.* New York, NY: RoutledgeFalmer.

Darling-Hammond, L., Berry, B., & Toreson, A. (2001). Does Teacher Certification Matter? Evaluating the Evidence. *Educational Evaluation and Policy Analysis,* 23(1), 57-77.

Deming, W. E. (1986). *Out of the crisis.* Cambridge, MA: MIT Press.

Dickinson, T. (Ed). (2001). *Reinventing the middle school.* New York, NY: Routledge Falmer.

DuFour, R., & Eaker, R. (1998). *Professional learning communities at work: Best practices for enhancing student achievement.* Alexandria, VA: Association for Supervision and Curriculum Development.

Eaker, R., DuFour, R., & Burnett, R. (2002). *Getting started: Reculturing schools to become professional learning communities.* Bloomington, IN: National Educational Service.

Educators in Connecticut's Pomperaug Regional School District 15. (1996). *A teacher's guide to performance-based learning and assessment.* Alexandria, VA: Association for Supervision and Curriculum Development.

Ellis, A. K. (2001). *Teaching, learning, and addressing together.* Larchmont, NY: Eye on Education, Inc.

Elmore, R. F. (2000). *Building a new structure for school leadership.* Washington, DC: The Albert Shanker Institute.

English, F. W. (2000). *Deciding what to teach and test: Developing, aligning, and auditing the curriculum.* Thousand Oaks, CA: Corwin Press, Inc.

Falk, B. (2000). *The heart of the matter: Using standards and assessment to learn.* Portsmouth, NH: Heinemann.

Fullan, M. (2001). *Leading a culture of change.* New York, NY: Jossey-Bass/Pfeiffer.

Fullan, M. (2002). *Changing forces with a vengeance.* New York, NY: RoutledgeFalmer.

Garmston, R.J., & Wellman, B.M. (1997). *The adaptive school: A sourcebook for developing collaborative groups.* Norwood, MA: Christopher-Gordon Publishers, Inc.

Glatthorn, A. A. (1999). *Performance standards & authentic learning.* Larchmont, NY: Eye on Education, Inc.

Glatthorn, A. A., & Fontana, J. (Eds.). (2000). *Coping with standards, tests, and accountability: Voices from the classroom.* Washington, DC: National Education Association.

Gredler, M. (1999). *Classroom assessment and learning.* Needham Heights, MA: Allyn & Bacon.

Gupta, K. (1999). *A practical guide to needs assessment.* San Francisco, CA: Jossey-Bass, Inc.

Guskey, T. (2000). *Evaluating professional development.* Thousand Oaks, CA: Corwin Press, Inc.

Guskey, T. R., & Bailey, J. M. (2001). Developing grading and reporting systems for student learning. In Guskey, T.R. & Marzano, R.J. (Series Eds.). *Experts in assessment.* Thousand Oaks, CA: Corwin Press, Inc.

Haladyna, T. M., Nolan, S. B., & Haas, N. S. (1991). Raising standardized achievement test scores and the origins of test score pollutions. *Educational Researcher,* 20(5), 2-7.

Haycock, K. (1999). *Results: Good teaching matters.* Oxford, OH: National Staff Development Council.

Henry, G. (1997). *Creating effective graphs: Solutions for a variety of evaluation data.* Editor-in-chief. New Directions for Evaluation, a publication of the American Evaluation Association..

Henry, T. (2001, June 11). Lawmakers move to improve literacy, the 'new civil right.' *USA Today,* pp. A1-2.

Herman, J. L., & Golan, S. (1991). *Effects of standardized testing on teachers and learning—another look.* (CSE Technical Report No. 334). Los Angeles, CA: University of California, Center for Research on Evaluation, Standards and Student Testing (CRESST).

Holcomb, E. L. (1999). *Getting excited about data.* Thousand Oaks, CA: Corwin Press, Inc.

Holly, P.J. (2003). *Conceptualizing a new path: Data-driven school improvement series.* Princeton, NJ: Educational Testing Service.

Isaac, S., & William, B. M. (1997). *Handbook in research and evaluation for education and the behavioral sciences* (3rd ed.). San Diego, CA: Educational and Industrial Testing Services.

Johnson, D. W., & Johnson, R. T. (2002). *Introduction: Cooperative learning and assessment.* Needham Heights, MA: Allyn & Bacon.

Johnson, R. S. (2002). *Using data to close the achievement gap: How to measure equity in our schools.* Thousand Oaks, CA: Corwin Press, Inc.

Joint Commission Resources. (2002). *Root cause analysis in healthcare: Tools and techniques.* Indianapolis, IN: Joint Commission Resources.

Kachigan, S. K. (1991). *Multivariate statistical analysis: A conceptual introduction* (2nd ed.). New York, NY: Radius Press.

Kain, D. L. (1996). *Looking beneath the surface: Teacher collaboration through the lens of grading practices.* Teachers College Record, Summer, 569-587.

Kifer, E. (2000). *Large-scale assessment: Dimensions, dilemmas, and policy.* Thousand Oaks, CA: Corwin Press, Inc.

Killion, J. (2002). *Assessing impact: Evaluating staff development.* Oxford, OH: National Staff Development Council.

Koretz, D., Stecher, B., Klein, S., & McCaffrey, D. (1994). The Vermont portfolio assessment program: Finding and implications. *Educational Measurement: Issues and Practice,* 13(3), 5-16.

Kosslyn, S. (1994). *Elements of graph design.* New York, NY: W. H. Freeman and Company.

Kouzes, J. M., & Posner, B. Z. (2002). *The leadership challenge: How to keep getting extraordinary things done in organizations.* (2nd Ed.). San Francisco, CA: Jossey-Bass Publishers.

Krueger, R. A. (2000). *Focus groups: A practical guide for applied research.* (3rd ed.). Thousand Oaks, CA: Sage Publications, Inc.

Kubiszyn, T., & Borich, G. (1996). *Educational testing and measurement: Classroom application and practice.* (5th ed.) New York, NY: HarperCollins.

Lambert, L. (2003). *Leadership capacity for lasting school improvement.* Alexandria, VA: Association for Supervision and Curriculum Development.

Lambert, L. (1998). *Building leadership capacity in schools.* Alexandria, VA: Association for Supervision and Curriculum Development.

Lazear, D. (1998). *The rubrics way: Using MI to assess understanding.* Tucson, AZ: Zephyr Press.

Linn, R. L., Baker, E. L., & Dunbar, S. B. (1991). *Complex, performance-based assessment: Expectations and validation guide.* (CSE Technical Report No. 331). Los Angeles, CA: University of California, Center for Research on Evaluation, Standards and Student Testing (CRESST).

Lissitz, R. W., & Schafer, W. D. (2002). (Eds.). *Assessment in educational reform: Both means and ends.* Needham Heights, MA: Allyn & Bacon.

Marzano, R. J. (2000). *Transforming classroom grading.* Alexandria, VA: Association for Supervision and Curriculum Development.

Marzano, R. J., Pickering, D., & McTighe, J. (1993). *Assess student outcomes: Performance assessment using dimensions of learning model.* Alexandria, VA: Association for Supervision and Curriculum Development.

Marzano, R. J., Pickering, D., & Pollock, J. E. (2001). *Classroom instruction that works: Research-based strategies for increasing student achievement.* Alexandria, VA: Association for Supervision and Curriculum Development.

McIntyre, C.V. (1992). *Writing effective news releases: How to get free publicity for yourself, your business, or your organization.* Colorado Springs, CO: Piccadilly Books.

McMillian, J. H. (2001). *Classroom assessment: Principles and practice for effective instruction* (2nd ed.). Needham Heights, MA: Allyn & Bacon.

McMillian, J. H. (2001). *Essential assessment concepts for teachers and administrators.* In Guskey, T.R. & Marzano, R.J. (Series Eds.). Experts in Assessment. Thousand Oaks, CA: Corwin Press, Inc.

McREL. (1995-2002). *Classroom assessment, grading, and record keeping.* Aurora, CO: Author.

McTighe, J., & Ferrara, S. (1998). *Assessing learning in the classroom.* Washington, DC: National Education Association.

Merrow, J. (2001). *"Good enough" schools are not good enough.* Lanham, MD: Scarecrow Press.

Microsoft. (2003). Available: http://www.microsoft.com.

National Staff Development Council. (2002, October). Scientifically-based research as defined by NCLB. *Results.* Oxford, OH: Author.

Northwest Evaluation Association (NWEA). (2002). Available: http://www.nwea.org.

O'Connor, K. (1999). *The mindful school: How to grade for learning.* Arlington Heights, IL: Skylight Professional Development.

Oshry, B. (2000). *Leading systems: Lessons from the power lab.* San Francisco, CA: Berrett-Koehler Publishers.

Oosterhof, A. (1999). *Developing and using classroom assessments* (2nd ed.). Upper Saddle River, NJ: Prentice Hall, Inc.

Parsons, B. A. (2002). *Evaluative Inquiry: Using evaluation to promote student success.* Thousand Oaks, CA: Corwin Press, Inc.

Patten, M. L. (1997). *Understanding research methods: An overview of the essentials.* Los Angeles, CA: Pyrczak Publishing.

Payne, R. K., & Magee, D. S. (1999). *Meeting standards and raising test scores when you don't have much time or money.* Highlands, TX: RFT Publishing Company.

Perone, V. (Ed.). (1991). *Expanding student assessment.* Alexandria, VA: Association for Supervision and Curriculum Development.

Peterson, K. D. (1999). *Shaping school culture: The heart of leadership.* San Francisco, CA: Jossey-Bass Publishers.

Peterson, R. A. (2000). *Constructing effective questionnaires.* Thousand Oaks, CA: Sage Publications, Inc..

Popham, W. J. (1999). *Classroom assessment: What teachers need to know* (2nd ed.). Needham Heights, MA: Allyn & Bacon.

Popham, W. J. (2001). Standardized achievement tests: Misnamed and misleading. *Education Week,* 21(3), 46.

Preuss, P. G. (2003). *School leader's guide to root cause analysis: Using data to dissolve problems.* Larchmont, NY: Eye on Education, Inc.

Quellmalz, E., & Burry, J. (1983). Analytic scales for assessing students' expository and narrative writing skills. (CSE Technical Report No. 5). Los Angeles, CA: University of California, Center for Research on Evaluation, Standards and Student Testing (CRESST).

Rauhauser, B., & McLennan, A. (1995). *America's schools: Making them work.* Chapel Hill, NC: New View.

Rauhauser, B., & McLennan, A. (1994). *America's schools: Meeting the challenge through effective schools research and total quality management.* Lewisville, TX: School Improvement Specialists.

Rauhauser, B., & McLennan, A. (1995). *Research design: Qualitative, quantitative, and mixed methods approaches.* Thousand Oaks, CA: SAGE publications.

Rogers, S., & Graham, S. (2000). *The high performance toolbox: Succeeding with performance tasks, projects, and assessments* (3rd ed.). Evergreen, CO: Peak Learning Systems.

Sanders, J. R. (2000). *Evaluating school programs: An educator's guide.* Thousand Oaks, CA: Corwin Press, Inc.

Schafer, W. D., & Lissitz, R. W. (1987). Measurement training for school personnel: Recommendations and reality. *Journal of Teacher Education,* 38(3), 57-63.

Schmoker, M. (2001). *The results fieldbook: Practical strategies from dramatically improved schools.* Alexandria, VA: Association for Supervision and Curriculum Development.

Senge, P., Cambron-McCabe, N. H., Lucas, T., Smith, B., Dutton, J., & Kleiner, A. (2000). *Schools that learn: A fifth discipline fieldbook for educators, parents, and everyone who cares about education.* New York, NY: Doubleday Dell Publishing Group, Inc.

Senge, P., Kleiner, A., Roberts, C., Ross, R. B., & Smith, B. (2000). *The fifth discipline fieldbook: Strategies and tools for building a learning organization.* New York, NY: Doubleday Dell Publishing Group, Inc.

Shepard, L. A. (2000). *The role of classroom assessment in teaching and learning.* (CSE Technical Report No. 517). Los Angeles, CA: University of California, Center for Research on Evaluation, Standards and Student Testing (CRESST).

Smith, J. K., Smith, L. F., & DeLisi, R. (2001). *Natural classroom assessment: Designing seamless instruction & assessment.* In Guskey, T.R. & Marzano, R.J. (Series Eds.). Experts in Assessment. Thousand Oaks, CA: Corwin Press, Inc.

Solomon, P. (2002). *The assessment bridge: Positive ways to link tests to learning, standards, and curriculum improvement.* Thousand Oaks, CA: Corwin Press, Inc.

Statistica. (2003). Available: http://www.statsoft.com.

Stiggins, R. J. (2000). *Student-Involved classroom assessment* (3rd ed.). Englewood Cliffs, NJ: Prentice Hall.

Stiggins, R. J. (1999). Assessment, student confidence, and school success. *Phi Delta Kappan*, November, 191-198.

Stigler, J. W., & Hiebert, J. (1999). *The teaching gap: Best ideas from the world's teachers for improving education in the classroom.* New York, NY: The Free Press.

Strong, R. W., Silver, H. F., & Perini. M. J. (2001). *Teaching what matters most: Standards and strategies for raising student achievement.* Alexandria, VA: Association for Supervision and Curriculum Development.

TetraData. (2002). Available: http://www.Tetradata.com.

Trice, A. D. (2000). *A handbook of classroom assessment.* Needham Heights, MA: Allyn & Bacon.

Tufte, E. R. (2001). *The visual display of quantitative information.* (2nd ed.). Cheshire, CT: Graphics Press.

Tufte, E. R. (1997). *Visual explanations: Images and quantities, evidence and narrative.* Cheshire, CT: Graphics Press.

Tufte, E. R. (1990). *Envisioning information.* Cheshire, CT: Graphics Press.

U. S. Department of Education. *No child left behind.* Available: http://www.ed.gov.

Visual Mining, Inc. (2003). Available: http://www.visualmining.com.

Wahlstrom, D. (1999). *Using data to improve student achievement: A handbook for collecting, analyzing, and using data.* Virginia Beach,VA: Successline Publications.

Whitaker, T., Whitaker, B., & Lumpa, D. (2000). *Motivating and inspiring teachers: The educational leader's guide for building staff morale.* Larchmont, NY: Eye on Education.

Wiggins, G. (1998). *Educative assessment: Designing assessments to inform and improve student performance.* San Francisco, CA: Jossey-Bass, Inc.

Wiggins, G., & McTighe, J. (1998). *Understanding by design.* Alexandria, VA: Association for Supervision and Curriculum Development.

Wilson, L. W. (2002). *Better instruction through assessment: What your students are trying to tell you.* Larchmont, NY: Eye on Education, Inc.

Wittrock, M. C., & Baker, E. L. (Eds.). (1991). *Testing and cognition.* Englewood Cliffs, NJ: Prentice Hall.

Wormeli, R. (2003). *Day one & beyond: Practical matters for new middle-level teachers.* Portland, ME: Stenhouse Publishers.

Worthen, B. R., White, K. R., Fan, X., & Sudweeks, R. R. (1999). *Measurement and assessment in the schools* (2nd ed.). Needham Heights, MA: Allyn & Bacon.

Yero, J. L. (2002). *Teaching in mind: How teacher thinking shapes education.* Hamilton, MT: MindFlight Publishing.

Yin, R. K. (2003). *Case study research: Design and methods.* (3rd ed.). Thousand Oaks, CA: Sage Publications, Inc.

Zemelman, S., Daniels, H., & Hyde, A. (1998). *Best practice: New standards for teaching and learning in America's schools* (2nd ed.). Portsmouth, NH: Heinemann.

Zmuda, A., Kuklis, R., & Kline, E. (2004). *Transforming schools: Creating a culture of continuous improvement.* Alexandria, VA: Association for Supervision and Curriculum Development.

Index

M

Matched Cohorts, 277
Maximum Score, 131, 277
Mean Score, 131, 277
Means, 277
Measures, 277
Median Score, 131, 277
Minimum Score, 131, 277
Mission, 201, 277
Mobility, 277
Mode Score, 114, 285
Multiple Measures, 277
    of data, 11

N

N, 277
National Percentile Ranks, 118
Needs Assessment, 278
No Child Left Behind (NCLB), 134, 137, 244, 278
Nominal Scale, 278
Normal Curve, 118-119, 122, 278
Normal Curve Equivalent (NCE) Scores, 117, 118, 278
Normal Distribution, 278
Normalized Standard Score, 278
Norming Group, 278
Norm-referenced Test, 117-119, 278
Norms, 278
Norms versus Standards, 279

O

Objectives, 174, 279
Observation, 279
On the CD
    chapter 2, 26
    chapter 3, 38
    chapter 4, 63-65
    chapter 5, 109-111
    chapter 6, 171-172
    chapter 7, 196-198
    chapter 8, 230-235
    chapter 9, 245

Open-ended Response Items, 80, 90, 279
Ordinal, 279
Outcome, 69, 259-260, 279
Over Time, 12, 279

P

Parameter, 279
Partnership Plan, 225-227
Partnerships, 279
Pearson Correlation Coefficient, 279
Percent Correct, 132, 279
Percent Mastery, 132
Percent Passing, 122, 132
Percent Proficient, 132, 139-167, 177-180, 280
Percentile, 122, 280
    rank, 122, 280
Perceptions Data, 77-94, 280
Performance Assessment, 126, 280
    arguments for and against, 127
Performance Standard, 280
Pie Chart or Graph, 280
Population, 280
Press Release, 280
Process Mapping, 280
Processes, 280
Professional Development, 281
    assessment, 100-103
    calendar, 221-223
    plan, 219-221
Program Evaluation, 281
Purpose, 201, 281
Purposes of this Book, 5

Q

Quality Planning, 281
Quality, 281
Quartiles, 122, 281
Query, 281
Questionnaires,
    parent, 91-94
    staff, 82-90
    student, 78-82
Quota Sampling, 281

W

Z

EYE ON EDUCATION and EDUCATION FOR THE FUTURE INITIATIVE
END-USER LICENSE AGREEMENT

READ THIS

You should carefully read these terms and conditions before opening the software packet(s) included with this book ("Book"). This is a license agreement ("Agreement") between you and EYE ON EDUCATION. By opening the accompanying software packet(s), you acknowledge that you have read and accept the following terms and conditions. If you do not agree and do not want to be bound by such terms and conditions, promptly return the Book and the unopened software packet (s) to the place you obtained them for a full refund.

1. License Grant

EYE ON EDUCATION grants to you (either an individual or entity) a nonexclusive license to use the software and files (collectively, the "Software") solely for your own personal or business purposes on a single computer (whether a standard computer or a workstation component of a multiuser network). The Software is in use on a computer when it is loaded into temporary memory (RAM) or installed into permanent memory (hard disk, CD-ROM, or other storage device). EYE ON EDUCATION reserves all rights not expressly granted herein.

2. Ownership

EYE ON EDUCATION is the owner of all rights, title, and interests, including copyright, in and to the compilation of the Software recorded on the CD-ROM ("Software Media"). Copyright to the individual programs recorded on the Software Media is owned by the author or other authorized copyright owner of each program. Ownership of the Software and all proprietary rights relating thereto remain with EYE ON EDUCATION and its licensers.

3. Restrictions On Use and Transfer

(a) You may only (i) make one copy of the Software for backup or archival purposes, or (ii) transfer the Software to a single hard disk, provided that you keep the original for backup or archival purposes. You may not (i) rent or lease the Software, (ii) copy or reproduce the Software through a LAN or other network system or through any computer subscriber system or bulletin-board system, or (iii) adapt or create derivative works based on the Software.

(b) You may not reverse engineer, decompile, or disassemble the Software. You may transfer the Software and user documentation on a permanent basis, provided that the transferee agrees to accept the terms and conditions of this Agreement and you retain no copies. If the Software is an update or has been updated, any transfer must include the most recent update and all prior versions.

4. Restrictions On Use of Individual Programs

You must follow the individual requirements and restrictions detailed for each individual program on the Software Media. These limitations are contained in the individual license agreements recorded on the Software Media. By opening the Software packet, you will be agreeing to abide by the licenses and restrictions for these individual programs that are detailed on the Software Media. None of the material on this Software Media or listed in this Book may ever be redistributed, in original or modified form, for commercial purposes.

5. Limited Warranty

(a) EDUCATION FOR THE FUTURE INITIATIVE warrants that the Software and Software Media are free from defects in materials and workmanship under normal use for a period of thirty (30) days from the date of purchase of this Book. If EDUCATION FOR THE FUTURE INITIATIVE receives notification within the warranty period of defects in materials or workmanship, EDUCATION FOR THE FUTURE INITIATIVE will replace the defective Software Media.

(b) **EYE ON EDUCATION, EDUCATION FOR THE FUTURE INITIATIVE, AND THE AUTHOR OF THIS BOOK DISCLAIM OTHER WARRANTIES, EXPRESSED OR IMPLIED, INCLUDING WITHOUT LIMITATION IMPLIED WARRANTIES OF MERCHANTABILITY AND FITNESS FOR A PARTICULAR PURPOSE WITH RESPECT TO THE SOFTWARE AND FILES, AND/OR THE TECHNIQUES DESCRIBED IN THIS BOOK. EYE ON EDUCATION DOES NOT WARRANT THAT THE FUNCTIONS CONTAINED IN THE SOFTWARE WILL MEET YOUR REQUIREMENTS OR THAT THE OPERATION OF THE SOFTWARE WILL BE ERROR FREE.**

(c) This limited warranty gives you specific legal rights, and you may have other rights that vary from jurisdiction to jurisdiction.

6. Remedies

(a) EYE ON EDUCATION's entire liability and your exclusive remedy for defects in materials and workmanship shall be limited to replacement of the Software Media, which may be returned to EDUCATION FOR THE FUTURE INITIATIVE with a copy of your receipt at the following address: EDUCATION FOR THE FUTURE INITIATIVE, ATTN: Brad Geise, 400 West 1st. St., Chico, CA 95929-0230, or call 1-530-898-4482. Please allow three to four weeks for delivery. This Limited Warranty is void if failure of the Software Media has resulted from accident, abuse, or misapplication. Any replacement Software Media will be warranted for thirty (30) days.

(b) In no event shall EYE ON EDUCATION, EDUCATION FOR THE FUTURE INITIATIVE, or the author be liable for any damages whatsoever (including without limitation damages for loss of business profits, business interruption, loss of business information, or any other pecuniary loss) arising from the use of or inability to use the Book or the Software, even if EYE ON EDUCATION, EDUCATION FOR THE FUTURE INITIATIVE, or the author has been advised of the possibility of damages.

(c) Because some jurisdictions do not allow the exclusion or limitation of liability for consequential or incidental damages, the above limitation or exclusion may not apply to you.

7. U.S. Government Restriction Rights

Use, duplication, or disclosure of the Software by the U.S. Government is subject to restrictions stated in paragraph (c) (1)(ii) of the Rights in Technical Data and Computer Software clause of DFARS 252.227-7013, and in subparagraphs (a) through (d) of the Commercial Computer—Restricted Rights clause at FAR 52. 227–19, and in similar clauses in the NASA FAR supplement, when applicable. ˙

8. General

This Agreement constitutes the entire understanding of the parties and revokes and supersedes all prior agreements, oral or written, between them and may not be modified or amended except in writing signed by both parties hereto that specifically refers to this Agreement. This Agreement shall take precedence over any other documents that may be in conflict herewith. If any one or more provisions contained in this Agreement are held by any court or tribunal to be invalid, illegal, or otherwise unenforceable, each and every other provision shall remain in full force and effect.

INSTALLATION INSTRUCTIONS

Windows

Step 1   Set up a folder on your desktop (or in your documents folder) labeled *Middle Data Tools* for capturing the files that you wish to download.

Step 2   Make sure your monitor is set to 800 by 600 or higher to view the entire CD contents. (When you are on the main menu page of the CD and cannot see the top menu bar, your monitor must be moved to a higher setting. Do this by going into *Start / Settings / Control Panel / Display.* Open *Display,* and click on *Settings.* Move the arrow on the screen area to at least 800 by 600 pixels.)

Step 3   The CD should start automatically. The introduction will run up to the *Main Menu* page. If the CD does *not* start automatically, follow steps 3a. and 3b. below:

     3a. Open/Explore *My Computer* and Open/Explore the CD *Middle.*

     3b. With the CD contents showing, click on *Click Here.exe.* The CD will begin.

Step 4   After the introduction, you will come to the *Main Menu.* If you do not have *Adobe Reader* v.5 or above, download it by pressing *Adobe Acrobat.* After installing, go back to the *Main Menu.*

Step 5   By placing your cursor on the section titles, you will be able to see what is on the CD. Click on the section that you want to know more about and read the descriptions of the files in that section.

Step 6   To download the tools from that section, press the *Download* button.

Step 7   When *Extract Archive Files* appears, click *Next.*

Step 9   Note: When *Destination Directory* appears, click *Browse* to locate the folder in which you want the files to download. If you put a folder entitled *Middle Data Tools* on your desktop, you will see it in the *Desktop Folder.* (This may vary slightly depending upon the version of *Windows* you are using.)

Step 9   Open *The Middle Data Tools* folder and click *Next.* The files will extract and ask you if it is okay to download. Click *Yes* and the files will extract into your *Middle Data Tools* folder. Click *Finish.*

Step 10   Go back to the *INFO* window. Select the *Back to Main Menu* button to return to the *Main Menu.*

Step 11   Continue exploring and downloading. You must quit the CD to view the documents that you download.

Mac

Step 1   Create a folder on your desktop (or your hard drive) labeled *Middle Data Tools* for capturing the files that you wish to download.

Step 2   Make sure your monitor is set to 800 by 600 or higher to view the entire CD contents. (When you are on the main menu page of the CD and cannot see the top menu bar, your monitor must be moved to a higher setting. Change the settings in the *Monitors Control Panel.*)

Step 3   The CD will start automatically. The introduction will run up to the *Main Menu* page. If the CD does *not* start automatically, follow steps 3a. and 3b. below:

     3a. Open the CD by double-clicking the CD icon on your desktop.

     3b. Select the icon for *Classic OS 9* or *OS X,* depending upon which operating system you use. The CD will begin.

Step 4   By placing your cursor on the section titles, you will be able to see what is on the CD. Click on the section that you want to know more about and read the descriptions of the files.

Step 5   To download the tools from that section, press the *Download* button.

Step 6   When a dialog box appears, click *Continue.*

Step 7   Note: A *Save* window will appear. Locate your *Middle Data Tools* folder, or if you did not make a folder when you started, create a new folder. Save the section's files to the *Middle Data Tools* folder.

Step 8   Go Back to *INFO* window. Select the *Back to Main Menu* button to return to the *Main Menu.*

Step 9   Continue exploring and downloading. You must quit the CD to view the documents that you download.

Please see our website for more information:

http://eff.csuchico.edu/home/

To contact *Education for the Future,* call:

(530) 898-4482